THE IRISH WHALES

THE IRISH WHALES

Olympians of Old New York

Kevin Martin

ROWMAN & LITTLEFIELD
Lanham • Boulder • New York • London

Published by Rowman & Littlefield
An imprint of The Rowman & Littlefield Publishing Group, Inc.
4501 Forbes Boulevard, Suite 200, Lanham, Maryland 20706
www.rowman.com

6 Tinworth Street, London SE11 5AL, United Kingdom

British Library Cataloguing in Publication Information Available

Library of Congress Cataloging-in-Publication Data

Name: Martin, Kevin, 1969–, author.
Title: The Irish whales : Olympians of old New York / Kevin Martin.
Description: Lanham, Maryland : Rowman & Littlefield Publishing Group,
     2020. | Includes bibliographical references and index. | Summary: "This book
     tells the fascinating story of seven Irish-American Olympians from the early
     twentieth century, who were sports heroes in their time yet are now largely
     forgotten. These decorated American athletes, who came to be known as the
     Irish Whales, dominated the Olympic track and field throwing events in the
     early 1900s."—Provided by publisher.
Identifiers: LCCN 2019059394 (print) | LCCN 2019059395 (ebook) | ISBN
     9781538142301 (cloth) | ISBN 9781538142318 (epub)
Subjects: LCSH: Olympic athletes—United States—Biography. | Irish
     Americans—New York (State)—New York—Biography. | Irish-American
     Athletic Club of New York—History.
Classification: LCC GV697.A1 M3399 2020 (print) | LCC GV697.A1 (ebook) |
     DDC 796.0922 [B]—dc23
LC record available at https://lccn.loc.gov/2019059394
LC ebook record available at https://lccn.loc.gov/2019059395

CONTENTS

INTRODUCTION

When you see a ballerina jump, she's like a bird, how she flies so easy. People are always excited when they see this. They cannot imagine how hard it is to come to this easy, the hundreds of hours of practice, practice, practice. This is also true for hammer.—Yuriy Sedykh, holder of the world hammer thrower record since 1986[1]

"The bottom line is that the hammer throw is a math equation."—Jud Logan, four-time U.S. Olympian[2]

On July 3, 1984, track and field fans at Mardyke Stadium in Cork City in the Republic of Ireland witnessed the greatest-ever, record-breaking feat in the history of the sport of hammer-throwing. On a beautiful sunny evening, two preeminent athletes, Russians Yuriy Sedykh and Sergey Litvinov, staged the weight-throwing equivalent of boxing's Ali–Frazier matches.

The rivalry between the two Russians defined the sport of hammer-throwing during the 1980s. Sedykh was a prodigy; he had taken the gold at the Montreal Olympics in 1976, at the age of twenty-one, with a throw of 77.52 meters, in a sport where participants are usually in their late twenties or early thirties before they reach their peak. Four years later he broke his own record twice, upping his mark to 80.64 meters. At the 1980 Olympics in Moscow, Sedykh took the gold medal again, breaking a two-month-old record set by Litvinov, by throwing 81.80 meters. This new record lasted a mere eight days: Litvinov, then twenty-two years old, threw a meter further. None of their peers could come close to them.

The men differed substantially in throwing style: Sedykh made three turns before releasing the hammer, while Litvinov, then the world record holder, was a disciple of a more conventional four-turn approach. While the four-turn method theoretically develops an extra 30 percent acceleration, it also means that a small mistake can significantly affect the result. At 5-foot-10, Litvinov was traditionally small for the discipline but was nevertheless the finest exponent of the sport in the Soviet system, primarily because of his uncanny explosiveness. While he did not have the long arms associated with stars of the discipline, his coordination was astonishing. The men were virtual opposites in facial appearance: Sedykh was bald with a walrus moustache and appeared dour and introverted; Litvinov, with his good looks, blonde hair, and lively eyes, had more of a star quality about him.

Just shy of 6:00 PM, Litvinov, the reigning world champion, stepped into the Mardyke throwing circle for his first effort. Conditions were absolutely perfect for hammer-throwing. There was not a breath of wind, and the lowering sun shone hazily on the proceedings. An infamously slow starter, Litvinov fouled his first throw. Sedykh took his place. Within seconds he exploded in a blur of motion, whipping the hammer around his head and spinning counterclockwise like a dervish. With his trademark guttural roar, the now-twenty-nine-year-old launched the hammer 86.34 meters—demolishing Litvinov's world-leading mark set thirteen months earlier by more than two meters. It was a monstrous throw and an astonishing effort in a low-key meet on the periphery of Western Europe.

Litvinov took his place in the circle and threw the hammer out to 85.14 meters, a full meter longer than his vanquished world record but not enough to pass the mark Sedykh set moments earlier. Neither man was to throw better than that, but during the course of the evening the record coming into the meet had been beaten with an astonishing six throws—four times by Sedykh and twice by Litvinov. Aficionadas of the sport agree that it was the single greatest day in the history of modern hammer-throwing. And it was fitting that these two great athletes fought such an epic battle on Irish soil, the land from which the sport is believed to have originated and from which arose the "Irish Whales"—the champions of the first five Olympic hammer-throwing competitions in the early twentieth century.

Hammer-throwing is dated to an ancient Irish sporting contest called the Tailteann Games, believed by some anthropologists to have been established as early as 1829 BC and held continuously through the twelfth century, when they ceased after the Norman invasion. The games were inaugurated as a tribute by King Lughaidh (also known as Lugh the Long-armed) to his foster mother, Queen Tailte, and staged during the last fortnight of July each year, culminating in the celebration of Lughnasadh on August 1. In the games, rival Celtic tribes competed against one another on the royal plains of County Meath, close to the Hill of Tara, the ancient seat of the Irish high king, where Lugh had buried his foster mother and raised a mound in her memory.

For the duration of the games a general truce was declared throughout the land, and personal feuds and animosities were put aside under the direct instruction of the high king. As well as honoring the dead, the games were used to proclaim new laws and as a place to find romance. Tailteann marriages—sometimes referred to as "handfasting" marriages—allowed couples to get hitched in a mass ceremony at the games, after which they were obliged to stay together for a trial period of one year to see if they were well suited; if not, they could divorce by going to the "separation hills" at the following games with no further obligations. Such marriages remained legal in Ireland until the thirteenth century.

Competitors took part in a host of sporting contests, including spear-throwing, boxing, sword-fighting, and chariot-riding; even "horse-swimming" was part of the annual schedule. One of the key events in the early versions of the games was wheel-throwing, in honor of the ancient mythological figure Cuchulainn, who could reputedly throw the wheel of a chariot a vast distance. In later times, a boulder attached to wood was used, and it is this event that evolved into the rudimentary version of hammer-throwing.

Although the vast majority of sources date the origin of throwing to the Tailteann Games, the Irish did not have an ancient monopoly on throwing. The event was also popular among Teutonic tribes at festivals held to honor their god Thor, a deity who had a remarkable addition to his armoury: a magic hammer, which, after he threw it and hit his target, returned automatically to his hand so he could then attack his next target. In Norse culture, Vikings reputedly threw hammers to ascertain how much land each individual could acquire when they pillaged new territories; the man was granted the amount he could cover with his throw.

In Britain, some kings of the Middle Ages were accorded epithets based on their hammer-throwing abilities: Charles Martel (688–741) was known as "Hammer Charles"; Edward I, who ruled from 1272 to 1307, acquired the nickname "Hammer of the Scots," while, later, Thomas Cromwell (1485–1540) was dubbed "Hammer of the Monks." On the other hand, Edward III of England, who held the crown between 1327 and 1377, prohibited his soldiers from weight-throwing because he believed it would impinge on their archery practice. Wary of Robert the Bruce and his Scottish foes, Edward III apparently believed throwing things at the enemy was an ineffective method of warfare.

Centuries later, Henry VIII of England, who ruled from 1509 to 1547, was reputed to have been a talented hammer thrower and enjoyed participating in competitions with members of his court in which they threw royally forged sledgehammers. Some athletic historians date to this period the change from a boulder attached to a stick to a sledge. Indeed, there is an extant drawing of Henry VIII throwing a sledgehammer.

Throwing events of various sorts had long entertained the Irish. Tribes and communities battled to see who among them could demonstrate supreme strength by throwing the longest or, in some cases, the highest. The objects thrown were various; stones, cart wheels, and crude versions of the hammer, among others. Sledgehammers were widely used; each local village had a forge. Different types of demonstrations of strength were popular throughout the country—in County Cavan, for example, competitors lifted cart wheels with their teeth—but it was the hammer that would become the most popular item to be thrown in Ireland.

In his seminal manual *How to Become a Weight Thrower*, James Mitchell, the first of the group of Irish American weight throwers to be known as the Irish Whales, described how the earliest versions of the discipline—rocks attached to a wooden handle—were of no prescribed weight, with handles varying in length from three to three and a half feet. The wooden handle was an inefficient throwing instrument and would break too frequently when it hit the ground, but Mitchell noted that "rumination on the subject was bound to produce some good fruit," and throughout time different materials were tried for the handles in different regions, including grapevines, whalebone, and iron, before wire became the standardized material in 1896.[3]

In his entertaining narrative, Mitchell alludes to past throwing feats in Ireland that would "make the modern giants gasp in awe."[4] He told the remarkable—or perhaps unbelievable—tale of one such throw at Oola Castle in Limerick, when a gigantic priest named Eliv Hanley engaged in a special match with an army officer. The object of the competition was to throw the hammer as high as they could against a one hundred-foot tower wall. Not only did the cleric win, but also he threw the hammer over the tower, and it was never seen again. Superstitious residents of the district believed it sailed into the clouds and up to heaven, but the more practical were certain that the hammer fell on the soft, boggy ground and sank below the surface. That the reverend athlete was a man of tremendous power was not in doubt because when he swung round in the throw, he wrenched the heels off of a new pair of shoes he was wearing.

The hammer throw continued to evolve during the course of the nineteenth century. In March 1864, Oxford and Cambridge Universities, the august English educational institutions that played a significant role in the codification of a number of sports in England, incorporated the hammer throw into their athletic programs. And, in 1866, the discipline became part of national athletic championships in England. In the first competitions, the athlete swung the hammer around his head and threw from a standing position to a distance measured from the forward foot; later, the hammer had to be released from behind a line marked on the field. The discipline was standardized by English athletic authorities in 1875; the hammer had to weigh 16 pounds and the handle had to measure 3 feet, 6 inches in length, and it had to be thrown from a seven-foot circle. (In 1887, the circle was extended to nine feet—probably in response to evolving techniques, but it was later returned to a seven-foot circle.) Early hammer-throwing simply involved revolving the hammer around the head before releasing it; subsequently, a turn and then a double turn became popular. The Scottish version of hammer-throwing—known widely for the part it plays in the Highland Games—as well as the international version, took different paths and have remained variations of the same sport.

In 1887, the National Association of Amateur Athletes of America adopted the same rules as Britain and set the overall length of the hammer handle at four feet. Beginning in 1891, the hammer had to consist of a spherical weight attached by a steel wire to a triangular handle, and in 1896, a flexible metal handle was legalized. With some further minor modifications throughout time, the discipline has remained essentially the same since.

Of all the athletic field events, the hammer is arguably the most esoteric and technically demanding. It requires an immense skill set from a participant. Upon first seeing the event, observers might be forgiven for thinking that the key to hammer-throwing is raw strength and power. It is much more than that, however. It requires an incredible degree of speed, agility, balance, and timing. It is little wonder that the great Yuriy Sedykh referred to his technique as "the dance."

The thrower's aim is to release the hammer at its maximum velocity and a specific angle, ensuring the greatest length possible. The most important and challenging requirement is to master the ballet-like steps required to make a number of turns—depending on the technique used—before the hammer is released. The technique is comparable to a pirouette in ballet—but performed, most often, by large, muscle-bound men. At the end of each turn the thrower must pause for a brief second, and before the release the hip is brought around with a strong thrust to increase the acceleration of the hammer and send it on its way. That is only a fraction of the movement principles required. The thrower must be conscious of keeping the radius of the hammer as long as possible, since the faster the athlete turns, the faster the hammerhead will go. Any reduction in the radius will result in a reduction in the hammerhead velocity. So the thrower gradually builds up his speed as he turns, reaching his top speed at the point of release. On top of all that, the thrower must bend his legs while keeping his back straight so that the pull of the hammer is counteracted by the athlete. For the beginner this seems counterintuitive. Finally, and crucially, the hammer must fly within a marked, narrow sector radiating from the U-shaped cage: the thrower has just six meters through which the hammer must be released. A small miscalculation can be calamitous, with the hammer ending up hitting the cage or going out of bounds.

The margin for error is tiny, and it requires a singular focus and dedication. Phil Conway, who represented Ireland at the Olympics and is the highest authority and top coach in the country, put it simply: "Hammer-throwing is a sport of repetition. It takes many, many throws before you achieve technical mastery."[5] Conway originally went to Boston University on a four-year athletic scholarship as a result of his shot-putting prowess but became interested in the hammer while there, recognizing the historical significance of the discipline to Ireland. "Irish people tend to identify more with the hammer than the shot . . . there would be a lot more interest in a 200-foot hammer throw than a heave of 65 feet in the shot."

The story of hammer-throwing is deeply entwined with the story of Ireland, specifically the history of Irish emigration. When the sport was first made part of the Olympic schedule in 1900, it would be an Irish American, John Flanagan, who took the gold for the American team. Remarkably, he and the rest of the Irish Whales who would follow went on to annex the title for the next twenty-four years. James "Jim" Mitchell, John Flanagan, Matt McGrath, Pat McDonald, Martin Sheridan, and Paddy Ryan would win a remarkable 12 gold, 8 bronze, and 2 silver Olympic medals in various throwing disciplines for the United States. Con Walsh, the seventh Whale, would add another competing for Canada. Between them they would claim eighty U.S. Amateur Athletic Union titles during their tenure: 32 in the hammer, 37 for throwing the 56-pound weight, 7 in shot put, and 4 in discus. Now largely forgotten, they were among the biggest international celebrities of their time. And for the newly arrived Irish, fighting for a piece of the American Dream, they were considered closer to gods.

I

EXODUS

Isle of Hope, Isle of Dreams

When Ellis Island opened on January 1, 1892, the first person to cross the threshold to register as an American citizen was Annie Moore, a seventeen-year-old girl from County Cork, Ireland. She had departed on board the steamship *Nevada* from Queenstown (now Cobh), County Cork, on the previous December 20th along with her younger brothers. At the time it was reported in the American press that Annie Moore was only fifteen years old and had arrived in the United States on the day of her birthday. Neither story was true. The birthday headline was creative license to enhance the story—her actual date of birth was in May, and she had given her age as fifteen in Cobh to obtain a cheaper passage, despite approaching her eighteenth birthday.

At 10.30 AM on that New Year's Day morning, a flag on Ellis Island was dipped three times, providing a signal to the waiting barge to bring the transatlantic passengers ashore. As it ferried in to the dock with the first of the third-class steerage passengers from the *Nevada* on board, the *John E. Moore* immigrant transfer barge, covered in red, white, and blue bunting, was encouraged along its way by a cacophony of foghorns, bells, whistles, and cheering spectators. After Annie Moore stepped on American soil, she immediately proceeded through the huge double doors of the new three-story wooden building, climbed the main staircase, and was directed into one of ten aisles, where she had to walk up to the registry desk to start the process of becoming an American citizen. As the first person to use the new facilities, she was officially registered by Charles Hendley, the former private secretary to the secretary of the U.S. Treasury. Annie and her brothers were then escorted into another room and presented with a $10 gold piece by John B. Weber, the superintendent of immigration, who wished them a happy New Year. There the three Moore children were reunited with their parents, who had traveled to the United States four years previously.

For many decades it was believed that Annie Moore had married a relative of famous Irish politician Daniel O'Connell, then moved to New Mexico and later Fort Worth, Texas, where she was thought to have met a tragic end in a traffic accident in 1923. For years, people assumed to be her relatives attended events at Ellis Island and in Ireland to celebrate the links between the two countries forged by immigration. But in 2002, Megan Smolenyak, a genealogist researching a documentary on Ellis Island for the Public Broadcasting Service, uncovered evidence, with the help of New York City's commissioner of records, Brian Andersson, suggesting that the Texan Annie Moore might have been another woman with the same name. After another four years' research by Smolenyak and her colleagues, the *New York Times* revealed that the Irish woman's life story had been confused with an Annie Moore born in Illinois, and that the Annie Moore of Ellis Island fame had never moved beyond the boundary of New York City. The famous Annie Moore, according to the genealogists' detective work, had married Joseph Augustus Schayer, a German American who worked at the Fulton Street Fish Market. The couple had settled down on the Lower East Side of Manhattan, where Annie had at least ten children, five of whom died before they reached three years of age and another three of whom survived until adulthood.[1] After living the typically impoverished life of many Irish immigrants of the era, Annie Moore died of heart failure in 1924, at the age of fifty, and was buried in an unmarked grave. Despite her impoverishment, it was said that she was so obese firemen had to remove her body from an upstairs window of her apartment on Cherry Street after her sudden death.

Today, Annie is honored by two statues, one at the Cobh Heritage Centre in Cork and the other at Ellis Island, while her unmarked grave in Calvary Cemetery, Queens, was eventually located in 2008, and a headstone erected and dedicated to her memory. During the ceremony a letter from the then-candidate for president—and a man with Irish heritage—Barack Obama, was read out to the assembled crowd, which included

Annie's descendants—Dominican Americans, Chinese Americans, Jewish Americans, and Italian Americans among them.

Annie Moore and her fellow transatlantic passengers were following in a long and difficult tradition of immigration to the United States from Ireland. Until 1830, the majority of Irish immigrants to North America were Protestants, leaving behind the northern part of Ireland, where their Scottish forbearers had been transplanted from their homes in lowland Scotland. Variously referred to as Scots-Irish or Scotch-Irish in the United States, they predominantly made their homes in rural America; by 1790, 300,000 Scots-Irish called the country home. The Ulster-Scots, as they are most commonly referred to in Ireland and Great Britain, had found poor agricultural returns and discrimination in the north of Ireland and settled largely in poorer southeastern areas of the United States, predominantly in Appalachia. Typically, settlers were given free land for the first five years and subsequently allowed to rent it at the peppercorn rate of a shilling per acre. Here there was no one to discriminate against them; they had land at a reasonable price, and there would be no more extortionate rents, condescending landlords, or religious discrimination. Here they could play their beloved music, distil their moonshine whiskey, and keep their pigs in peace.

Ulster-Scottish immigrant John Dunlap from County Tyrone, a man who would later become the printer of the Declaration of Independence, wrote to his brother-in-law in Ireland, telling him that any young man who wanted to be free and happy should immediately go to America. There was, he wrote, "no place in the world where a man meets so rich an award for good conduct and industry."[2] This early Protestant stock would make significant contributions to America; among those born in Ulster were the fathers of presidents Andrew Jackson, James Buchanan, and Chester Alan Arthur, while presidents James Polk, Andrew Jackson, Ulysses Grant, Grover Cleveland, William and Benjamin Harrison, William McKinley, and Woodrow Wilson had Ulster-Scottish ancestry.

Throughout time the Ulster-Scots came to form a smaller percentage of Irish immigrants to the United States. By 1840, they accounted for a little more than 10 percent; however, from the 1840s to the end of the nineteenth century, Catholic immigration to the United States became a torrential flood. Beginning in 1845, a fungus called *Phytophthora infestans*—potato blight—brought tragedy to Ireland on an unprecedented scale. The population of Ireland had doubled from 4 to 8 million between

1800 and 1845; the vast majority were rural peasants who rented their lands from absentee British or Anglo-Irish landlords and lived at a subsistence level almost totally dependent on the potatoes they grew for food and payment of rent. Through the process of subdivision, the individual land holdings of tenants were pitiful; by 1841, a full 563,153 of 691,114 farms consisted of less than fifteen acres. Potatoes were nutritious and easy to grow; the Irish consumed 7 million potatoes a year, with the average adult working male in Ireland eating a staggering 14 pounds of potatoes per day, while the average adult Irish woman ate 11.2 pounds. It was a precariously balanced situation—lives lived on the outer edges of subsistence.

In 1845, half the crop failed; the following year, it was decimated. The potato crop had partially failed in the past, but this was unprecedented. The infamously harsh winter of 1846 saw people dying in droves from a combination of hunger, typhus, and dysentery—the latter frequently referred to as famine fever. The peak of the death toll occurred in the winter of 1847–1848, where in some districts as much as a quarter of the population perished. While the potato crop did not fail completely, in 1847 the majority of farmers had not sown seeds because they presumed it would fail again; others did not have any seeds to sow, while tens of thousands were evicted from their land for nonpayment of rent. Workhouses, set up to provide employment for the destitute, could not cope. In 1845, 6,000 had perished in the workhouses; two years later the figure was 66,000.

It was not just the failure of the potato crop that decimated Ireland; a laissez-faire capitalism employed by British authorities compounded the issue. Free markets, they believed, would solve the crisis, not food aid. Under armed guard, wheat, oats, and barley were exported to England while the Irish peasants starved. Charles E. Trevelyan, the British civil servant in charge of the relief efforts, viewed the famine as a divine solution to Irish overpopulation and believed God had visited the calamity on the country to teach the people a lesson. Exact figures are not possible, but most estimates suggest a million people died of starvation and illness during the course of the Great Famine of 1845–1847, while another million left the country—most of them fleeing to the United States.

The *Mayo Constitution* newspaper of October 31, 1848, reported that 143,632 immigrants had entered the port of New York through September of that year, of which 72,896—more than half—were Irish. Germany provided 40,731 people, while 17,223 noted their point of origin as England. Italy, synonymous with immigration to the United States during later periods of the nineteenth century, had a mere 241 immigrants, while a solitary Chinese person is marked on the register.

From 1840 to 1900, 3.6 million Irish people immigrated to the United States, with more than 1.7 million coming between 1840 and 1860. In each decade between 1820 and 1869, the Irish accounted for more than 35 percent of the total immigration to the United States, and in the four years after 1847—the very height of the famine in Ireland—1.8 million immigrants landed in New York, of whom 848,000 were Irish. After 1860, the figure gradually dropped, but the Great Famine had triggered a drastic demographic decline from which Ireland would never recover.

For the overwhelming majority of those who managed to survive the Atlantic crossing, there was no going back. Catholic emigrants overwhelmingly had a more difficult time establishing themselves in the United States compared to their Protestant predecessors. Many crossed the Atlantic Ocean as indentured servants; the vast majority of those who were lucky enough to arrive alive only had the clothes on their backs, never mind the resources to set up on their own holding like their earlier Protestant counterparts. Irish Catholic immigrants mostly settled in the urban area of the Northeast. Some moved on, but many could not. Apart from a lack of resources to get any further, they had seen too many of the limitations imposed by the vagaries and hardships of trying to make a living off the land: The Irish rejected the land because the land had rejected them.

While the Irish streamed to U.S. cities—particularly Boston and New York—America itself was experiencing dramatic urbanization. In 1830, only 10 percent of Americans lived in cities, while New York was the only urban center in the country with a population of more than 100,000. By 1900, 40 percent of Americans lived in cities, of which thirty-eight had a population of more than 200,000. During a span of a hundred years—from 1820 to 1920—19 million immigrants entered the United States, of whom 4.5 million were Irish.

The contrast between the environments the Irish had left behind and the urban maelstrom in which they found themselves upon arrival could not have been starker. Here there were dishonest money changers and brokers, people selling tickets for onward journeys that did not exist and others offering to carry the passenger's luggage and disappearing with it.

In the mid-1800s a majority of children living in New York City had at least one foreign-born parent. Neighborhoods throughout the city were frequently drawn along ethnic lines, the whole a complex mosaic of Russian, Polish, Jewish, Italian, African American, German, Bohemian, Chinese, Irish, and a host of others. Between 1847 and 1851 alone, 848,000 Irish entered the United States through the port of New York—the same number that had entered all the ports of North America combined in the previous two decades.

These staggering numbers of Irish immigrants to New York presented huge logistical difficulties for city authorities, and for all of the glories of the United States, the living conditions of many immigrants in New York were nothing short of a humanitarian crisis. Many of the Irish gravitated toward Lower Manhattan, the notorious crime-ridden Five Points area in particular. In 1835, renowned frontiersman Davy Crockett visited the area and compared the Irish of his acquaintance in the western states, who were "first-rate gentlemen," to the Five Pointers, who he thought "worse than savages . . . too mean to swab hell's kitchen."[3] Author Charles Dickens passed the same way in 1852, and noted the "hideous tenements which take their names from robbery and murder."[4] The popular press consistently portrayed the area as one dominated by public drunkenness, prostitution, and continual public violence.

The Irish Catholics in New York City were housed in abysmal tenements, often little more than outhouses. In the late nineteenth century, a report on tenement life in Five Points counted one bathtub for 1,321 families and one water tap for a floor of apartments. Five Points was an area heavily polluted by industry, where businesses using naphtha, benzene, and other flammables made fire a constant threat. Raw sewage and rodent infestations were endemic, while arbitrary eviction was common and disease rampant.

Irish immigrants suffered disproportionate health problems and bore the highest rates of cholera, typhoid, and typhus in the city. While some in the contemporary press had ascribed this to the Germans being cleaner and more orderly in their living habits, the reality was so many of the Irish arrived in the United States with their health already broken and did not have the financial resources of their German counterparts.

While the Five Points area stood out because of the sheer numbers living in the area, similar tenements were located in other parts of the city, virtually dominated by the Irish. Conditions were frequently little better than the notorious "coffin ships" that had carried the Irish immigrants across the Atlantic Ocean during the famine years. Poverty among Irish immigrants was endemic and grinding. In 1858, 64 percent of the admissions to the city's almshouses were Irish. They were also overrepresented in charity hospitals, lunatic asylums, and prisons.

The predominant view among American white Anglo-Saxon Protestants—the power brokers in American society who could, or claimed they could, date their arrival to the coming of the *Mayflower* to the country—was that the Irish were the very worst of incomers. These Irish Catholic immigrants were not like the industrious Scots-Irish who had arrived generations earlier during the colonial period: those hardworking and God-fearing folk of solid Protestant stock who had helped America fight for freedom and tame the frontier. These recent arrivals were poor, unskilled refugees who huddled together in their squalid urban tenements and—worst of all—were of the wrong religious persuasion.

The earlier Protestant immigrants had escaped the papists of Europe and an Ireland they had so despised, and now here were those very religious enemies turning up in their multitudes on their shores. Feelings toward the Vatican had softened little since the sailing of the *Mayflower* two centuries earlier. Stories circulated that the pope was sending his army to overthrow the American government, establish a new Vatican, and impose canonical law. Violence between Irish Catholic and Protestant nativist gangs was to become a central motif in the nineteenth-century American city. Until 1806, Catholics were barred from public office in the United States unless they swore a Test Oath renouncing the authority of the pope and Catholic doctrines. The abolition of the oath by New York State Assembly member David De Witt inevitably annoyed such nativist street gangs as the True Blue Americans and the Order of the Star-Spangled Banner, and on Christmas Eve of that year, St. Peter's Church was the first Catholic edifice to come under attack in the city. In 1831, St. Mary's Church—the third oldest in New York—was torched, while 1834 witnessed brutal and incessant street fighting in the Five Points area. When nativist groups threatened to burn the original St. Patrick's Cathedral—the most significant Catholic citadel in the city—the fiery Archbishop "Dagger" Hughes told Mayor John Harper that if it came to pass, New York would become another Moscow—the Russian city having recently been burned down during the course of the Napoleonic Wars.

Fights were often launched for the most spurious of reasons. On June 21, 1835, a riot broke out when an Irishman overturned an apple cart owned by a local vendor in the heart of the Five Points area. The Irish combatants claimed the argument had started when a native had earlier insulted an Irishman about drinking on the Sabbath. The discrimination against Irish immigrants in nineteenth-century America was not subtle, nor did it only involve physical violence.

The "No Irish Need Apply" advertisements and simian caricatures—most notoriously by cartoonist Thomas Nast—were imported wholesale to the United States from Victorian Britain, where they long had currency. Various anti-immigrant groups coalesced around the political party known as the "Know Nothings"—so called because they claimed to know nothing when questioned about their political viewpoints. Only native-born citizens could be elected to office in the Know Nothings, as long as they were not Roman Catholics. Protestantism defined the best of American society, and Catholicism was incompatible with American values. The Irish Catholic immigrants were an economic hindrance by taking jobs from "real" Americans and pushing down wages. Yet, despite this, or perhaps because of it, the Church loomed large in the lives of the recently arrived Irish Catholics during the course of the nineteenth century. Moreover, the parochial structure of the official church reinforced the clannish nature of Irish communities.

Of all the stereotypes propagated by the nativist-oriented media, it was the Irish as drunkards that was the most dominant and proved the most enduring. Nast—considered the father of the American cartoon and the inventor of the modern image of Santa Claus—despised the Irish and frequently represented them as dirty, riotous, monkey-like, and ill-educated in *Harper's Weekly*, but it was as drinkers he most frequently depicted them in his infamous sketches. *His First School*, for example, depicted a young Irish boy sitting at a bar surrounded by a fearsome looking group of men. The less-than-subtle implication was that Irish immigrants only learned what they knew from attending drinking establishments, not the educational institutions of the nation. *His Paddy-gree*, another of Nast's drawings on a similar theme, depicted a child in a pig sty brandishing a bottle of whiskey.

Nast converted from Catholicism to Protestantism, and his anti-Irish sentiment, it has been suggested, may have been a result of bullying during his childhood. He also witnessed the violence between Irish immigrants and African Americans in the New York Draft Riots, during which the Colored Orphan Asylum near his home was burned down. This has also been suggested as a motivating factor in his virulently anti-Irish ideology. Perhaps his most famous, or infamous, representation of the Irish is *The Day We Celebrate*, a portrayal of Saint Patrick's Day dating from 1867. The drawing depicts a mass brawl between a group of simian-faced men, a number of whom have bottles sticking out of their pockets; the word *blood* is written at the bottom left side, with *rum* scrawled on the other. And Nast influenced others to come: In 1860, Charles Kingsley described the Irish as "human chimpanzees," while three years later Charles Loring Brace published *Races of the Old World*, with illustrations depicting the Irish as ape-like in countenance, noting that the difference between the English and Irish skull was nine cubic inches, while it was only four between the average African and Irish.

Discrimination against the Irish Catholic in the workplace was commonplace. The vast majority ended up in low-paid, low-skilled jobs, for instance, longshoremen, canal diggers, hod carriers, quarry workers, and railroad and factory workers, thus providing a substantial amount of the cheap labor required to advance the booming American economy. Much of the work was degrading and dangerous, with frequent falls, crush injuries, and even drownings. Upward mobility in the work force for the Irish was slow. In 1860, 46 percent of male Irish immigrants worked in such low-paid, unskilled jobs as day laboring; by 1880, the figured remained steady at 47 percent. White-collar jobs were a rarity among Irish emigrants; in 1860, only one in a thousand Irish immigrants worked in the professions. The workplace proved an equally difficult environment for many Irish women. The majority of employed female Irish immigrants worked as household help in 1860, a proportion that grew only larger by 1880. Sometimes they were not even considered for such positions because of their nationality. An advertisement for a housekeeper from the *Daily Sun* in 1853, noted that the employer would consider applicants of any color and from any country, except Ireland. Such was the economic disenfranchisement of the Irish in American cities at the time.

The overwhelming majority of Irish immigrants, male and female, had come to the United States with no skills apart from their desire to work at anything to get a foothold in American society. They were ready to start at the bottom, a place that also happened to be occupied by many African Americans. The Irish were frequently referred to as "nigger Irish" or "white negro," and African Americans "smoked Irish." Still, while the racism experienced by Irish emigrants was unrelenting and brutal, the treatment of African Americans by some of the new Irish Americans cannot be overlooked. In one sense, it was out of kilter with the Irish temperament.

Daniel O'Connell, the leading voice for Irish nationalists in the United Kingdom, and Theobald Matthew, a famous cleric and leader of the temperance movement, both frequently voiced their abolitionist views. Frederick Douglass, former slave and African American abolitionist, had traveled throughout Ireland for four months in 1845 and 1846, during which time he gave more than fifty lectures to appreciative audiences: Douglass had found the Irish "warmhearted, generous, and sympathising with the oppressed everywhere."[5] But when it came to competition for resources in the New World, Douglass noted that the picture was different. Because the Irish had been persecuted so badly for so long in their own country, they were taught by "real" Americans to do the same to African Americans. In the American city, Douglass wrote, the Irish learned to "believe that we eat the bread that which of right belongs to them . . . that our adversity is essential to their prosperity."[6]

In North America, it was purely a matter of survival. Many Irish, struggling for jobs and acceptance, soon distanced themselves from African Americans, driving them from the workplace and neighborhoods like Five Points. This racism displayed by some Irish Americans toward African Americans—and other ethnic groups who subsequently came to the United States—was indicative of the greasy pole American society was proving to be. It was a dog-eat-dog battle to climb the social ladder, and the Irish were grimly determined to make their way up from the bottom; the African Americans and others who suffered at their hands were collateral damage in the often-brutal process of assimilation and advancement.

From the start, Irish immigrants demonstrated a strong propensity to stick together in the cities of their new home; clubs and societies like the Irish Emigrant Society of New York, established in 1841, provided assistance to the impoverished who continued to flood into the city on a daily basis. It provided advice to immigrants looking for employment and attempted to achieve redress for those who had been conned into buying bogus drafts when sending home money to others who wished to cross the Atlantic.

The strong sense of ethnic identity brought to the United States by the native Irish was perhaps most famously demonstrated in the establishment of parades on Saint Patrick's Day each March 17, with the first iteration held as far back as 1732, in Boston, followed by a New York version in 1762. The choice of date for Saint Patrick's Day had historical resonance; until the practice was banned in 1802, straw effigies were burned on "Pope Day"—March 17. This unique celebration grew and grew in subsequent decades; by 1872, the New York City parade attracted 50,000 participants and a crowd of 500,000.

The American branch of the Ancient Order of Hibernians, longtime organizers of the parade, proved to be the most enduring of the benevolent societies formed for the support of Irish immigrants. Originally founded in May 1836, in St. James' Church near the Five Points area, it had as its original purpose the protection of churches from attack by nativist gangs and other anti-Catholic elements.

Not all of the societies formed were motivated by the desire to materially help the incoming Irish, however; others were more interested in political agendas. The Fenian Brotherhood was formed in New York in 1858, by John O'Mahoney and Michael Doheny, with the avowed aim of advancing the nationalist cause in Ireland, primarily among the legions of embittered immigrants. John Devoy became the driving force behind Clan na Gael, the most significant nationalist body in the United States, which was successful in fundraising and, to a lesser degree, recruiting members in the United States. Many Irish men, who had fought in the American Civil War on the Union side, were deeply embittered by the treatment they had experienced from British authorities in Ireland and eager to provide training to new Clan na Gael recruits. Not only would these often-impoverished former soldiers be instrumental in helping Ireland achieve its long-standing wish for freedom for the people left behind, but also these men believed their activities would enhance their status in the New World.

Nineteenth-century New York was a hive of Irish nationalism. County societies abounded: The first to be formed was the Sligo Young Men's Association in 1849, providing social outlets, employment assistance, and disability and death benefits to members. In 1856, the New York Catholic Library Association was founded, and in 1860, a branch of the Ossianic Society of Dublin opened in New York with the aim of promoting the translation and publication of manuscripts in the Irish language. Arguably, no other ethnic group in the city concerned themselves as much with their mother country as did the Irish.

While clubs and fraternal organizations provided solace to the Irish in a foreign land, the greatest triumph of the Irish Catholic immigrants in New York and other cities in the United States was through the ballot box; they overwhelmingly supported the Democratic Party and voted in greater numbers than any other ethnic group. Long accustomed to the political machinations that for centuries had engulfed their native country and upheld the power of the British colonizer, the Irish knew the power of politics; they managed to turn their disadvantage to their advantage. Irish emigrants had been politically seasoned by the struggle to disestablish the Anglican Church, repeal the hated Act of Union with England, and, perhaps most of all, implement land ownership reforms.

The machinations of the Democratic Party machine in New York in the late nineteenth century and the first decades of the twentieth century are often referred to as Tammany Hall, in honor of its original incarnation as the Society of Saint Tammany, or the Sons of Saint Tammany. And the history of Tammany Hall mirrors the development of the Irish community: The Irish had to literally break into it to become members. In 1817, a group of Irish immigrants stormed Tammany headquarters to protest discrimination against them by the then-nativist body. Although they were grudgingly accepted in the beginning, the hordes of Irish poor became valuable commodities and were welcomed with open arms when New York State abolished the property vote and conceded universal franchise in 1821. Thereafter, Tammany evolved from a bastion of nativism to a high church of Irish power in New York. With its labyrinthine structure, its tentacles reached into all corners of the community. At its height, the political structures of the organization comprised thirty-two thousand people.

Political involvement for the Irish had little to do with ideology or morality: It was a means to make a living and obtain a foothold in American society. In the early years, the Irish achieved a succession of symbolic victories through Tammany; it pressured legislators to overturn a ban on Catholic chaplains ministering to Catholic inmates in prisons and Catholic patients in hospitals, and engineered a situation where the King James Bible was no longer the only version that could be used in schools. Postfamine Irish immigrants flocked to the Democratic Party, and by 1880, Tammany Hall had achieved what had previously been thought impossible and maneuvered William R. Grace—a son of Irish Catholic immigrants—into position as mayor of New York.

Throughout time, it was the control of the public purse that would become the biggest weapon in an increasingly Irish Catholic–dominated Tammany Hall. The number of public works contracts awarded to Irish men increased dramatically, while the numbers of teachers, firemen, and policemen of Irish birth and extraction in service to the city grew exponentially.

This uniquely American tapestry of Catholicism, clannishness, Irish nationalism, poverty, and fealty to the Tammany political machine defined the paths taken by the majority of Irish immigrants to New York in the latter half of the nineteenth century. Moreover, as the new century dawned, it also gave rise to what would become another central component of the social fabric in the United States, as well as the image of American identity itself: sports.

2

AMERICAN SPORTS

Irish Whales

Irish immigrants have long been synonymous with sporting achievement in the United States. The role played by the Irish in the history of American boxing, for example, is astounding. Between 1853 and 1899, twelve of America's thirteen undisputed heavyweight champions were Irish-born or had at least one Irish parent, while nine world champions between 1870 and 1920 were first-generation Irish or of Irish extraction. Such was the reputation of the Irish as boxers that many non-Irish pugilists changed their names to those typically found in the old country. World heavyweight champion Jack Sharkey, for example, was born Joseph Paul Zukauska, a son of Lithuanian immigrants.

Baseball also saw a multitude of Irish participants, many of whom reached the highest level of the game. Among famous names of nineteenth-century players celebrated in the Baseball Hall of Fame in Cooperstown, New York, are Mike "King" Kelly, Cornelius McGillicuddy, known as "Connie Mack," and "Smiling Mickey" Welch. The great Connie Mack reputedly acquired his shortened designation because his full name would not fit on the scoreboard. An estimated one-third of major-league players in the 1890s were Irish, and they were also prominent in management as the game developed; by 1910, Irish managers made up a little less than two-thirds of those in both the National and American Leagues. At the opening of the 1915 season, nine of the sixteen managers in the leagues were Irish, while eleven of the sixteen most successful managers in the 1920s were of Irish descent.

When Bill Joyce, manager of New York Giants, was asked which nation made the best baseball players, he pointed to the Irish. "Give me a good Irish infield and I will show you a good team," he said. "I don't mean that it is necessary to have them all Irish, but you want two or three quick-thinking [Irish] . . . to keep the Germans and others moving. I don't want to be accused of casting reflections on any nationality, but there is no question that it takes the Irish to keep the world agoing."[1] It was a commonly expressed sentiment in many quarters, so much so that Jerrold Casway termed the 1890s the "Emerald Age of Baseball." The number of Irish-born baseball players was truly extraordinary for a country that did not have a tradition of playing the game. Until 2009, Ireland still had more major-league players than Japan; however, it was an early flourishing that would not last. Thirteen Irish players debuted in the 1870s, nineteen in the 1880s, seven in the 1890s, six in the 1900s, and two in the 1910s: Just two debuted in the twentieth century, and there have been none since Joe Cleary made one appearance for the Washington Senators in 1945.

Boxing and baseball were not the only sports with a strong Irish connection. Pedestrianism—now known as ultra-running—was a particularly popular sport in nineteenth-century America in which the Irish were prominent; the multitudes were intrigued to see how long athletes could keep going until they had to give up. As far back as 1835, Patrick Mahoney from Kenmare, County Kerry, came in third in the "Great Foot Race" held on Union Course Race Track on Long Island on April 24. Competitors were offered $1,000 to run 10 miles in an hour, and 20,000 spectators saw the 33-year-old Irishman finish behind American Henry Stannard and Prussian athlete George Glauer. Later on, Daniel O'Leary from County Cork was a noted practitioner and famously once defeated Edward Payson Weston—the so-called "Champion Pedestrian of the World"—in a six-day walk held in Chicago. O'Leary went on to beat records established by Weston, most notably by once covering 116 miles in less than twenty-four hours. Those involved in the sport were not universally appreciated: One newspaper referred to participants as the "worst class of New York."[2]

In 1896, Irish immigrant John J. McDermott won the first marathon held in the United States when he ran from Stanford, Connecticut, to the

Columbia Oval in the Bronx, in a relatively leisurely time of 3 hours, 25 minutes, and 55 seconds, and on April 19 of the following year, he went on to win the inaugural Boston Marathon, beating another Irishman, J. J. Kiernan, into second place.

Other professional sports also had a rub of the green. James "Squire" Butler was a leading jockey, going on to own the Empire City racetrack in Yonkers, where he found himself waging constant warfare against the patrician New York Jockey Club. Irish Americans Michael Phelan and Dudley Kavanagh were two of the early big stars in billiards, instrumental in transforming it from a novelty barroom pastime to a popular spectator sport. Phelan was widely considered the most "scientific" of players and wrote the first book about the sport, while Kavanagh was known as the "Champion Billiard Player of America" and played in the first-ever game where admission was charged. Phelan would have a lasting legacy in American—and world—popular sporting culture with his invention of the game of pool. The Irishman designed it to be played in the smaller spaces of saloons where the working classes congregated. Billiards was generally played in gentlemen's clubs or large private homes, although billiards halls later became popular.

In the more genteel world of tennis, Maurice McLoughlin, a son of Irish immigrants, was a highly regarded champion credited as the man who made it a sport of the common man. Henry Chandler Egan, John J. McDermott, Mike Brady, and Tom McNamara, all of Irish immigrant stock, were highly talented golfers, with McDermott winning the U.S. Open in 1911 and 1912, while Egan won an Olympic gold medal for the team at the 1904 games in St. Louis. Egan also took silver in the individual golf competition.

However, despite the riches many participants acquired from their sporting participation, professional athletes were not viewed in a positive light by blue-blooded white Anglo-Saxon Protestant Americans; even the word *sport* was used derogatorily to describe a person with a flamboyant lifestyle. The respectable classes glorified the Corinthian ideals of amateur sports and looked askance at any sport that involved payment to the athlete or, even more objectionably, betting. It was in the amateur arena that the real values befitting a gentleman were forged, these arbiters of morality believed. Sportswriter Caspar Whitney, an early proponent of the Olympic movement in the United States, infamously wrote that the "vermin" of the professional athletic class had no place in amateur sports.

Whitney, most famous for coming up with the concept of an All-American team in college football and as president of the American Olympic Committee between 1906 and 1910, bemoaned the idea of bringing together in sports two divergent elements of society that never met elsewhere on even terms. [3]

Of all the sports in which the Irish participated boxing was particularly reviled, with the moral bona fides of the many boxers of Irish extraction constantly questioned. John L. Sullivan, an Irish American heavyweight boxing champion of the world, might have been a hero to the immigrant masses, but there were plenty in Boston who did not warm to his exploits. That Sullivan was famous for wearing green shorts and often expressed his dislike of the English did not help his case. After a fight in Canada he once refused to toast Her Majesty because a "true Irish man never drinks to the health of a British ruler, king or queen." [4]

When it came to Irish American sporting endeavors, critics did not limit themselves to professional sports. Elements of the American press were quietly happy to point out the violence in the native sports of Gaelic football and hurling, which the Irish had brought across the Atlantic. The *Gaelic American* was never a newspaper to take accusations of brutality in Irish sports lightly and once responded to an article in the *New York Times* that suggested Gaelic footballers only kicked the ball when they could not kick the man, with a stinging retort, damning American football in the process. Gaelic footballers, it pointed out, did not have to wear "ear or nose protectors, shoulder or hip pads, masks, or leather" to guard themselves against injury, and there had never been a fatality among those who played the game in the United States. Irishmen played with earnestness, and any anger displayed was just a "burlesque," it claimed.

As well as their native sports of Gaelic football and hurling, the Irish had brought traditions of amateur athletics—particularly in the throwing disciplines—to the United States, but they were not welcomed with open arms in the rarefied milieu of organizations like the famed New York Athletic Club (NYAC), dominated as it was by Anglocentric white Protestants. The NYAC, the preeminent amateur athletic club on the East Coast, dated back to 1868, when John Babcock, Henry Buermeyer, and William Curtis gathered at the Knickerbocker Cottage, a popular bar on Sixth Avenue and 28th Street in Manhattan, to discuss the establishment of a sporting organization where gentlemen amateurs could practice the popular amateur sporting pursuits of the day. Among other things the

NYAC introduced bicycle racing and the sport of fencing to the United States; hosted the country's first indoor track meet; and organized the first American championships in track and field, boxing, and wrestling. From the start, its members included the great and the good of New York society. When the NYAC's first branch was established in 1885, on 55th Street and Sixth Avenue, the opening gala was a glamorous occasion attended by most all of Mrs. Astor's famous "400," a list of New York's social elite created by Caroline Webster Astor in about 1872, consisting of those of old, moneyed stock and others who had become recently rich as a result of the Industrial Revolution. There were, needless to say, no Irish Catholic names on the prestigious list.

The ostensible shunning of Catholic Irish from the likes of the NYAC was for the supposed predilection of the Irish to professional sport; the real reason was bigotry. The Irish were equally interested in participating under the amateur ethos but throughout time would be forced to do so largely under their own flags of convenience. If an Irish immigrant—and those of other ethnic groups—was to become involved in athletics, it would prove easier to do so in settings other than these exclusive environments typified by the NYAC, with its roll call of Belmonts, Roosevelts, and others of the cream of New York Knickerbocker society. It would be almost three decades before the NYAC would openly have members from outside their own select elites. This led to a situation where athletes from the same country often formed their own clubs to compete in amateur athletics. It would be in such clubs that Irish Americans would make their single biggest contribution to American sports.

Above all other men who crossed the Atlantic Ocean from Ireland in search of a better life and an amateur sporting outlet in the United States, it would be a group of weight throwers—subsequently to become known as the "Irish Whales"—who would shine brightest on the New World stage. James "Jim" Mitchell, John Flanagan, Matt McGrath, Pat McDonald, Martin Sheridan, and Paddy Ryan would win a remarkable 12 gold, 8 bronze, and 2 silver Olympic medals for the United States. Con Walsh, the seventh Whale, added another competing for Canada. Between them they would claim 80 Amateur Athletic Union titles in the throwing disciplines: 32 in the hammer, 37 for throwing the 56-pound weight, 7 in the shot put, and 4 in the discus.

The origins of the term *Irish Whales* is not entirely clear, but it was first recorded in John Tiernan's famous *New York Times* column "Sports of the Times," written in a piece by John Drebinger, who was deputizing for the absent Tiernan. Longtime sports correspondent Arthur Daley later wrote in the same column how he believed the name dated to the U.S. team's journey to the 1912 Stockholm Olympic Games. Dan Ferris, an American athletics official who had traveled with the team, told Daley how the Irish throwers were sitting at a table together when a tiny waiter came to take their order. The employee had the misfortune of having the job for the duration of the journey, and by the time the athletes reached Stockholm he had lost twenty pounds, according to Ferris. Each man took five plates of soup as a starter and then had "three or four steaks with trimmings."[5] At one point, as the exhausted waiter walked by Ferris, he supposedly uttered the immortal words, "It's whales they are, not men." Daley considered it an appropriate designation, claiming they never worried about their waistlines or their training, ate an enormous amount of food, and drank vast quantities of beer, which never affected their performances.

In 1964, Daley again wrote of the Irish weight throwers, once more placing emphasis on their eating habits. He noted, "Some of their greatest feats were at the table."[6] He recounted a time when a number of the group were competing at an athletics meet in Baltimore. One of the Whales placed an order for a postmeet snack with the head waiter at a local restaurant, requesting "twenty-seven dozen oysters and six huge T-bone steaks." The waiter set the table for a party of thirty-three and was surprised when only three men turned up to consume the food. He asked them if they wanted to wait for the rest of their party, but they just laughed and started to tuck into the food. This may well be how this unprecedented group of athletes derived their name. It might simply have been that so many of them were so big or they wore the blue uniform of the New York Police Department. Wherever the name came from, there is no doubting that they truly were whales of men. The first of these behemoths to cross the Atlantic Ocean was Jim Mitchell.

3

JAMES "JIM" MITCHELL
AND THE IRISH INVASION

On September 16, 1888, fifty-three athletes and officials left the port of Queenstown (now Cobh), County Cork, in the southernmost part of Ireland (then part of the British Empire) aboard the SS *Wisconsin*, bound for fabled New York City. The plan for this so-called "Irish Invasion" was the brainchild of Maurice Davin, cofounder of the Gaelic Athletic Association (GAA) and the man who, along with Michael Cusack, wrote the first set of rules for the native Irish sports of Gaelic football and hurling. The organization had been formed only three years earlier by a group of like-minded cultural nationalists who looked askance at the continued encroachment in Ireland of such British codified sports as soccer, rugby, and cricket, to the detriment of native pursuits. Their avowed desire was to codify and promote Gaelic football, hurling, and athletics in an Ireland they hoped would soon be free.

At a meeting of the Central Council of the GAA held at Limerick Junction in County Tipperary on July 6, 1888, Davin first addressed the members about his bold idea of a transatlantic visit. For some time, he told them, he had been considering sending a body of representative Gaels to the United States to showcase the association there and afford immigrants and American native Irish an opportunity to see Irish pastimes played by the best. The traveling group he envisaged would include two hurling teams selected from the greatest exponents of the game in the country, as well as a number of men considered the most able all-round athletes in the nation; in the end the touring party would be comprised of

25 hurlers, 18 athletes, and 10 officials. The hoped-for result of the trip was to further strengthen the nascent GAA in the United States among the immigrant Irish communities and pave the way for an annual athletics and hurling contest between the two countries. If all went well, hurling could even become one of the great American sports, Davin believed. Additionally, it was envisioned the trip would allow the organization to pay off some of its existing debts, with the surplus used to fund a revived version of the Tailteann Games, the ancient Irish sporting festival and a project close to the heart of the nationalistically minded Davin.

In a time of burgeoning political and cultural nationalism the trip appeared to be a perfect plan for the youthful organization. The project would not only demonstrate the athletic abilities of the Irish, but also showcase the GAA's—and by extension the Irishman's—ability to organize a complex logistical task. It was a project worthy of a race of people who no longer should be under the jackboot of the oppressor. It would, they believed, bring pride to the generations of Irish men and women who had long made the United States of America—particularly the great cities of the East Coast—their home. The Gael was rising once again to try and overthrow the mantle of oppression that had been cast over his beloved homeland for seven hundred years by the British Empire. The hour of freedom was coming; the clouds would soon part and let the sun shine brightly on the green fields of Erin. These fine men, Davin and his associates believed, would be in the vanguard of the new dispensation. Famed U.S. cities like New York, long home to generations of Irish men and women, could only have been impressed by the venture. The GAA estimated the "Invasion," as it was called from the start, would net the organization an estimated £5,000 from gate receipts. It was a lofty ambition and an exciting plan.

The endeavor got off to a great start. As the Irish party sailed out of the port, bands played and huge crowds on the quays wished them a safe voyage. Pat Davin—a brother of Maurice—kept a diary of the proceedings. Pat was a talented athlete himself; in 1878 alone, he captured national Irish titles in the high jump, long jump, and 120-yard hurdles. When the invasion team landed in the United States, he had hoped to compete in an all-around athletic competition against the best in the land. After no suitable candidate could be found he placed an advertisement in American newspapers calling on a suitable adversary to come forward, but no one did—a fact he later bemoaned in his autobiography as one of the great disappointments of his athletic career.

The first evening aboard the SS *Wisconsin* was idyllic; the Irishmen danced late into the night with their fellow passengers from Germany, Sweden, and Russia, according to Pat Davin's diary. It was to prove too good to be true. In the middle of the night a vicious storm arose; many of the Irishmen had never before been at sea and were badly affected. Davin noted that this was particularly the case with the majority of the hurlers, as they came from inland parts of Ireland. The hurlers, he wrote, remained up, saying their prayers, and "expected every minute to be their last."[1] Passengers were thrown about the deck like "dead dogs," with men, women, and children heaped together. Things did not get any better when the passengers saw a small boat bobbing in the sea with only the stump of its mast remaining. Nine days later, the weary seagoers disembarked in New York, where the *Herald* eulogized the new arrivals:

> It would prove a difficult task to bring together at short notice a more impressive assemblage of specimens of manhood that the half-hundred clear-complexioned and clean-limbed, stalwart, bright-eyed, muscular, strapping, and fine-looking young fellows who were grouped on the deck of the steamship "Wisconsin" at noon yesterday. The crowd would have inspired an artist in quest of a model for "a picture of health." They were the representatives of Ireland's muscular Christianity called from every county from the Emerald Isle—literally the flower of Erin's manhood.[2]

The journalist was equally impressed by the Irish athletes' clothing:

> Their attire was as characteristic as their appearance, their "reefers," cutaways, Ulster, and Inverness capes were of soft, warm, national frieze. Most of them wore knee-breeches, and all carried blackthorn or furze sticks, that would more than pose a match for the hickory or "locust" [police nightstick] of one of the finest.

Here was a group of men the Irish immigrant could be proud of.

The tour got off to a rocky start when one of the Irish athletes lost control of a hammer at a practice session in Manhattan and seriously injured a spectator, but proceedings improved after that, albeit temporarily. According to Davin's diary, the hurling exhibition matches drew huge praise in the New York press and created a "veritable hurricane of excitement and applause."[3] The matches may have been called exhibitions, but there were some ferocious encounters. In the Manhattan Grounds, at least a dozen hurling sticks were broken in one match.[4] Not long into the tour, the hurlers ran out of sticks and had to get some made; the only wood available was hickory, widely used to make baseball bats at that time. The "clash of the hickory" did not have the same ring to it as the "clash of the ash." (Hurling sticks are normally made from ash wood, and the phrase "clash of the ash" is frequently used to describe the game.) Hurling sticks made from hickory were not as durable as those made from Irish ash, and supplies had to be continually renewed. But problems with the equipment aside, elements of the American press were greatly impressed by the spectacle of the games. News about the trip even made the headlines in Australia, where the *Freeman's Journal* eulogized the "men of nerve and muscle" and the "splendid shoulders and arms" of James Mitchell.[5]

Pat Davin made some wonderful observations in his diary about the effects the tour had on Irish people who had made the United States their home. On one occasion where one of the hurlers gave a hurling stick to three old Irish women, it brought back such memories that each of them took it in turn and "kissed it with reverence," while "all three wept copiously." It was a proud moment for those Irish immigrants to see the talented athletes from the old country coming to perform in their adopted home. Now they could show their fellow Americans the athletic glories of the Gael and the proud heritage of their forbearers. The majority of Irish immigrants may have come to the New World with nothing but the clothes on their backs, but they had a proud history and sports were an important part of it.

Upon arrival in each city, the Irish group was met by pipe and brass bands, and paraded to their hotels, but unfortunately, the adventure was blighted by ill luck. American athletics was divided by two competing administrative bodies at that time, and despite the GAA trying to remain neutral, the disharmony resulted in only fifteen exhibition hurling matches, while the athletes only competed on nine occasions, much fewer than Maurice Davin and his fellow organizers had anticipated. The United States was also preoccupied with the presidential election between Republican nominee Benjamin Harrison and Democratic incumbent Grover Cleveland, and the athletes did not gain as much attention in the press as they had been led to believe they would, even among publications oriented toward the Irish American community.

The Irish invaders made appearances in New York; Boston; Philadelphia; Newark and Paterson, New Jersey; Providence, Rhode Island; and Lowell, Massachusetts. In addition to the U.S. fixtures, the group had planned a two-week tour of Canada; however, it had to be cancelled due to adverse weather conditions. The unfortunate combination of factors resulted in the touring group running out of money halfway through the venture, and Maurice Davin was forced to rely on the good offices of Michael Davitt—founder of the Land League political movement in Ireland and a patron of the GAA—to send the impoverished athletes £450 to get them through the rest of their time in North America. Davin hoped he would be able to raise sufficient funds to at least pay off the loan from Davitt by having an end-of-tour spectacular exhibition at Madison Square Garden in New York, but despite drawing a huge crowd, this too proved ill-fated.

After the exhibition the American organizers presented the touring party with a bill for $75, which, they claimed, was the net loss they had suffered from the night. It was, according to Davin, a "cruel and shameless trick." The whole venture had proven a major disappointment for the Irish group. To add salt to the party's wounds, there had been an earlier American tour by Irish sportsmen with a much smaller group of athletes in 1885, which had proved a success; the big "Irish Invasion" of 1888 could only be termed a failure in financial terms. The touring party not only lost money, but also men. When Davin's diary turned up for sale in 2016, the true extent of the diminution of the party was highlighted in the media. When the returning group turned up at the port to board the *City of Rome* on October 31, Davin was taken aback. The ship, he wrote, sailed away "bearing the sad remnant" of the fifty-three hurlers and athletes who had landed on U.S. soil five weeks earlier, with only twenty-four men returning to their native sod.

Some of those who stayed in the United States went on to have further success in the sporting arena. John J. Mooney from County Cork joined the Xavier Athletic Club and had a successful career as a long jumper, even setting an unofficial world leading mark on a trip back to Ireland in 1894. Fellow Cork man William McCarthy competed as a middle-distance runner with the Manhattan Athletic Club, while J. J. Connery was a pole vaulter of note with the Star Athletic Club. Still, of those who chose to remain, it was James "Jim" Mitchell—the first of the group of Irishmen who would later become known as the "Irish Whales"—who would create the greatest impression on the world of American sports.

Jim Mitchell's ascension to the top of the sport of throwing was meteoric and unprecedented. Within four days of his stateside arrival he smashed three existing records by throwing 125 feet, 10 inches in the unlimited run and follow hammer at Brooklyn; 58 feet, 2 inches in the 14-pound weight throw at Boston; and 118 feet, 11 inches from the 9-foot hammer circle in New York.[6] From 1889 to 1896, he went on to win eight American hammer championships in a row while holding the 56-pound throw title from 1891 to 1896, inclusively. It was an astounding achievement.

Mitchell was unassailable, and wherever he went he was the subject of intense fascination, his size alone intimidating other competitors. His throwing brought the sport into a new dimension. Born on January 30, 1864, in Bartoose, a townland near the small village of Emly in County Tipperary, James Sarsfield Mitchell was, like the other Irish Whales, of rural farming stock. He had served notice of his athletic prowess as a fourteen-year-old, competing predominantly in the quarter-mile foot race and the high jump; by seventeen he was able to clear 5 feet, 10 inches. Given the physical colossus he would become in later life, it is difficult to imagine Mitchell as a high jumper and almost impossible to believe he was once a specialist in long sprints.

Photographs of his time as a competitive hammer thrower in his later career in the United States show him to be as wide as a barn gate—a man who in all likelihood would struggle to run a hundred yards. After Mitchell broke both of his ankles in 1882, competing in a high-jump competition—easy to believe given the effects a man his size might suffer under the pressure of his own body weight—he turned his attention to the hugely popular sport of throwing and, like other men of his time, regularly competed in a range of events in the discipline. He first served notice of his prowess on June 3, 1885, when he threw the 14-pound weight—sometimes referred to as the "winding weight"—a little more than fifty-one feet. At the first-ever GAA national athletic championships, held on October 5 of the same year in Tramore, County Kerry, the young Mitchell was narrowly beaten in the 28-pound throw but was awarded the challenge cup in the 16-pound hammer for a throw of 106 feet, 6 inches. It was a fantastic start to the young man's throwing career.

Speaking in 1887, Mitchell ascribed his ardor for the throwing events in athletics to the inspirational fictional character of Matt "The Thresher," hero of the hugely popular novel *Knocknagow* (1873)—subtitled *The Homes of Tipperary*—by Charles Kickham, a fellow Tipperary man. It was an appropriate choice. The hero of Kickham's novel, Matt "The Thresher" O'Donovan, was an avowed nationalist, a talented sledge thrower, and a man of the common people. In a key scene in the novel Matt defeated Captain French, a son of the local landlord, in a hammer-throwing competition. If the description of Captain French's throwing is an accurate representation, the techniques used then were not a world removed from today:

> He took the heavy sledge, and placing his foot to the mark, swung it backwards and forwards twice, and then wheeling rapidly full round, brought his foot to the mark again, and flying from his arms as from a catapult, the sledge sailed through the air, and fell at a distance that seemed to startle many spectators. [7]

Mitchell identified with a hero who represented the ordinary tenant farmers of the nation—a broth of a boy who brought glory to his people through sporting achievement and demonstrated the power of the native Gael to the British landowning class. It was a motif that was to follow the Irish Whales throughout the course of their illustrious careers, both in Ireland and the New World.

Jim Mitchell pursued a relentless path to the top of the throwing events in Ireland. In November 1885, he broke the existing Irish record held by Doctor William J. M. "Jumbo" Barry—a highly regarded all-round athlete and medical doctor from Cork, and a man so intellectually able he was said to have passed his medical examinations in one year at Edinburgh University. Barry is rightly considered the first great competitive Irish hammer thrower and won the British Amateur Athletic Association (AAA) title five times between 1885 and 1895, but was soon overhauled by Mitchell in the record stakes. In the next three years, Mitchell went on to dominate throwing in the British Isles, and by the time he arrived in the United States as part of the Irish invasion at the age of twenty-four, he had won a remarkable seventeen national titles in the GAA All-Ireland Athletics Championships between 1885 and 1888, and also the Irish Amateur Athletic Association (IAAA) shot put title in 1887. His fame had also spread to Britain, where he had won three successive

AAA hammer titles between 1886 and 1888, in addition to shot put titles in 1886 and 1887.

There is no doubting that the GAA played a central role in the development of the Irish weight-throwing tradition; when the organization was formed in 1884, athletics absorbed much of its initial energies. Its main concern was wrestling control of athletics from existing British influence; at the organization's first meeting, Gaelic football and hurling only came up for discussion after a prolonged debate on athletics and the continual encroachment of the British athletic authorities on the track and field system in Ireland. Of particular concern to GAA authorities was the ongoing establishment of new athletic clubs, primarily in the eastern region of the country, under the auspices of British authorities. The British had brought their increasingly codified sports with them wherever the writ of empire ran, using schools, in particular, to aid in the development of cricket, soccer, athletics, and rugby, among other sports. Industrialization had brought new systems of regulation, with games moving from informal recreation to strictly regulated competitions. The Football Association and the Rugby Football Union, for example, introduced standardized rules that would apply throughout the country and the empire, to replace the variants played in different communities. The Corinthian values developed in sporting participation according to systematic regulations on the playing fields of England, the ideology went, shaped the character of the right sort of man to ensure the empire was well administered in distant parts. Here the qualities of discipline, leadership, strength, vitality, and loyalty could be developed, a worldview typified by the views of J. E. C. Weldon, principal of the illustrious Harrow School between 1881 and 1895:

> The pluck, the energy, the perseverance, the good temper, the self-control, the discipline, the cooperation, the esprit de corps, which merit success in cricket or football, are the very qualities which win the say in peace or war. . . . In the history of the British Empire it is written that England has owed her sovereignty to sports. [8]

Many of the richest of the upper echelons of Irish society—largely the Anglo-Irish—sent their children to be educated in schools like Harrow, from where they returned with knowledge of these newly codified sports, which they passed on through their social networks. The military—also controlled by British authorities as the colonial overlords—provided a secondary vector for the spread and codification of athletics in Ireland. That there was a considerable overlap between the officer class in the army and attendance at British public schools copper-fastened the socioeconomic administration of athletics; the sport was largely monopolized by those from the elite classes in Ireland, particularly in Dublin.

On February 28, 1857, the Dublin University Football Club Races were held for the first time at Trinity College; such was the popularity of the event that ten years later, the races became a two-day festival. The College Races were attended by the political power brokers of the city and country, including the Lord Lieutenant—the most powerful political figure in Ireland—and leavened with novelty with the inclusion of such events as dropping the football, throwing a cricket ball, and a "cigar race," where the competitors had to keep lit cigars in their mouths for the duration of a short sprint.

The races even attracted competitors from England, and student athletes from Trinity College were so motivated to win they saw fit to hire professional trainers to prepare them for the proceedings. The august college had no pavilion at the time, but marquees and reserved enclosures were provided for the notable attendees, who included army and naval officers, members of the judiciary, and important landowners, all of whom were given complimentary tickets for the occasion. It was a world far removed from the lives of the rural Irish peasantry, who were extensively involved in the "Land Wars" during that time, fighting tooth and tail to get better rights and protection from summary evictions off their land.

The social profile of entrants in the College Races might best be judged by the prizes awarded to winners. In 1883, among the goodies given out were a silver salver, a Gladstone bag, a crocodile ink stand, and an oak salad bowl—not prizes that the average country peasant would aspire to owning. Trinity College was a bastion of Anglo-Irish and Protestant culture; the Catholic Church did not allow its members to attend without a letter of dispensation from their local bishop until 1904, although Trinity had allowed Catholics to attend beginning in 1793, but few took them up on the offer.

Class distinction was also a serious barrier in the annual civil-service games; only competitors coming under the heading "gentleman athletes" were allowed to participate. The rules were explicit in outlining those who were barred from competing:

Any person who has ever competed in an open competition, or for public money, or for admission money, or with professionals, for a prize, public money, or admission money, or at any period of his life taught or assisted the pursuit of athletic exercise as a means of livelihood; or is a mechanic, artisan, or laborer.[9]

It was the last clause that gave away the Victorian ideology—and snobbery—underpinning these athletic meets. The rules of the 1878 Henley Regatta, for example, were virtually identical: "No person shall be considered an amateur oarsman or sculler . . . who is or has been in trade or employment for wages as a mechanic, artisan, or laborer."[10]

Codified sports were the preserve of the amateur gentleman, and if you did not fit the definition as decided by the elites, you were not welcome. In a society like Ireland, overwhelmingly made up of small-holding rural farmers and low-paid workers, this substantially narrowed the potential number of competitors.

The spread of such "foreign games" as rugby, soccer, and athletics organized according to rules codified by the British did not sit well with cultural nationalists like Michael Cusack and Maurice Davin, who viewed this move as further evidence that Great Britain wished to control every aspect of Irish society—a further form of cultural colonization.

Davin and his followers had experienced enough British encroachment on organized sports in Ireland. Thus, the primary mission of the GAA was to gain a form of cultural "home rule"—the ever-longed-for political aspiration for the entire country—through the promotion of native Irish sports, and the resistance to increasing Anglicization through sporting organizations, including athletic clubs, was paramount to achieving this goal. From its establishment, the GAA consistently encouraged local sports days throughout Ireland—throwing events, in particular—and Maurice Davin was a several-time national hammer-throwing champion when competitions were regularized. He believed there was no better exercise than weight-throwing and even had a rudimentary gym with weights made at his home in Clonmel, County Tipperary.

Davin kept a notebook during the 1870s outlining his meticulous preparations for competitions, noting his daily diet and the particular dangers of cigarette smoking, which he believed would result in a man amounting to nothing. He famously came out of retirement in 1881, at the age of thirty-nine, to compete in the British Amateur Athletic Championships after becoming annoyed when the English press suggested there were no talented athletes left in Ireland. After training for two weeks, Davin took the hammer and shot put titles. Michael Cusack was also a weight thrower of some proficiency, and it is likely that the two men's paths first crossed at the 1875 Irish athletic championships.

As well as viewing the encroachment of the British Amateur Athletic Association in Ireland as an extension of colonial powers, Davin and Cusack did not like the emphasis the British put on track events to the detriment of the field. They believed the field events of jumping and throwing were better suited to the Irish temperament, a fact Cusack alluded to in a historically significant article called "A Word about Irish Athletics," published in the *United Ireland* and the *Irishman*—both nationalistically orientated journals—in October 1884. Cusack called on Irish people to "take the management of their games into their own hands, to encourage and promote in every way every form of athletics which is peculiarly Irish, and to remove with one swoop everything that is foreign and iniquitous in the present system."[11] He believed the Irish should no longer have to compete under the rules of a body he considered to be unrepresentative of Irish interests. It was time to end the situation whereby athletic meetings in Ireland were held according to the rules of the AAA of England, and he believed any person competing at any meeting not held under these rules should be ineligible to compete elsewhere. Cusack claimed that even the aesthetics of the meetings held under the AAA's auspices were colonial in appearance—a little part of England transferred across the Irish Sea with "foot races, betting, all flagrant cheating being their most prominent features. Swarms of pot hunting mashers sprang into existence."[12]

In an article in the *Shamrock* newspaper in February 1883, he was even more scathing of athletic meets held under the auspices of the British-influenced IAAA. It is not quite clear what he is getting at, but there seems to be a conflation of confused sexuality and limited sporting ability. He wrote, "In the English parts of Ireland, the term 'athletics' has of late been applied to that thing which a number of older young persons of doubtful gender do in fine weather after having undergone several weeks of careful nursing and when nobody outside their own class is allowed to compete."[13] This intermixing of sexual orientation and British sport was not confined to Cusack. Archbishop Croke, the first patron of the GAA, bemoaned the governing of sports in Ireland:

If we continue traveling for the next score years in the direction that we have been going in for some time past, condemning the sports that were practiced by our forefathers, effacing our national features as though we were ashamed of them, and putting on, with England's stuffs and broadcloths her masher habits, and such other effeminate follies as she may recommend, we had better at once, and publicly, abjure our nationality. [14]

Maurice Davin also wrote of the writ of the IAAA in Ireland. While acknowledging the efficiency and fair play inherent in the way English authorities governed athletics, he subtly pointed out the overemphasis of track in their events, noting that at leading meets there was a lack of jumping and weight-throwing, which he believed was inimical to widespread participation. From his experience, he wrote, "For one bystander who takes off his coat to run a foot race, forty strip to throw weights or try a jump of some kind." [15] The Irishman was a natural weight thrower, a man given to demonstrations of physical strength, and should athletic meetings and sports day organizers put more emphasis on throwing events, there would be a higher rate of participation, he believed. It was a substantially subtler argument than the one put forth by Cusack.

After the foundation of the GAA, the fledgling organization spent almost eighteen months formulating rules for its own athletic meets. They happily accepted the IAAA's rules pertaining to the running of track events but set about putting in place a body of rules for throwing competitions to be held under its own auspices. Additionally, the GAA allowed their athletic competitions to take place on Sundays—the IAAA did not—thus opening up the arena to a swath of people who would have had only the Sabbath to rest from their labors. In January 1885, the governing body of the GAA passed a new law making it illegal for any of their members to partake in an athletic event run according to rules other than their own, a decision that would cast a long shadow over international participation by Irish athletes in the coming years.

The IAAA, established in 1885, with rules identical to its English ancestor, had the support of the GAA at first; Michael Cusack even attended the inaugural meeting at the Wicklow Hotel in Dublin, although differences of opinion and interpretation were evident from the beginning. While the GAA allowed winners to receive small monetary awards to offset their traveling expenses, the IAAA was strictly opposed to financial compensation. Cusack would later observe that there seemed little sense in giving a young Irishman a fish knife or butter cooler, as it would be much more practical for a "poor Irish youth to accept his traveling expenses and a sovereign or two than get the fish or butter."[16] When the IAAA instituted a rule that any athlete who competed under the auspices of a different organization could no longer take part in their competitions, the gloves came off.

Inevitably, the GAA made political capital of this, portraying itself as a democratic and nationalist organization, in contrast to the elitist nature of the IAAA, which Cusack once graphically described as a "ranting, impotent West British abortion."[17] After Cusack's tempestuous outburst, John Dunbar of the IAAA wrote to him to see if they could hold a conciliatory meeting, but the GAA man's response was abrupt: "Dear Sir, I received your letter this morning and burnt it."[18]

It was only a matter of time before the two competing bodies faced off in the athletic arena. On June 17, 1885, the County Kerry Amateur Athletic and Cricket Club held its annual sports day in Tralee on the same day the local branch of the GAA held theirs. Cusack had made it his business to travel to Kerry to help the locals organize the logistical details, ensuring that local nationalists and religious figures were brought on board to help out. Understandably, the day proved a great success. Ten thousand people showed up to watch the GAA sports, while only a few hundred saw fit to attend their rival's version.

The IAAA was the first to get a national championship off the ground when its inaugural meeting was held at the Royal Dublin Society showground in Ballsbridge, Dublin, on July 11, 1885, while the GAA had its first showpiece championships at the race course in Tramore, County Waterford, on October 6 of that same year. The GAA gained rapid ground, and at the association's Annual General Meeting in late October, Michael Cusack was pleased to announce that almost 150 athletic meets took place under its auspices the previous year. For such a young entity, it was a hugely impressive start. Athletics in rural Ireland were now predominantly under the control of locals with nationalist sympathies, many of whom were also politically active.

The impasse between the rival athletic bodies ended in April 1886, when the GAA rescinded its rule allowing financial awards as prizes; the IAAC reciprocated by allowing all athletes to compete in their events provided they had not previously competed for money. This uneasy rapprochement held together for twenty years, allowing Irish athletes to compete consistently, a major factor in the many finely honed athletes that would subsequently leave the country's shores to compete for the United States and other countries.

Athletes like Jim Mitchell, who had cut his teeth at the many athletic events in Ireland, were seasoned competitors at a young age, and the variety of titles on offer was reflected in how heavily garlanded most of them were by the time they crossed the Atlantic Ocean, despite almost all of them still being of tender years.

Shortly after his arrival in New York, Jim Mitchell joined the Manhattan Athletic Club—formed in 1878, and famous for its "Cherry Diamond" emblem—because they were the first to promise him a job; for this he was banned by the Amateur Athletic Union, which purported to keep the sport from being tainted by any hint of professionalism. After being reinstated in March 1889, he spent a short time with the New Jersey Athletic Club before joining the preeminent New York Athletic Club. By 1897, he was so far ahead of the field that many in the athletic fraternity believed him unbeatable, and through his throwing feats he became an iconic figure in popular American culture. When newspaper magnate William Randolph Hearst weighed the threat posed by the Spanish military in Cuba, he opined in the *Journal* that it would be simple to defeat the invaders: Send some of the best athletes in the country, including Mitchell. He said, "All we have to do is send a regiment of our best athletes. Such men as the world's heavyweight boxing champion, 'Fighting Bob' Fitzsimons, boxer James J. Corbett, expert baseball player 'Cap' Anson, champion hammer thrower Jim Mitchell. . . . They would scorn Spanish bullets."[19]

Mitchell's list of achievements is staggering. From 1889 to 1896, he won eight successive USA hammer titles. In addition, he held the 56-pound weight title from 1891 to 1897, and went on to win a further four at varying intervals. Mitchell extended the hammer record from the 119 feet, 5 inches he set at Limerick in 1886, to 145 feet, .75 of an inch in New York in 1892. In so doing he broke the world record on eleven occasions. When the term *Irish Whales* later came into vogue to describe the group of Irish American athletes who would dominate the world stage in throwing events for three decades, James "Jim" Mitchell was considered the first.

Later in life, Mitchell came to be revered as an eminent authority on weight-throwing after his *How to Become a Weight Thrower* was published in 1916, as part of the much-praised Spalding "Red Cover" Series of Athletic Handbooks. It was immediately recognized as a fine practical training manual for aspiring throwers and an excellent model for instructional sporting literature. Mitchell cleverly got an expert in each of the throwing events to contribute a chapter, in addition to his own detailed preamble on the nature and origins of throwers. It was to become the bible for a generation of weight throwers.

James "Jim" Mitchell was in the vanguard, but like all great athletes, he would eventually meet his match. With the arrival of John Jesus Flanagan from Kilbreedy, County Limerick—later dubbed the "Modern Hercules"—to New York, the sport of hammer-throwing would move to a whole new level.

4

JOHN "THE MODERN HERCULES" FLANAGAN AND OLYMPIC GOLD

Olympism is a philosophy of life, exalting and combining in a balanced whole the qualities of body, will, and mind. Blending sport with culture and education, Olympism seeks to create a way of life based on the joy of effort, the educational value of good example, social responsibility, and respect for universal fundamental ethical principles.— Baron Pierre de Coubertin, founder of the International Olympic Committee

In 1860, 46 percent of male Irish immigrants in the United States worked in such low-paid unskilled jobs as day laboring. By 1880, the figure remained consistent at 47 percent. In 1900, it had inched up slightly, to 51 percent. During that forty-year period, the number of Irish who owned their own businesses only increased from 5 to 6 percent, but there were some slight indicators of upward mobility. In 1860 and 1880, only one in a thousand Irish immigrants worked in the professions, but this figure had moved up to seven by 1900. The percentage of Irish in lower-paid white-collar jobs went from 6 percent in 1860 to 11 percent in 1900. Upward mobility for Irish women by employment type had not yet started. Sixty-three percent of employed female Irish immigrants worked as household help in 1860, climbing to 69 percent in 1880 and 73 percent in 1900.

Fraternal organizations continued to be a significant part of the fabric of immigrant life. By 1898, the New York branch of the Ancient Order of Hibernians (AOH) had 200,000 members. The Daughters of Erin—a female auxiliary of the AOH founded in 1894—had a membership of

20,000 by 1897. Clan na Gael continued to have an attraction to the Irish immigrant community. As far back as 1871, it had been organizing picnics that doubled as sports days where teams from different cities competed; by 1878, the New York picnic was attracting 13,000 people, and in 1904, 15,000 attended a Brooklyn Clan na Gael athletic meeting held in Ridgewood Park on Long Island.

Jim Mitchell's reign as the greatest thrower in the United States had been long and glorious, a decade of dominance gilded with baubles and marked by lavish encomiums on the continent. Mitchell had been the apogee of physicality; the might of contemporary Irish America–made flesh, unassailable in a discipline that required a tightly balanced coordination of power and skill, and an exacting degree of technical acumen. He had proved unassailable. Then along came the second of the Irish Whales, John "The Pocket Rocket" Flanagan, bringing the sport to a whole new level.

By the time Flanagan immigrated to the United States in 1896, he had been demonstrating his athletic ability from a young age, winning his first title at a sports day organized by the Royal Irish Constabulary—the name given to the police force in Ireland at that time—in 1894, when he took the 56-pound weight throw title. In April 1896, Flanagan set a record in the hammer thrown from a seven-foot circle of 147 feet at the Gaelic Sports in Stamford Bridge, London, beating the existing record of Jim Mitchell by two feet; in May of that same year, he established a new world record in the unlimited run and follow version of the hammer—which subsequently became obsolete—at Kensal Rise, London, with a throw of 156 feet. Shortly thereafter he departed for the United States. First joining the New York Athletic Club (NYAC), Flanagan took his first title in late May when he smashed his own record for throwing the 16-pound hammer from the seven-foot circle in Bayonne, New Jersey, but it was at the New York Metropolitan Championships of 1897, held in the heat of August in Columbia Oval, that the reign of the great Mitchell finally came to an end.

A new Irish American of spectacular ability had entered the throwing arena in the shape of John Flanagan, and Jim Mitchell finally had to give way to a young pretender, another proud Gael who would carry forward the mantle of the Irish as the dominant force in weight-throwing events. In the second half of 1897, Flanagan went on to further burnish his reputation as the preeminent new hammer thrower on the North

American stage with wins at the American and Canadian championships; in the latter, he beat Mitchell's existing Dominion's record by a massive nine feet. At the same meet he also took gold in the 56-pound weight throw. Flanagan was on his way to complete dominance.

For a hammer thrower, John Flanagan was small—only 5-foot-9.5—but he perfected the three-turn technique first used by Californian athlete Alfred Plaw to bring the discipline to a new level of technical efficiency. Up to that point throwers had used a double rotation, but the addition of a further turn meant additional speed could be generated before the hammer was released. It was basic science but not an easy technique to master, particularly for those who had learned their trade using the double-rotation style. One of the obvious difficulties was trying to release the hammer directly out from the circle to land in the field; the danger was that inexperienced athletes could throw it anywhere.

"Pocket Rocket" was the perfect sobriquet for John Flanagan. In an era when the vast majority of throwers were huge men, Flanagan was a much more compact athlete. His throwing style was an aesthetic wonder of the age, and many New Yorkers went to watch him train in Travers Island, the home of NYAC, for an evening's entertainment. In a discipline where it was commonly thought that the bigger the man, the farther he could throw, here was a man of average height who, through developing a new technique based on superior biodynamic principles, had outmaneuvered the colossal Jim Mitchell. In an era of constant technological development, it was a further triumph of the ability of the human mind to advance a process through the application of brain power—albeit with athletes who had traveled across the Atlantic Ocean. Such was Flanagan's ability and reputation in the discipline that he worked as a consultant to the Spalding Athletic Company in designing hammer equipment.

John Flanagan, like Jim Mitchell before him, joined the New York Police Department (NYPD). The story of the NYPD is closely entwined with that of the Irish immigrants to the city in two major respects: The forces of law and order were expanded and regularized to deal with the increasingly uncontrolled interethnic feuding and associated violence that continued to engulf the city and heavily involve Irish immigrants, while, somewhat ironically, it became a significant source of employment for Irish men, including all but one of the Irish Whales, largely through the patronage system honed by the Tammany Hall Democratic Party–led administration.

By the 1840s, it was clear to New York City administrators that the existing policing system based on night watchmen was no longer fit for the purpose. The population was continually expanding, and crime was becoming evermore rife. In particular, the ongoing warfare between the nativist and immigrant gangs was spiralling out of control. On May 7, 1844, the state of New York passed the Municipal Police Act, authorizing the creation of a standing police force and abolishing the outmoded night watchmen system. Due to internal wrangling, it took more than a year for the law to be put into effect. Modeled on the Metropolitan Police Service in London, the NYPD had a military-like organizational structure complete with rank and order, and after protracted debate the department adopted a blue uniform.

Things did not run smoothly from the start. In 1857, there was a major rent in the fabric of the fledgling organization when Republican reformers in the state capital of Albany created a new Metropolitan police force, abolishing the Municipal force in an effort to curtail the influence of the Democrat-run New York City government. Mayor Fernando Wood did not accept this new dispensation, and for several months there were two rival police forces and an increasingly farcical face-off. The newly created Metropolitans included three hundred odd men who had left the Municipals, but the remainder were raw recruits with minimal training. Wood directly controlled the Municipals, which by then consisted of a remaining cohort of eight hundred policemen and fifteen officers who had stayed loyal to him. The division of manpower, reflecting the wider milieu, broke down along ethnic lines: Immigrants mostly stayed loyal to the Municipals, while those of Anglo-Dutch Protestant heritage—the people who viewed themselves as the "real Americans"—went to the Metropolitans. The inevitable result was chaos and a further upsurge in criminality.

High farce ensued in mid-June when a group of Metropolitan officers, complete with a warrant, attempted to arrest Mayor Wood but was rebuffed by his loyal Municipal forces. The Metropolitans regrouped and, armed with an updated warrant, once again marched on City Hall—this time with a superior force. The Municipals were lying in wait and, aided by a significant number of public supporters, went to battle with their enemies. The Metropolitans were forced to call on the services of the state-controlled seventh regiment, and after a bloody encounter, the warrant was eventually served on Mayor Wood, who would suffer a double whammy when the Court of Appeals ruled in favor of the state on July 2. The chastened politician was left with no choice but to disband the Municipal police force.

From the afternoon of July 3, the Metropolitans were the new top dogs in Gotham, but the start of their reign was to prove less than auspicious. The following day—Independence Day—the woefully inexperienced Metropolitans were unable to control rioting in the city and had to be rescued by the nativist Bowery Boys when they were besieged by the infamous Dead Rabbit gang, along with their fellow Irish American criminal gangs, the Roach Guards and the Mulberry Street Boys.

The opening days of the reign of the newly established Metropolitan Police Force continued to be far from successful. On July 12, German immigrants in the Little Germany section of Manhattan rioted when the infant Metropolitans tried to enforce newly drawn up liquor laws by closing down saloons. In the course of the resultant fighting, a blacksmith was killed, prompting ten thousand members of the disgruntled public to march up Broadway the following day carrying a large banner proclaiming, "Opfer der Metropolitan-Polizei" (Victim of the Metropolitan Police).

The lot of the Metropolitan police officer would continue to be a difficult one in the ensuing years. In July 1863, the New York state militias were helping union troops in Pennsylvania when rioting broke out in the city as a result of discontent concerning new legislation passed by Congress pertaining to the drafting of men for the army to fight in the ongoing American Civil War. With the militia missing in action, the unfortunate police were left on their own to quell the riots, the largest civil and racial disturbances in U.S. history outside of the Civil War. The instigators of the riots were overwhelmingly working-class white Irish immigrants who feared black workers—exempt from the draft—would take their jobs, while also being deeply resentful of wealthier men who, through a provision in the legislation, could buy their way out of compulsory military service by paying a commutation fee of $300 to hire a substitute. By the end of a week of ferocious fighting, 120 people were dead in what subsequently became known as the Draft Riots.

Numerous public parks, two Protestant churches, many private residences of blacks and sympathizers, and, infamously, the Colored Orphan Asylum at 44th Street and Fifth Avenue were destroyed. As a result of the trouble, the demographics of Lower Manhattan changed dramatically, with many black inhabitants moving out; by 1865, the number of black residents in Manhattan was less than ten thousand for the first time since 1820. Leading up to the Draft Riots, the atmosphere in New York had been a tinder keg. In March, white longshoremen—predominantly Irish—had rioted, refusing to work with black laborers, and attacked more than two hundred men. Further controversy about the methods of the NYPD arose after January 13, 1874, when officers crushed thousands of people demonstrating about the poor economic conditions and high unemployment in the Tompkins Square Park Riots.

Throughout the years, the NYPD would become a feeding trough for Democratic Party political loyalists, particularly Irishmen. Thankful for the chance in life given to them by their political masters, Irish members of the force were often given to corruptive practices to further advance the cause of the Democratic machine. Police officers responsible for manning voting booths turned a blind eye to systematic ballot stuffing amid a plethora of other fraudulent activities; "votes were recorded for the dead, the departed, and even the unborn."[1] As well as providing assistance to political allies of the machine, the police harassed, arrested, and interfered with the activities of political opponents. Political machines were the primary means through which crime was organized in urban areas, and politicians frequently ran or supervised gambling, prostitution, drug distribution, and racketeering. Organized crime and the dominant political parties of American cities had become one and the same.

At the dawn of the twentieth century, police were acting as the enforcement arm of organized crime. In return for providing services to the political bosses, the police force had carte blanche in the use of force and was more concerned with the solicitation and acceptance of bribes than any law control. The police had become primary instruments for the creation of corruption in the first place, and the Irish were in the vanguard; by the end of the nineteenth century, 70 percent of the NYPD was Irish. Such was the persistent level of flagrant corruption among members of the police force that the Lexow Committee was established in 1894, to try to instigate a degree of reform, and it was only under the stewardship of future U.S. president Theodore Roosevelt, who came to lead the committee in 1895, that any effective inroads into the endemic corruption started to be made. The Lenox Committee found that gambling and police extortion were widespread and promotion required bribery; a promotion to sergeant could be bought for $1,600, while captaincy cost as much as

$15,000. The police force of New York City had become rotten to the core, and the process of rehabilitation would prove long and slow.

It was a proud boast for the NYPD to have such exceptional physical specimens as Jim Mitchell and John Flanagan on the force; physical fitness was encouraged among officers. Police bosses facilitated those officers who strove to compete at a high level, allowing them latitude with their work schedules to maximize their athletic potential. Involvement in Police Athletic Leagues provided further opportunities to hone their athletic abilities. These police athletes were regarded as the cream of the NYPD. They had the requisites required to make good officers: discipline, physical strength, and courage.

Immediately after his defeat of Mitchell, John Flanagan's abilities caught the attention of the national governing body of athletics, and he was invited to join the American team; a little more than two years later, he would travel to the 1900 Olympic Games in Paris, the second iteration of the modern Olympics. Above all other competitions, the revived Olympics were to bring the Irish Whales to the center of the American sporting narrative and cement their place in history.

The first modern Olympic Games were held in Athens in 1896. The city had been chosen to host the games by a congress—the first meeting of what would subsequently become the International Olympic Committee (IOC)—organized by French historian and teacher Pierre de Coubertin in Paris, in June 1894. De Coubertin had been inspired by a sports demonstration he had seen while touring the 1889 Paris Exhibition and first proposed the Olympic concept in 1892, at a conference, where it was summarily rejected despite a stirring oration by the Frenchman:

> It is clear that the telegraph, railways, the telephone, the passionate research in science, congresses, and exhibitions have done more for peace than any treaty or diplomatic convention. Well, I hope that athletics will do even more. . . . Let us export rowers, runners, and fencers: There is the free trade of the future, and on the day it is introduced within the walls of old Europe the cause of peace will have received a new and mighty stay. This is enough for your servant to dream now . . . to continue and complete, on a basis suited to the conditions of modern life, the grandiose and salutary task, namely the restoration of the Olympic Games.[2]

Despite the initial rejection of his idea, de Coubertin did not give up on his quest and, at an international conference in Paris in 1894, organized to discuss the principles and problems of amateurism in sport, he once again forwarded his case, playing on the worries of the representatives of the elite and aristocratic amateur athletic associations from throughout the world in attendance. He put forth the theory that the newly moneyed industrial classes were encroaching on their sports and clubs, threatening the social exclusivity and moral purity of their pursuits. De Coubertin suggested in a letter sent to the delegates prior to the conference—which eventually came to be called the Paris International Congress for the Re-establishment of the Olympic Games, after having earlier being termed an International Amateur Congress and then an International Athletic Congress—that his idea of a revived Olympic Games could provide the solution and create a necessary climate of internationalism in a troubled world, and ensure that the threat of war would be subsumed by a focus on healthy sporting competition. This time his imprecations fell on fertile ground, and plans were soon made for the reestablishment of the games.

Initially, de Coubertin hoped to hold the first iteration of the games in his home city of Paris in 1900, but Greek support for the concept was so positive that the plan was moved forward, and it was decided that the first games would be held in Athens in 1896. It was an appropriate and popular choice. Greece was the original birthplace of the Ancient Olympic Games, believed to have started in 776 BC in Olympia, in which athletes competed in just one event—a footrace. Chariot racing, wrestling, boxing, and the pentathlon were added throughout the years. In the Ancient Olympics, the competitors were young men from Greek city-states and colonies who often participated naked to celebrate the beauty of the human body. The last Ancient Olympics took place in AD 393, and were subsequently banned by Roman emperor Theodosius I in his ill-fated quest to suppress paganism.

The Athens Olympic Games of the modern era—officially known as the Games of the I Olympiad—held between April 6 and April 15, 1896, were, given the many logistical problems posed by the choice of location, a great success. The help of Crown Prince Constantine was a major factor in making the games work. As the head of the Greek Organizing Committee, he oversaw the extensive sales of souvenir stamps and medals to fund proceedings, and also managed to solicit a donation of 1 million drachmas from wealthy businessman Georgious Averoff. From the start, de

Coubertin was at pains to point out to members of the IOC that he was not merely trying to recreate the Ancient Olympics and its pageantry, but also make them modern and relevant. Panathenaic Stadium in Athens played host to the biggest-ever gathering to view a sports event to that date. The games included competitions in 9 sports, 10 disciplines, and 43 events, in which 14 nations were represented by 241 male athletes,[3] who with the exception of the clean-cut American college boys had the "signature waxed moustache of the young scions of the haute bourgeois and aristocracy, aped by the middle classes."[4] Not every American was impressed by the idea of their country traveling to Europe to compete in Athens. The *New York Times* was particularly condescending, opining that the athletes were taking an expensive journey to a third-rate capital where they would be devoured by fleas.[5]

The sports included in this first iteration of the modern Olympic Games were athletics, cycling, fencing, gymnastics, sailing (cancelled due to bad weather), shooting, swimming, tennis, weight lifting, and wrestling. Sports that had been tainted by professionalism—in the eyes of the organizers—like baseball, soccer, cricket, and boxing, were not deemed worthy of inclusion. At the time of the games there were few fixed international standards for the included sports, leading to inevitable confusion at some junctures in the proceedings. The track built by the Greek hosts, for example, was 330 meters long with an almost rectangular layout, while track races were run anticlockwise in most countries, but the Greeks insisted on clockwise progression. American sprinters were using a crouched start by this time, but the other nations were still employing a standing start. While American hurdlers were able to run and cross the barriers without breaking stride, the Greeks still jumped, stopped, and starting running again.

In 1896, athletes technically represented athletic clubs or competed as individuals—with the exception of Hungary, which entered an official national team—although medals are now credited to the country from which the athletes come. The highlight of the games was the marathon, and the Greeks were ecstatic when their countryman, Spyridon Louis, a previously unheralded water carrier, won the race on front of one hundred thousand adoring fans who lined the route. In addition to the awarding of his laurels, Louis was chosen to lead the parade of medal winners at the closing of the games.

The first Athens Olympic Games were, as de Coubertin and his fellow organizers had hoped, characterized by true amateurism. Employees working at the British Embassy were strongly encouraged to participate by their betters, while other nonnatives who happened to be on holiday or business in Athens were roped in by enthusiastic organizers. Australian competitor Edwin Flack had only come to Athens to watch the games but ended up winning the 800 and 1,500 meters races. The only professional athletes who competed at the games were the fencers. While women were not allowed to participate, the intrepid Stamata Revithi ran the marathon course in five hours and thirty minutes—albeit it the day after the men had done so—and although not allowed to enter the stadium at the end of her odyssey she commandeered witnesses to sign their names and verify her achievement; unfortunately no record of this document remains.

Although the United States was outnumbered by competitors from France, Greece, and Great Britain, they still managed to win eleven titles, the most of any nation. Greece had approximately 170 athletes at the games and came second in the medal table with ten wins. The U.S. team had 27 entries in 16 events, with 20 of the 27 resulting in top-three finishes. The Americans were lucky to have gotten there on time, as they failed to realize the Greeks were using the old Julian calendar, which meant the games began on April 6. The Americans had been planning for an April 18 start and didn't arrive until the opening morning after an overland dash from Naples. Despite that close shave it was an overwhelmingly positive experience for the Americans.

Irish American James Connolly was the star of the show. He took the first title of the games when he won the hop, skip, and jump—subsequently the triple jump—with a leap of more than forty-four feet. Connolly added a second-place finish in the high jump—tying him with American compatriot Robert Garrett—and a third in the long jump during the course of the games. Connolly was treated as a star upon his return to Boston, where he was presented with a gold watch by his adoring fans. Victory in international sporting competition would become hugely important to the United States in developing its own sense of identity, and the American contingent was justly proud of their achievements in Athens.

With Pierre de Coubertin being a Frenchman, it was inevitable that the Olympic circus would roll into his home city of Paris in 1900, despite the imprecations of the Greeks, who believed Athens would be the perfect location for a permanent home for the championships. It was to prove a difficult and fraught venture, and de Coubertin later wrote, "If there was a place in the world that felt indifferent about the Olympic Games, Paris was the first."[6]

In their misguided wisdom, the IOC ceded the running of the games to the Union of French Societies for Athletic Sports (USFSA), which wanted to run them in conjunction with the World Fair—called the Exposition Universelle Internationale by the French—which was being held in Paris that year, a decision de Coubertin later came to regret. The USFSA published a different schedule of events than was originally planned by the IOC, resulting in the withdrawal of many athletes, while others simply refused to deal with the organization. Organizers did not even use the term *Olympic Games*, preferring to call them the *Concours International-aux D'exercices Physiques et de Sport* (International Physical Exercises and Sports), while the press reported the competitions variously as the "International Championships," "International Games," "Paris Championships," "World Championships," and "Grand Prix of the Paris Exposition." De Coubertin later ruefully commented to friends that it was a miracle the Olympic movement survived the games. Some sports historians have even suggested that athletes died without knowing they had an Olympic title to their name from the Paris games. At the crux of the difficulty were the differing viewpoints of de Coubertin and Alfred Picard, the head of the exposition; the latter later described many of the plans of the former as "cheap and unfit to represent the nation" and his sporting ideas as "absurd anachronisms."[7]

Twenty-four nations competed in nineteen sports between May 14 and October 28, in an Olympic Games of firsts and lasts in Paris. It was the first and last time medals were awarded for automobile and motorcycling racing, ballooning, equestrian high and long jumps, cricket, croquet, Basque pelota, swimming obstacle racing, and underwater swimming. The Paris games were also notable as the only Olympics to use live animals—pigeons—as targets for the shooting event, and most significantly of all, women were allowed to compete, although of the 997 athletes participating, only twenty-two were female. Among the highlights of the championships was the winning of four gold medals in three days by American hurdler Alvin Kraenzlein—the man who is credited with the leg-extended style of the discipline—and the remarkable achievement of fellow American Ray Ewry, who having overcome polio in his childhood won three gold medals on the same day in the now-obsolete standing jump events. Frenchman Constantin Henriquez de Zubiera, a member of both the gold medal–winning rugby team and the tug-of-war team, became the first black athlete to compete in the Olympic Games.

The French scheduled track and field competitions for Sunday, which was not considered de rigueur in the United States in 1900. The Americans threatened not to compete, and the French considered moving some competitions to July 14. When they realized that was Bastille Day, they moved the events back to July 15—a Sunday. The Americans were annoyed, and a number of athletes failed to show up for the competition.

Ireland did not have an Olympic team—it was not yet a free nation— and those resident in Ireland had to compete with the British team, but it was the United States that would be the greatest beneficiary of Irish talent in Paris, with John Flanagan in the vanguard. The hammer throw final took place on July 16, at the Calvary Cross in the Bois de Boulogne— once the hunting grounds of the French royal family—with five competitors, three Americans and two Swedes, in the starting lineup. Truxtun (frequently misspelled Truxton) Hare, a renowned American football player for the Penn Quakers football team of the University of Pennsylvania—still one of only a handful of players to have been chosen as an All-American player in each of his four years at college—placed eighth in the shot put at the games and competed in the discus without recording a mark, but the hammer was his strongest discipline and he was expected to provide Flanagan with some degree of challenge. Josiah McCracken, another gifted American college footballer of Ulster-Scots extraction, was the only other competitor considered likely to provide a realistic threat to Flanagan. McCracken had taken silver in the shot put despite not competing in the final round of throws because they took place on a Sunday and ran counter to his religious beliefs.

On the day of the hammer competition the athletes were presented with the unusual sight of an oak tree in the middle of the field in the Bois de Boulogne. It was thought by many that none of the competitors would throw anywhere near the distance Flanagan could manage, but connoisseurs were impressed when Hare threw 151 feet, 9 inches with his second effort, bettering his previous best mark; however, the competition was quickly decided when Flanagan threw 167 feet, 4.5 inches with his second throw. There was no chance whatsoever that any of the other four athletes would be able to come anywhere close to the Limerick man's mark, and by virtue of it being the first time the event was held as part of an Olympic Games, it was a new record. Hare took the silver, while McCracken finished in the bronze medal position with a throw of just less than 143 feet. The distances thrown by the Swedish competitors—Eric Lemming and Karl Gustav Staaf—went unrecorded. It was the first great triumph of the remarkable John Flanagan.

The *New York Times* pointed to the superiority of the Americans in the event, as well as the health and safety concerns posed by the erratic throwing of the Swedes, who "caused some amusement among the spectators, not unmixed with a certain amount of apprehension."[8] It also commented on the relative lack of interest in the proceedings by natives, in keeping with Pierre de Coubertin's subsequent criticisms, and seemed happy to report that those in attendance were largely American. At one point the crowd thought Flanagan had broken the world record and became momentarily enthusiastic, but the throw proved three inches short and spectators quickly settled back into their Parisian hauteur. Flanagan also took part in the discus competition, where he finished seventh.

The two Swedish athletes would find success elsewhere. Karl Staaf took gold as part of the Swedish tug-of-war team at the games, while Eric Lemming would later become a renowned javelin thrower, taking gold medals in 1906, 1908, and 1912. If the javelin had been included on the Paris schedule, he would have been the likely victor, as he had set a world record the year before at nineteen years of age, going on to increase that mark thirteen times during the course of his career.

Truxtun Hare went on to compete for the United States at the St. Louis Olympic Games, where he took a bronze medal in the all-around event and a gold medal as part of the American tug-of-war team. A true Renaissance man, Hare found later success as a lawyer, painter, and author. *The Graduate Coach*—one of the two series of books he wrote—appropriately consisted of five volumes celebrating the importance of sports in a man's life. Hare died in 1956, at the age of seventy-seven. Josiah McCracken subsequently studied medicine, after which he spent more than forty years in China educating trainee doctors. After retiring to the United States in 1952, he spent his retirement fundraising for his beloved Chinese medical system before dying at the age of eighty-eight in 1962.

The United States had once more demonstrated its remarkable sporting capabilities on the world stage, taking 16 of the 23 track and field titles on offer and competing in all but one event, the 5,000 meters team race. The Americans failed to win a medal in only three events—the marathon and the two steeplechase races. They brought home 48 medals: 19 gold, 14 silver, and 15 bronze. Theodore Roosevelt had challenged them to prove that they were the world's "strongest and boldest people," and they had.[9] The *Chicago Tribune* complained that the ease with which the American athletes carried off prizes "finally grew monotonous."[10] Caspar Whitney, editor of *Outing*, gloated that the entire event was like an American intercollegiate competition.[11]

It was a fantastic start to the Olympic career of John Flanagan, but it was only the beginning of an odyssey that would bring him to a level that had never been thought possible, and he would go on to achieve something that has only been outdone by two track and field athletes in the history of the Olympics. He might have been a relatively small man, but Flanagan's eventual achievements would prove gargantuan. In addition to the man from Kilbreedy, County Limerick, there were more Irish Whales lurking in the waters; the production line was about to become even richer.

5

AMERICAN FIASCO, IRISH AMERICAN TRIUMPH

The St. Louis Olympic Games, 1904

The important thing in the Olympic Games is not to win, but to take part; the important thing in life is not triumph, but the struggle; the essential thing is not to have conquered, but to have fought well. To spread these principles is to build up a strong and more valiant and, above all, more scrupulous and more generous humanity.—Pierre de Coubertin

Baron de Coubertin had high hopes for the first American hosting of the Olympic Games in 1904. He urged members of the International Olympic Committee (IOC) to do everything they could to make the championships a great success and expressed the hope they would draw across the ocean qualified representatives of the sporting societies of the world for a manifestation that would be "both worthy of the noble and ancient Olympian past and the glorious future of the great American republic."[1] He would be badly disappointed.

The history books remember the 1904 Olympics as a comedy of errors characterized by farcical mismanagement, poor attendance, horrendously hot weather, and general apathy. Originally the games were scheduled to take place in Chicago, but St. Louis was hosting the World's Fair—officially called the Louisiana Purchase Centennial Exposition—that year, and a reluctant de Coubertin was prevailed upon to move the competition. The Olympic founder chose not to attend the games and later famously wrote in his memoirs that he "had a sort of presentiment that the Olympiad would match the mediocrity of the town."[2] The IOC was anxious to demonstrate to the world that the concept of the modern Olympics was not an entirely European one and opted for the United States, hoping they would take place in one of the great cities, but after efforts by Philadelphia, New York, and Chicago were scuppered by various political shenanigans, the games were awarded to St. Louis; it proved to be a terrible choice, and criticism would become universal afterward.

De Coubertin dismissed the city out of hand, contending that "its drinking water was a muddy brown—too thick to drink, too thin to plough . . . and summer was a humid inferno." He wrote that the city "seemed to have no gravitation of its own, serving instead as a pestilential hub traveled by hordes of people going somewhere else." The worst thing was that it had no athletic tradition or organization, which would result in the "aristocrats of the eastern sports establishment" looking down "their blue-blooded noses" at the entire event.[3]

It could have been so much different. There was no doubting the impressive infrastructure put together for the exposition: more than 1,500 buildings, 50 miles of walkways, and pavilions from 62 nations, and 43 of the then-45 states of the United States were part of the extravaganza. It was, according to the promotional literature of the organizers, an "exhibition of human progress . . . the newest and noblest achievements, its triumphs of skills and science, its most approved solutions of social problems."[4] Even an "Irish Village" containing reconstructions of the Irish Parliament, a miniature version of Blarney Castle complete with the famous kissing stone, a restaurant, and a small theater where Irish dance, music, and drama were performed were included in the exposition.

Whatever about the demonstration of scientific development at St. Louis, the sporting dimension of the proceedings proved extremely disappointing. A total of 651 participants—of whom only 6 were female—representing 12 different countries attended the games, which had a program consisting of 91 events in 15 different sports. The U.S. team won 239 medals, the largest number by a country in a single games. American athletes won 70 of the 94 gold medals on offer and 22 of the 24 events in track and field. The U.S. team was even criticized for fielding athletes who had not attained citizenship; as recently as 2012, Norway called for the IOC to change the nationality of two medals awarded to wrestlers who had competed under the U.S. flag but, they argued, were Norwegian nationals at the time of the 1904 games.

The competitions dragged on for almost five months, starting on July 1 and ending on November 23. Most of the athletic events were held between August 29 and September 3—the original schedule for the games—but the rest of the proceedings were scattered and held during a succession of sports showcases that included a military athletic festival, an Irish sports festival, and a YMCA basketball championship. As organizers used the term *Olympic* for the athletic competitions, confusion later became rife as to which competitions were official and which were not. The low profile of the sporting events added to the problem. Virtually all the events were held in the small and inconspicuous Francis Field stadium and gymnasium—part of Washington University—which were located in a section of the fairgrounds hidden behind the aeronautical concourse, one of the most popular exhibits in the program. The swimmers had to compete in an artificial lake created by the Palace of Agriculture. The crowds at the sporting events were poor, while national press coverage was limited and international coverage virtually nonexistent.

One element of the festival that has been largely lost in the mists of time was the holding of demonstrations of the Irish sports Gaelic football and hurling, as well as various weight-throwing competitions of Celtic derivation. The original ambitious plan had been to hold a three-day festival of Irish sports as part of the proceedings. Elements in the press were delighted that the American public would witness such disciplines as the rarely seen 42-pound weight throw and a demonstration of hurling. In the end, the proceedings were limited to the morning of Saturday, July 21, when competitions were held in running, triple jump, throwing, Gaelic football, and hurling. In the football match, the Chicago Fenians beat the St. Louis Innisfails on a score line of ten points to one, while the latter also won the hurling, but there is no opposition or score listed in any record, suggesting there may have been a walkover. There was an additional Irish dimension to the games as the Ancient Order of Hibernians organized their annual convention on the same day. It attracted more than 2,000 delegates representing 250,000 members, some of whom had even traveled from Australia and New Zealand.

Highlights and positive Olympic milestones were limited in St. Louis. Women were confined to archery, although there were a number of female exhibition boxing matches. Len Tau and Jan Mashiana, Tswana tribesmen who came to the city as part of the Boer War exhibit at the World's Fair, became the first Africans to compete in an Olympics when they took part in the marathon, while on August 31, American athletes George Poage and Joseph Stadler became the first African Americans to win Olympic medals; Poage took a bronze in the 400 meters hurdles, with Stadler taking silver in the standing high jump. The achievements of American gymnast George Eyser provided perhaps the most heartening story from the games. Eyser won a total of six medals—three gold, two silver, and a bronze—despite being at the distinct disadvantage of having to compete with a wooden left leg; his original limb had to be amputated after it was mangled when he was run over by a train.

Strange things happened at the St. Louis Olympics. The games were the only time the sport of "plunge for distance" diving featured on the schedule, whereby the diver leapt from an eighteen-inch platform and had a minute to travel as far across the pool as possible without moving his arms or legs. It was essentially competitive floating. The event was subsequently removed from the schedule because, understandably, it was judged to have little appeal to spectators.

The games also included a bizarre side event called Anthropology Days, in which "uncivilized tribes" from throughout the world were recruited from the World's Fair "human zoo" and encouraged to compete in different Olympic sports. Ainus, Patagonians, Pygmies, Igorot Filipinos, and Sioux were paid to participate in such traditional Olympic events as the long jump, archery, and javelin throw, as well as invented disciplines—adjudged suitable to backward people—like the pole climb and mud-throwing. Anthropology Days was billed as a "display of the tribesmen's natural athletic ability," but the participants received almost no instruction, and most performed poorly as a result, leading the chief organizer, the indefatigable James E. Sullivan, to conclude that the events were proof that the "savage has been a very much overrated man from an athletic point of view."[5] Sullivan completed his own report on the games as part of the *Spalding Almanac Series*, in which he reported on a 56-pound weight-throw competition between three Patagonian tribesmen where the best mark recorded was 10 feet, 6 inches. Sullivan was scathing and compared their performance to John Flanagan, who threw the weight many feet farther than the combined total of the tribesmen. Pierre de Coubertin later called Anthropology Days an "outrageous charade" and noted presciently that it would lose its appeal when "black men, red men, and yellow men learn to run, jump, and throw, and leave the white men behind them."[6] At the end of his lengthy discourse on Anthropology Days, Sullivan fulminated that those who considered themselves authorities on athletics should omit references to the "natural ability of the tribesmen" from then onward unless they could prove otherwise.[7]

Sullivan had played a central part in the political maneuverings that had brought the games to St. Louis, and it was on him the opprobrium expressed by those who had seen the farcical events during the course of the marathon race rested. In his wisdom, Sullivan only allowed two water stations on the race course despite the fact that the competitors had to deal with temperatures of ninety degrees and unpaved roads swirling with dust. Sullivan made these arrangements because he wanted to conduct research on what he termed "purposeful dehydration," although he was well aware that dehydration could prove fatal. The result of his meddling was inevitable chaos. Of the 32 athletes who started the race, only 14 managed to finish, while the winning time of 3 hours, 28 minutes, and 45 seconds was farcically slow. Further controversy arose shortly after the end of the race when it became apparent that Fred Lorz, the first to cross the line, had traveled eleven miles by car. Lorz was given a one-year ban, and the title was awarded to Thomas Hicks, an English athlete who had begged his trainer to let him drop out earlier but rallied after being given a mixture of strychnine, egg whites, and brandy, and managed to finish second.

Despite the haphazard nature of the games, they provided some Americans with an opportunity to express their jingoistic sentiments. Author Charles Lucas poured particular scorn on France, which showed its ingratitude by not sending a team even though the Americans had made the Paris games a success and without the English they would have been a farce; however, he believed it did not matter, as any Frenchman would have managed to finish fourth in St. Louis. Additionally, the English athletic scene was infested with professional athletes. Thus, they would not have been welcomed had they deigned to turn up.[8]

Lucas took pains to point out the fine facilities the Americans provided for the games, where the "conditions were ideal," whereas the Paris event had been "contested on grassy plots" with "part of the course lying in a clump of trees," while the course of the sprints was wet and soggy. At St. Louis, by contrast, the running track was the perfect shape and constructed in the most modern manner; the apparatus used by the athletes was of the most modern manufacture, while the "field arrangements and acoustics . . . were a revelation to Americans themselves."[9]

Whatever about the limited nature of the competition and the quality or otherwise of the facilities available for the 1904 games provided John Flanagan with a relatively straightforward opportunity to retain his hammer title. In 1903, Flanagan had joined the New York Police Department, where his cushy job in the Bureau of Licenses had afforded him the time he needed to hone his spectacular hammer-throwing skills. The intervening period between the 1900 Paris Olympics and the St. Louis Olympic Games had seen him surge farther ahead in the event despite other athletes copying his three-turn technique.

On September 2, 1901, he had established a new world record, appropriately as part of the annual Irish American Athletic Club (IAAC) Games held at Celtic Park, where he threw 171 feet, 9 inches, beating his own world-leading mark of 169 feet, 4 inches. On October 4, Flanagan threw the hammer 170 feet and a half-inch at a meeting under the auspices of the American Athletic Union (AAU) in Louisville, Kentucky, but it was his performance in the discus on the day that turned heads when he threw 119 feet, 6 inches, a full 20 feet ahead of the second-place athlete. A little more than a fortnight later, Flanagan claimed another world record when he threw the 56-pound weight a distance of 36 feet, 9.5 inches at the IAAC games in Celtic Park, beating the existing record of Jim Mitchell of 35 feet, 10 inches. He now held the world records for throwing the hammer, with 171 feet, 9 inches; the discus, with 120 feet, 11 inches; and the 56-pound weight for distance with 36 feet, 9.5 inches. John "The Pocket Rocket" Flanagan was now master of everything he surveyed in the throwing domain, and the era of James Mitchell had long been buried.

Going into the 1904 Olympics, Flanagan was the overwhelming favorite for the hammer title. Friday, August 29, was a scorching-hot day at Francis Field. All six competitors were American, with John DeWitt and Ralph Rose pencilled in as the most likely threats to Flanagan. DeWitt, from Philipsburg, New Jersey, was a highly rated college football player with the Princeton Tigers, standing at 6-foot-1 and weighing more than 200 pounds; however, he, like the others in the field, was dwarfed by the giant Ralph Rose. Of the two, Rose was considered the most likely to provide Flanagan with a realistic challenge. Ralph Rose was a sensation and an American who many thought would challenge the hegemony of the Irish American throwers. From Healdsburg in California, he was an absolute beast of a man, standing 6-foot-5.5 and weighing more than 250 pounds. Photographs show a man with normally proportioned arms and legs, and a giant torso. Like many of the throwing athletes of the era, his muscularity was hidden beneath his immense bulk.

Until Rose came to public prominence, the only thing most people knew about Healdsburg was its importance as a center of prune production. During his first college year at the University of Michigan, Rose had set a new world mark in the 12-pound shot and an American record in the 16-pound version of the discipline. By all accounts, he was an ungainly thrower, but his sheer bulk and power made up for his technical shortcomings. Coming into the games Rose had won the shot and the discus at the U.S. Student Athletic Championships, known as the Big Ten Championships. Here was a man for the nativist-inclined Americans to get behind, a man born and raised on American soil, a man other than the Irish Catholic immigrants who had made the throwing events their own the previous few years.

There were reports that Rose had thrown 190 feet during the course of training in California, and his supporters had high hopes he would provide a stern challenge for John Flanagan, who had now won more than ten national titles in the United States. Alfred Plaw, who had beaten Flanagan at the AAU national championships—one of the few times the Irishman was ever beaten—did not make it to the games, further shortening the odds on the Irish athlete. James Mitchell was in attendance but past his best by then and substantially overweight.

John Flanagan opened the proceedings in the hammer-throwing final. He stepped into the seven-foot circle, carefully measured his distance, and swinging the weight around his head three times, made two lightning-like turns and sent the hammer whistling through the air in front of the appreciative crowd. After carefully measuring, the judges announced his throw as 168 feet, 1 inch long, a new Olympic record. DeWitt followed up with a throw of 164 feet, 11 inches, while Rose only managed to throw a disappointing 150 feet in his first attempt. In the adverse conditions, none of the athletes would improve on their marks; the competition was viewed as a disappointing display of hammer-throwing and all too easy for the superlative Flanagan. Rose's unorthodox technique let the giant American down on the day, and he deliberately fouled a number of times by stepping through the ring. The ever-competitive Jim Mitchell, now forty-four years old, finished a distant fifth.

Flanagan did not confine his throwing to the hammer at St. Louis; on September 1, he competed in the 56-pound throw from a seven-foot circle, an event that turned out to be one of the few at St. Louis that had an international dimension. Flanagan was considered joint favorite with Canadian Etienne Desmarteau, a police officer from Quebec who had obtained hero status when he saved a family from a potential arson attack on their shop while working his beat. Despite Desmarteau's high standing in his native city, the police had refused to allow him time off to compete in the games and duly fired him from the force when he insisted.

Flanagan and Desmarteau had met once previously at the AAU championships in 1902, where the Canadian had prevailed, but in July 1904, Flanagan had established a new world record in the discipline and was throwing exceptionally well in practice. Ralph Rose and Jim Mitchell were once again in the lineup; Rose opened the proceedings with a foul throw; Desmarteau followed with an effort of 34 feet, 4 inches. Flanagan was third into the circle and landed the weight at a mark of 33 feet, 4 inches. These proved to the best marks either could manage, and they took the gold and silver medals, respectively.

Desmarteau was one of only two non-Americans to take a gold medal at the games; the other was Tom Kiely, the great Irish athlete who won the all-around event competing as a nonaligned entrant.

Upon his return to Canada, Desmarteau was rehired by the police force and went on to set a new world record for the 56-pound throw from the seven-foot circle in July of the following year, before sadly succumbing to typhoid fever in October. His name lives on in Canadian sporting circles, as the basketball arena used for the 1976 Montreal Olympics was named in his honor.

John Flanagan had done the unprecedented when he took his second successive hammer throw and was rightly hailed a hero, but St. Louis also saw the emergence of another Irish Whale, considered by some to have been the greatest all-around athlete to have ever lived. The time had arrived for Martin Sheridan to take the stage.

6

PEERLESS ATHLETE AND INTREPID AMERICAN

Martin Sheridan and the Forgotten Olympics

When the New York Police Department (NYPD) was considering a suitable epitaph to engrave on the Celtic cross gravestone of Martin Sheridan in Calgary Cemetery, they came up with the words, "Peerless Athlete: Intrepid American." It was an appropriate tribute to the man some aficionadas still consider the greatest all-around athlete of all time. Sheridan, born in the small village of Bohola, County Mayo, would become a revered figure in the United States—and Ireland—and his life story encapsulates many of the themes and tropes that render the story of the Irish Whales so special.

The Bohola of Martin Sheridan's youth was one of open countryside, agricultural pursuits, and innocent games, albeit painted against a background of rumbling political strife centred on the burning question of land ownership and, for many, endemic, grinding poverty. Gaelic football, pitch and toss, and banging buttons had wide appeal, but it was to throwing that Martin Sheridan and his brothers were drawn. Local police officers were the wellspring of interest in the discipline among the youth of the area. In a field adjacent to the barracks, directly across the road from the Sheridan's homestead, the youngsters received instruction in the finer points of throwing techniques from members of the Royal Irish Constabulary, and it was Martin Sheridan who was able to outthrow all comers from a young age.

Like the rest of the west of Ireland, Bohola had suffered profoundly from the 1845–1847 famine. Between 1841 and 1851, the population of the area dropped from 4,301 to 2,970. Postfamine times were only marginally better, and employment opportunities were few. Government work schemes were put in place to try to alleviate some of the suffering. One of the projects was the making of the Treenduff road in front of the Sheridan homestead; the hard labor the men were forced to do for the reward of one stone of Indian meal per week may have influenced the young Sheridan that his future lay elsewhere.

Martin Sheridan was born on March 28, 1881, to Martin Sheridan Sr. and Jane Sheridan (née Durkin), the second youngest of seven children. Sheridan Sr. worked a ninety-acre farm inherited from his father Patrick, a significant landholding at that time, setting him at an economic and social remove from the vast majority of the local citizenry. Sheridan Jr. was born at the height of the land wars in a time of widespread privation among the agricultural classes, and it is little wonder that he would go on to hold strong nationalist sympathies for the rest of his life. Despite not suffering as badly as many of his schoolmates, Martin Sheridan was surrounded by the appalling vista of the grinding poverty and constant immigration that was the lot of the native Irish peasantry in the latter part of the nineteenth century. Like so many others, he followed a well-worn path when in 1899, he immigrated to the United States at the tender age of eighteen to join his brothers, Richard and Andrew.

A number of years later, Martin told journalist and fellow Olympic hammer thrower Robert Edgren of how he had stopped off at Southampton in England and spent a few weeks working with an Italian laboring gang before crossing the Atlantic. It is an account that deserves to be taken with more than a small handful of salt, if the style in which the story is written is an indication of its veracity. The story was published in *Munsey's Magazine* in the winter of 1909.

Upon arriving in the British port, the young Mayo man had no money and looked about for work. According to Edgren, a lifelong booster of Martin Sheridan, the Irishman saw a group of Italian laborers laying cables and carefully observed the techniques the men were using. Judging them laborious and inefficient, Sheridan undertook to do better. He knocked each spike into the ground with one blow of a sledge where the Italians had taken four or five.[1] The foreman of the laboring gang was duly impressed and employed the young Irishman, who proceeded to do three men's work. Throughout the day he swung his sledge without stopping. The other laborers tried in vain to keep up with the pace he set. When the day was through, Sheridan, "with an untamed Irishman's desire to proclaim himself as fresh as a daisy," jumped over the double railway tracks with a standing jump and back again.

Sheridan worked with the gang for a further number of weeks until he was happy he had enough money to continue onward to the United States. Everyone, except for the foreman, was happy to see him go. Edgren's story was most likely another example of the mythmaking that would become a significant part of the treatment given to the Irish Whales in the American press; they were consistently portrayed as characters who could manage feats beyond the ability of the mere mortal. There is no information from any other source to back up this story.

Not long after his arrival in the United States Martin joined his brother Richard and John Flanagan at a training session on the grounds of the Pastime Athletic Club in New York. Richard was a prominent athlete by then. At the end of the session the three men held an impromptu discus-throwing competition. The two experienced throwers were shocked at the natural ability of the younger Sheridan, who had limited prior exposure to the discipline. It was the start of an incredible athletic career. Like Jim Mitchell and John Flanagan before him, Martin Sheridan joined the NYPD after spending a short time working as an electric streetcar driver and instructor at the Pastime Athletic Club. His tram-driving days were once immortalized in a cartoon in the *New York Evening World* showing him reaching over the front of the vehicle throwing people out of the way and suggesting that this was the way he had developed his impressive physique.

There is little doubt that his brother Richard contributed significantly to Martin's rapid ascent through the ranks of throwers. Richard, also a NYPD officer, who went on to reach high rank, won American discus titles in 1898, 1899, 1901, and 1902, but by the time he won his third, Martin had become a talented thrower and it was he who was destined for greatness with his unique combination of strength, speed, and determination. Sheridan achieved his first competitive success in the discus in the United States when he threw 120 feet, 7.75 inches at Paterson Stadium, New Jersey, in September 1901. After trading the record with John Flanagan in a number of athletic meets, Sheridan set a new world-leading mark of 129 feet, 3 inches at the Pastime Autumn Games the following year.

Sheridan's ascent to the top of the shot put was also rapid. He took the American Athletic Union (AAU) Junior title in 1902, with a throw of 32 feet, 6 inches, a relative paltry effort in comparison to what was to come later. In 1904, he threw 40 feet, 9.5 inches to take the senior title, adding it to his discus title, and was well on his way to becoming one of the best athletes in the world. It was scarcely credible that Ireland had now provided all three athletes who dominated the throwing events on the world stage.

At 6-foot-2 and 220 pounds, Sheridan cut an impressive figure and would later be famously assigned personal bodyguard to the governor of New York in the course of his police duties. Robert Edgren frequently compared Sheridan to Phayllos of Croton, an ancient Greek athletic hero considered the greatest all-arounder of his day, and it was as an all-arounder that Sheridan would later find his greatest fame.

At the Olympics in St. Louis, at the age of twenty-three, Martin Sheridan went head-to-head with American teammate Ralph Rose in the discus and shot put. Going into the games, Rose was the favorite to take the gold in both events. The first half of Rose's mission was accomplished when he took the gold in the shot put, with Sheridan placing fifth. The giant American was set to double up in the discus in what would be a competition for the ages. With his first throw, Rose flung the disc to a new world record of 128 feet, 10.5 inches. Greek athlete Nicholas Georgantas threw an impressive 123 feet, 7.5 inches with his second attempt in a less-temperamental performance than his outing in the shot put, from which he had withdrawn in high dudgeon after his first two efforts were adjudged foul throws.

By the end of the third round, Sheridan found himself in the bronze medal position after a throw of 121 feet, 10 inches. With his fourth throw of 125 feet, the Irishman moved up one place, but it was his fifth that would prove decisive. Summoning all his energy he remarkably threw the exact same distance as Rose to balance the competition on a knife edge. This was an unprecedented situation; to throw an object such a long distance and have it land at the exact same distance was a rare outcome.

With their sixth and final throws, neither man improved on the tied distance, forcing a throw-off. It was, by any estimation, a remarkable turn of events that had never before happened at an Olympics. Each man was now required to throw three more times. In keeping with the shoddy record keeping of the games only the longest throw of each athlete is listed in the annals, but there was no doubt about the winner; with one of his throws reaching 127 feet, 10.5 inches compared to Rose's best effort of 120 feet, 6.5 inches, Martin Sheridan was the new Olympic discus champion. The manner of Sheridan's victory would become characteristic of his championship performances throughout his illustrious career.

Often a slow starter, he invariably rose to any challenge. He had that most desirable of abilities all athletes seek: When the chips were down, when he was backed into a corner, when defeat was staring him straight in the face, Sheridan was able to find an extra gear. Time and time again throughout his career, Martin Sheridan would demonstrate his unparalleled fighting abilities; he was a man who was never beaten until the final shot was thrown, and oftentimes, as at St. Louis, one of those final shots would be the one to decide the outcome. In any walk of life, but particularly in sports, the individual who does not countenance defeat as an option when the stakes are highest is the one who takes the laurels. Sheridan was the very definition of a championship athlete.

One of the many strange happenings at the St. Louis Olympic Games was the handicap competition in the throwing events in addition to the standard tournament. No longer considered valid Olympic medals, those awarded were subsequently removed from the all-time medal tables. Chief James E. O'Sullivan ostensibly programmed events to give high school boys and foreign athletes a chance to win a prize, but it did not work out like that. In the handicapped hammer, John Flanagan carried a zero handicap and took the title, followed by fellow American Albert Johnson, who carried a thirty-foot handicap, while the gallant Jim Mitchell finished in the bronze medal position with a handicap of twenty-three feet; however, it was Martin Sheridan who would provide the greatest demonstration of his sublime skills in the handicapped events with a throw of 132 feet in the discus. There was no doubt about the Irishman's ability.

Only three weeks after winning his gold medal in St. Louis, Martin Sheridan established a new world record of 133 feet, 6.5 inches for the discus, but it would be the unique occasion of the no longer recognized 1906 Intercalated Olympic Games that would prove his crowning glory. At the time they were referred to as the "Second International Olympic Games in Athens" by the International Olympic Committee (IOC), and medals were distributed to the winning athletes; however, these awards are no longer recognized by the governing body and are not displayed at the Olympic museum in Lausanne, the arbiter of all things Olympian.

Pierre de Coubertin did not think the games were a good idea but was overruled by other members of the committee who were anxious to resuscitate the flagging venture after the less-than-convincing American iteration. After the decision was made to proceed with the championships, de Coubertin did his best to ignore them; when the baron printed the program for the games in his *Revue Olympique*, he failed to mention the dates on which the games were to be held. Previewing the forthcoming event in a later edition, he included fourteen pages of text inviting readers to explore Greek art and history but only made one reference to the games, while leaving out the Olympic stadium as part of his recommended itinerary of the city. In the end, de Coubertin did not travel to the games, preferring to stay in Paris to attend a conference on arts, letters, and sports.

The IOC considered Athens a safe choice: It had the infrastructure and accommodations from the first games in 1896, and could surely be trusted to organize proceedings better than they had been in St. Louis or Paris. It had the history and heritage that, the organizers hoped, would lend credibility to a concept that had been badly rocked by the two dismal recent outings. The Greeks pulled out all the stops; even the royal family lent their organizational might to the games. Famous Italian decorator Alberto Fauntapier was commissioned to refurbish the streetscape of the adjacent port of Piraeus and design a pageant with the theme of a night in Venice, complete with gondolas. A towering colonnaded arch, which had been planned for the 1896 Olympic Games but never built, was erected in front of the stadium. Nathaniel Perry, an event organizer from the London Athletic Club, was brought in to oversee the redesign of the stadium seating and entrances, while many of the main streets of Athens were paved for the first time.

Even James E. Sullivan was impressed by the Greek approach, discerning an "atmosphere which is foreign to athletic followers either in America, Great Britain, Australia, or elsewhere."[2] Sullivan noted that the games meant a lot to the country and "brought reminiscences of the days of the Greek splendors and supremacy" with this spirit of sacredness pervading people from "the peasants to the royal family." It was the direct involvement of the Greek royal family that did much to make the games a success. In the first instance, King George I was related to a number of other European royals, being the second son of the late King Christian IX of Denmark and a brother of Queen Alexandra of Great Britain, who brought her husband, King Edward V, to the games—a major coup for the Greeks. King George's four sons adopted a hands-on approach during the championships and were frequently on the field keeping an eye on the proceedings or going to other venues to ensure everything was going according to plan. Crown Prince Constantin was in charge of the games; his brother, Prince George, acted as a referee and was in charge of the appeals committee; Prince Andrew directed the fencing contests, while Prince Nicholas helped out in general.

The 1906 Intercalated Games were viewed as a considerable success and created a number of firsts: They marked the first time the opening was held as a separate event, the first time athletes marched as a team behind their national flag, and the first time there was a designated athletes' village. They were also the first games with a closing ceremony, and for the first time national flags were raised for the victors, while the javelin and pentathlon were added to the schedule. The games were also notable from an American point of view, as the Americans formed the first semblance of a properly unified team. They were no longer a collection of athletes from a few elite clubs and universities, but a properly selected unit carefully managed by the capable American Olympic Committee, whose honorary president was none other than President Theodore Roosevelt.

This time the illustrious members of the New York Athletic Club were not wearing the winged foot on their singlet; it was replaced by a shield decorated with stars and stripes. It was clear the United States was now standing behind its athletes. A nationwide fundraising effort had brought in $14,000, which the Athens committee topped up with a further $1,500, while more than 2,000 people had come to Hoboken, New Jersey, to see the athletes off when they left aboard the *Barbarossa* on April 3. It was a great start to the American Olympians' venture, but the journey would prove unlucky for one Irish Whale.

Jim Mitchell had continued to compete until 1905, specializing in the 56-pound weight, and he had taken his final title at the age of forty-one at a meet in Portland, Oregon, where he defeated the fabled Ralph Rose. Astonishingly, Mitchell decided, just after his forty-second birthday, to compete in Athens in the stone-throwing competition, but after training ferociously for six months and losing fifty pounds in body weight, he suffered a cruel and unusual misfortune. While in transit to Athens, the *Barbarossa* was hit by a freak wave, causing Mitchell to fall and dislocate his shoulder, restricting his ability to compete. If not for his shoulders being so broad, it was reported, he would have been washed overboard. To add insult to injury, a Greek won the stone throw with an effort a full thirteen feet shorter than Mitchell had thrown in practice. Mitchell also gamely competed in the hammer, but by this time the piano wire hammer had replaced the old wooden version with which Mitchell had developed his formidable skills, and he no longer had the speed of his younger days. Despite the inevitable restrictions imposed by his injury, advancing age, and the changed nature of the implement, the veteran athlete managed to throw 147 feet, 6 inches with the 16-pound version of the hammer and 175 feet with the lighter 12-pound implement at Athens. The end of a wonderful career had finally come for the proud Irishman and the first of the Irish Whales.

Without any shadow of a doubt, the 1906 Intercalated Games belonged to Martin Sheridan. A new development in his burgeoning career had come in 1905. Until then, he had primarily been known as a discus thrower, and there was little public knowledge of his overall athletic ability. That changed dramatically when he entered the 1905 American All-Around Championships after encouragement from his colleagues in the Irish American Athletic Club (IAAC). The two favorites for the title, Ellery H. Clarke and Adam B. Gunn, were expected to have a closely fought battle; Sheridan did not figure high on the list of favorites.

The formidable Ellery Harding Clarke, born in March 1874, in West Roxbury, Massachusetts, had won both the high jump and long jump titles at the 1896 Olympic Games in Athens—still the only athlete to complete this double—and previously taken the AAU all-around title in 1897 and 1903, although he never managed to take a national title in either jumping event. Ellery's appearance was deceptive; at 5-foot-11 with a medium build, his bespectacled, quizzical face and unruly hair made him look more like an academic than a sportsman, but his mien belied a fiercely competitive instinct. His performances in the 1897 all-around event were of such a standard that he would have taken gold at the previous year's Olympics in the high jump, long jump, shot put, 100 meters sprint, and 110 meters hurdles. Ellery had also competed in the all-around competition at the 1904 games in St. Louis but was forced to drop out after five events due to bronchitis; despite only having points from those five events he still managed to finish in sixth position.

Adam Beattie Gunn, originally from the village of Golspie in the Scottish Highlands, had immigrated to Buffalo, New York, where he found a job with General Electric and athletic fame. In 1901, he had taken the all-around title when the American Athletic Championships were held in his hometown. The following year, he retained the title and went on to take the silver behind Tom Kiely—the great Irish all-arounder.

Ellery and Beattie did finish close to one another in the 1905 all-around competition—only four points separated them—but neither took the gold. Their fight was for silver and bronze, with the unheralded Sheridan usurping the two precompetition favorites in sensational fashion. Of the ten events listed in the program, the Mayo athlete finished first in five, joint first in another two, and third in the remaining three. It was a level of sustained excellence in the combined track and field event that had never before been seen on American soil and heralded the arrival of an outstanding new talent. When the points were added up, Sheridan had established a new record with a combined score of 6,820.5 points, a full 460 points ahead of the previous mark, set by Henry Gill of Toronto. It was a truly astonishing performance.

Coming into the 1906 Intercalated Games, Greek thrower Nikolaos Georgantas was, the Greek nation believed, a certainty for the discus title. The event had long been a sporting discipline held in the highest esteem by the Hellenes. The ancient Greeks considered the throwing of a discus a perfect test of an athlete's precision, coordination, and physical strength, and it was a central part of the schedule of the Ancient Olympics. In its earliest outings, the discus was one of the five events that made up the pentathlon; the other four were versions of jumping, wrestling, running, and javelin. The ancients variously used discuses made from lead, bronze, iron, and stone in different weight increments, depending on whether the competitions involved adult men or youths. Archaeologists have uncovered versions that weigh as little as four pounds and as much as thirteen pounds, and between eight and thirteen inches in diameter.

The centrality of the discipline in the sporting lives of the ancient Greeks is famously evidenced in Homer's *Iliad* in the section describing the funeral games for Patrockolus. Following the death of the Achaean hero, Achilles declared to the assembled Achaean army that there would be a special games held in honor of their dead comrade. The schedule for the games included chariot racing, boxing, wrestling, foot races, duelling with spears, archery, spear-throwing, and discus. The centrality of the discus to Greek sporting life is also evidenced in a work of art considered one of the greatest of its kind. The *Discobolus* of Myron—also known as the "discus thrower"—is a Greek statue completed in the late Severe Period, which ran from circa 460–450 BC. Sadly, the original statue, cast in bronze, has not survived, but it is known to the world from subsequent Roman copies cast mostly in marble with some miniature versions in bronze, for example, the *Palombara Discobolus*—the first such statue to be discovered.

The *Discobolus* of Myron has frequently been cited as the first piece of art to attain "rythmos"—harmony and balance; however, harmonious and balanced as it may appear to the art critics of the world, the throwing motion captured in the statue would be considered biomechanically inefficient by today's standards. The other trademark embodied in the sculpture, according to art historians, is "symmetria"—the proportioning of the body. The potential energy expressed in the sculpture's tightly wound pose, expressing the moment of stasis just before the release, showcases the advancement of classical sculpture from archaic times, according to experts, although some critics with knowledge of athletics have noted the lack of muscular strain shown in the statue despite the outflung limbs.

Palombara Discobolus, the first copy of the original statue to be found, turned up in 1781, in a private home in Rome. Dating from the first century BC, it was to have a remarkable journey. The prized artifact was sold to Adolf Hitler in 1938, by Italian foreign minister Galeazzo Ciano, despite vociferous opposition from scholars and many of his cabinet colleagues. In spite of the hue and cry, the priceless work of art was shipped to Munich, where it remained on display until 1948, when it was returned to the Italians, who chose to install it at the Palazzo Massimo in the National Museum of Rome—where it can still be seen in all its glory. During its time in Germany, *Discobolus* featured prominently in the opening sequence of the 1938 film *Olympia*, made by Leni Riefenstahl, which documented the Berlin Olympics of two years earlier.

From the extant statues it is possible to deduce how the Greeks threw the discus. The right-handed thrower brought his left foot forward and shifted his weight mainly to his right foot. With his right hand, he swung the discus a few times back and forth, slightly turning his body with the movement of the swing. After the last preliminary swing, the athlete moved his weight onto his left foot and, with a powerful swing, threw away the discus. Unlike modern athletes, Greek discus-throwers probably did not turn several times around their own axis. For that reason, they would have thrown significantly shorter distances.

After the discontinuation of the Ancient Olympics in AD 393, the discus mysteriously disappeared from view. German Christian Georg Kohlrausch is credited as the man who rediscovered and reintroduced the discus to the world as a competitive sport. In 1880, Kohlrausch was appointed as a gymnastics teacher at the Klosterschule Pädagogiumzum Kloster Unser Lieben Frauen, a former cloistered school in Magdeburg, and he gradually became known throughout the world through his experiments with pupils to rediscover the discus and the technique of throwing it, based on the available statuary and drawings. He became so well known in Germany that the sporting pioneer would receive letters from people worldwide addressed simply to "Christian Kohlrausch, Germany."

As the discipline regained its former popularity, the technique evolved. The first modern athlete to throw the discus while rotating the entire body was František Janda-Suk from Bohemia, in the present-day Czech Republic, who reputedly invented his technique when studying the position of the famous statue *Discobolus*. After a year of honing his skills, the Bohemian won the silver in Paris at the 1900 Olympic Games.

The 1906 discus final took place on Wednesday, April 25, the opening day of the championships. Martin Sheridan led from his first throw, followed by the two hulking figures Georgantas of Greece and Järvinen of Finland. Robert Edgren later described the details of the competition in what may be fantastic or fantastical detail. Sheridan's fourth throw sailed across the field and landed on the edge of the running track. The prince was duly impressed and pointed to a wall behind the running track: "That was a magnificent throw. It will be told for many years that Sheridan, of America, threw the discus into the running-track. If you could send it to the stone wall, now, you'd have a monument there to measure the throw for centuries."[3] This was a challenge Sheridan could not refuse, and he told the prince he might even be able to throw it over the wall and land it in a creek flowing on the other side. The creek was the famous Ilissus, much written about in Greek mythology. Sheridan managed to throw the discus to the foot of the wall, breaking the world record with three consecutive throws. The competition proved to be a one-sided affair. Sheridan threw 136 feet, while Georgantas only managed 118 feet, 3 inches, a shocking result for the natives looking on. Järvinen of Finland took the bronze medal. Martin promised the king he would come back some day and throw the discus over the wall.

Edgren described one of Sheridan's throws as follows:

> He put all the strength of his perfect body, all the determination of his stout Irish heart into it. As he swung to get his balance, his gray eyes shot fire, and the play of his muscles was like the writhing of snakes. There was a gasp of astonishment as the dish-like missile left his hand . . . it sailed, and sailed, and sailed. We knew long before it landed that no other man alive could equal the throw. [4]

The discus was only the start of Sheridan's remarkable medal haul at the 1906 Intercalated Games. That same day, he took the silver medal in the standing high jump, and on Friday he repeated the feat in the standing long jump, finishing behind compatriot Ray Ewry in both. In the shot put two days later, the best throw Sheridan could manage was 40 feet, 4.5 inches, well behind that of Järvinen of Finland, but fortuitously for the Irish American, the Finn was disqualified for throwing the shot illegally and the Irishman was awarded his second gold medal.

With two gold and two silver medals in his pocket, Martin Sheridan was not finished. In 1906, it was the sole outing in Olympic history for the stone-throwing competition; Sheridan only decided to enter it at the last minute as a replacement for the unfortunately injured Jim Mitchell. Sixteen athletes from eight countries entered the event, which simply involved throwing a 14-pound stone as far as possible using a technique of the athlete's choosing. Sheridan managed to throw 52 feet, 10 inches, good enough to take the silver medal behind Georgantas, who threw it 62 feet, 4 inches. It must have taken Sheridan back to his early days in Bohola when the police encouraged the local young boys to throw stones as an introduction to the techniques of discus and shot put.

If Sheridan had not injured his right leg while practicing for the standing long jump—he put the spikes from his left foot into his right calf muscle—he most likely would have taken the pentathlon title too, as he had been the overwhelming favorite for the event. In comparison to the ten-event all-around discipline Sheridan had dominated at the American championships, the five-event pentathlon, with the exception of wrestling, would have played to his strongest suits. The other four events—the standing long jump, javelin, Greek-style discus, and 600 feet foot race—

were all well within his comfort zone. Wrestling was the last event of the five to be held, and it was virtually a certainty Sheridan would have compiled enough points after the first four events to make his lead unassailable. But it was not to be, and he would later refer to it as the greatest disappointment of his illustrious athletic career.

Sheridan's individual points total in track and field at the 1906 Intercalated Olympic Games was more than that achieved by any other national team, with the exception of the United States. Two American athletes, Ray Ewry and Paul Pilgrim, finished on ten points each—the next-best individual score of the games—a full nine points behind Sheridan. His achievements so impressed King George that he awarded the Irishman a ceremonial javelin and erected a statue in his honor in Athens that is still extant; appropriately, it is a copy of *Discobolus* of Myron.

Sheridan had caught the eye of the world press at Athens. A journalist from the *Redmond Palladium* of September 1906 described him as such:

> [His] chest was unusually broad and deep, his shoulders square, the muscles of his legs having their greatest development in their long sinews rather than in circumference. His repose was the most striking thing about him after his muscular development, for he rarely moved, talked little, and laughed and smiled less. It was plain he took his work seriously.

The writer went on to describe Sheridan's throwing technique:

> It seemed he must necessarily leave the ground and fly up into space, so full of the suggestion of flying was the tense, beautifully graceful figure. Any sculptor that can create that effect in bronze is likely to be ranked among the masters of his kind and will create something far above the tinkling golf players and football warriors that represent our sculptors in the field of sport.[5]

The *Los Angeles Herald* noted his legs were "like rods of iron" and that "his firm face, his blue eyes, and brown hair make him an ideal of masculine development, and in his field he is worthy of the finest models carved by the ancient Greek sculptors."[6] The *Grand Forks Herald* described him as follows:

> Sheridan strips an Apollo. His face is tanned a ruddy bronze, but his body is as white as a baby's. As he steps about or raises his arms his

muscles spring and move like live things under the white sheath. As he steps into the circle his body unconsciously draws itself together, tense and alert, the muscles softly crawling and shaping themselves about the back, along the shoulders. His fingers clinch the weight, and as he raises his arms the ridges and mounds of muscles writhe and bunch under the skin. What a picture he makes raising for his throw! Sheridan's pose is worthy of the work of a great sculptor. [7]

The Intercalated Games were a triumph for the Greek nation and boded well for the future of the Olympic movement. That they had attracted athletes from nineteen competing nations was a major achievement and a balm for the wounds that had been opened by the two previous efforts. King George was effusive in his speech at the reception held to mark the closing of the games, expressing the hope that subsequent iterations of the games might return to his country. It did not come to pass, and the games have been wiped from the records.

In 1949, a three-man commission headed by IOC president Avery Brundage concluded that the games were not official, and the issue has never been subsequently broached. Given the similarities between de Coubertin's original vision for a modern Olympics and what transpired in Athens, it is ironic that this has remained the case. With a well-organized and executed program of sports, minus the shabby commercialism the World's Fair had brought to the two previous games, they were the best realization of the founder's dreams up to that point. They had also attracted more competitors than the Paris and St. Louis games combined, and did much to keep the Olympic idea alive.

An incident in Athens involving Irish athletes competing for Britain prefigured a controversial issue that would involve some of the Irish Whales at the 1908 Olympic Games in London. Con Leahy, Peter O'Connor, and John Daly were entered in the Athens games by the Irish Amateur Athletic Association and the Gaelic Athletic Association; they were even given green blazers and caps emblazoned with a gold shamrock and an Irish flag (the "Erin Go Bragh" version, which preceded the tricolor); however, the rules governing participation were changed just before the games commenced, and only athletes nominated by national Olympic committees were deemed eligible to compete. The British Olympic Committee saw an opportunity and immediately claimed the three Irish athletes, who were less than pleased but could not have competed otherwise. Encouraged by James E. Sullivan, head of the American delegation, the athletes asked members of the IOC if they could march under an Irish banner, but their request was summarily dismissed. O'Connor and Leahy took gold and silver, respectively, in the hop, skip, and jump—now the triple jump. At the flag-raising ceremony O'Connor saw his chance when two Union Jacks went up the pole. He scaled the flagpole in the middle of the field in front of 55,000 spectators, including members of the British royal family, and held an Irish flag aloft, while Leahy protected him from the authorities. It was arguably the first example of the politicization of sports at an international level.

In 1956, O'Connor told a journalist from the *Irish Times* about a letter of protest he had written to the organizing committee in which he noted that Pierre de Coubertin was happy to recognize Bohemia and Finland separately from their respective imperial overlords of Austria and Russia but unwilling to make a similar exception for Ireland, most likely because he was afraid to offend Britain. O'Connor went on to describe his actions at the presentation ceremony.[8] O'Connor asked Prince George of Greece if it would be possible to raise the Irish flag at a subsequent medal presentation ceremony but was politely rebuffed when the royal stated, "When Ireland has a parliament of its own you can hoist the flag but not before."[9] This time, instead of observing the two Union Jacks ascending the flagpoles, the Irish athletes walked around the stadium waving their Irish flags, letting spectators know where they really came from.

Athens was a triumph for the United States. The country had sent thirty-six men to the championships and brought home twenty-four medals. James E. Sullivan was proud to report that President Roosevelt had cabled him to congratulate the team, noting, "Uncle Sam is all right."[10]

It was also a fantastic triumph for members of the IAAC of New York. Tammany Hall politician Daniel F. Cohalan led the speeches at a banquet at the Astor Hotel welcoming back the victorious club athletes. He noted the contradiction of holding the celebration in such a rarefied environment when it was a "poor man's club that had won 32 points of the 75 of the American team at Athens."[11] For Martin Sheridan, from the tiny village of Bohola in the county of Mayo, the most poverty-stricken outpost on the west coast of Ireland, it was an unparalleled triumph. He owed a debt to the IAAC.

Cartoon by Thomas Nast entitled "The Ignorant Vote: Honors Are Easy," taken from *Harper's Weekly, December 9, 1876. Library of Congress LC-USZ62-57340.*

Irishman in work clothes admiring a well-dressed Irishman's stickpin. *Library of Congress POS-TH-STO.*

J. E. Sullivan, chief of the Department of Physical Culture at the 1904 World's Fair and the Olympics. *Courtesy of the Missouri Historical Society, St. Louis.*

Martin Sheridan of the Greater New York Irish Athletic Association, winner of the discus event at the 1904 Olympics. *Courtesy of the Missouri Historical Society, St. Louis.*

John Flanagan of the Greater New York Irish Athletic Association performing the 56-pound hammer throw at the 1904 Olympics. *Courtesy of the Missouri Historical Society, St. Louis.*

American athlete John Flanagan in the hammer throw competition at the 1904 Summer Olympics. *Crawford Family U.S. Olympic and Paralympic Archives, U.S. Olympic and Paralympic Committee.*

American athlete Martin Sheridan in the discus throw competition at the 1904 Summer Olympics in St. Louis. *Crawford Family U.S. Olympic and Paralympic Archives, U.S. Olympic and Paralympic Committee.*

Con Walsh throwing the hammer, possibly at the Cork Athletic Grounds, in 1906.
Courtesy Redmond Walsh.

1865-67   1904

Festival and Games of the

IRISH REVOLUTIONARY BROTHERHOOD VETERANS

At CELTIC PARK, Laurel Hill, L. I., Sunday, June 26, 1904

To Commemorate the 141st Anniversary of the Birth of Theobald Wolfe Tone.

GAMES COMMENCING AT TWO O'CLOCK   *MUSIC BY SOMERSET*

The following are the events to be contested for by some of the most noted athletes in the world:

BICYCLE RACES—Three and Five Miles.
FENCING CONTEST—Broadsword and Foils. For the Championship of America.
FOOTBALL MATCH—Irish Volunteers-Kerrymen.
IRISH PRIZE DANCING.
PUTTING HEAVY WEIGHT CONTEST—Between T. F. KEILY,
Ireland's Greatest Athlete, and JOHN FLANAGAN, Champion of America.

COMMITTEE OF ARRANGEMENTS:

P. J. CONWAY, Chairman   EDWARD WHELAN, Sec'y

TICKETS, 25 CENTS

Proceeds to be Devoted to the Erection of a Monument on the I. R. B. Plot in Calvary Cemetery to the Memory of the Men of '65 and '67 who Died in Exile.

Advertisement for sports day at Celtic Park, home of the Irish American Athletic Club. *Courtesy of Kevin McCarthy.*

Poster advertising an athletic competition between Martin Sheridan and Tom Kiely. *Courtesy of Kevin McCarthy.*

John Flanagan throwing the hammer at YMCA Brooklyn. *Library of Congress LC-B2-464-13.*

President Theodore Roosevelt standing with members of the 1908 U.S. Olympic team. *Library of Congress LC-USZ62-133049.*

Matt McGrath, American Olympic athlete, Bain News Service. *Library of Congress LC-B2-2210-11.*

John Flanagan cigarette card.

M. J. McGrath cigarette card.

Martin Sheridan cigarette card.

The 1912 Olympic Games in Stockholm. The United States sweeps the shot put. Left to right: **Pat McDonald (gold), Larry Whitney (bronze), Ralph Rose (silver).** *Graubergs Art Industry, Crawford Family U.S. Olympic and Paralympic Archives, U.S. Olympic and Paralympic Committee.*

Pat McDonald (USA, gold) at the 1912 Olympic Games in Stockholm, shot put. *Crawford Family U.S. Olympic and Paralympic Archives, U.S. Olympic and Paralympic Committee.*

Pat McDonald. *Library of Congress LC-B2-2404-11.*

The 1912 U.S. Olympic team takes the field in Stockholm, led by Matt McGrath and Ralph Rose. *Library of Congress LC-DIG-ggbain-12183.*

Pat McDonald examines the tape. *Library of Congress C-B2-2404-14.*

Irish American athlete Patrick Joseph "Pat" McDonald (McDonnell) (1878–1954). *Library of Congress LC-B2-2282-9.*

Irish Whales Pat McDonald and Matt McGrath, of the Irish American Athletic Club, posing for a 1912 U.S. Olympic team photo. *Library of Congress LC-B2-2542-8.*

Baron Pierre de Coubertin, founder of the Olympic movement. *Library of Congress LC-B2-3302-6.*

Officer McGrath on the beat near the Brooklyn Bridge, early 1900s. *Library of Congress LC-B2-3921-11.*

Paddy Ryan. *Library of Congress.*

James Sarsfield Mitchell, the first of the Irish Whales. *Library of Congress.*

Con Walsh representing the Seattle Police Department, probably in 1922, when he was forty-one. *Courtesy of Redmond Walsh.*

Con Walsh on his last visit home to Ireland. *Courtesy of Redmond Walsh.*

Monument for Pat McDonald at White Strand, Doonbeg, County Clare Ireland. *Courtesy of Night of the Big Wind.*

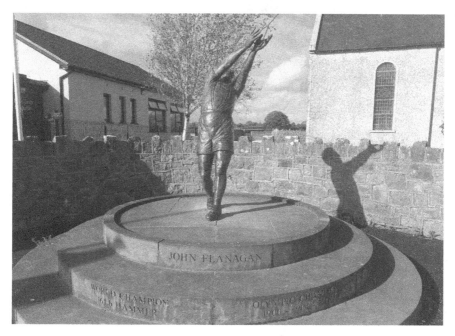

Statue of John Flanagan, Martinstown, County Limerick. *Courtesy of Kevin McCarthy.*

Statue of Paddy Ryan, Pallasgreen, County Limerick. *Courtesy of Kevin McCarthy.*

Statue of Matt McGrath, Nenagh, County Tipperary. *Courtesy of Kevin McCarthy.*

7

THE IRISH AMERICAN ATHLETIC CLUB
Home of the Whales

While the Irish Whales had developed their techniques in Ireland, it was the vibrant New York athletic system that would be their making. They were naturally gifted sportsmen, but it was the New World that honed their technical mastery. The New York athletic system was the most technically advanced in the world at the start of the twentieth century, and the northeastern urban centers of the country provided the keenest competition available anywhere. An estimated seven hundred athletic clubs catered to the masses in the Greater New York area. Each weekend clubs of various ethnic, religious, social, and political hues organized and competed in well-publicized track and field meets. It was the deep immersion of the Irish Whales in this ultracompetitive milieu that brought out the best in them.

The United States was the center of progress where science was rapidly transforming countless aspects of human endeavor, notably sporting performance. As the *Los Angeles Times* noted in 1908, "America trains her athletes as she does her racehorses. Our athletics are filled with technicalities and minute points of which British athletes do not dream."[1] For the majority of the Irish Whales, it was the Irish American Athletic Club (IAAC) of New York that would provide their scientific education.

The first of three incarnations of the IAAC of New York was instituted in April 1879, with the intention of providing a sporting outlet for Irishmen other than the patrician environments of such clubs as the New

York Athletic Club (NYAC). With their fellow countrymen, Irish athletes could practice their sport in a collegial and comfortable environment. The club held its first meeting the following month with a program of ten athletic events, in addition to a keenly contested tug-of-war between a team of bachelors and a team of married men. Despite holding four further annual meets, the first IAAC petered out in 1885.

With the Gaelic Athletic Association (GAA) tours of the United States in 1885 and 1888, the pride Irish immigrants had in their sporting abilities must have been reignited, as a second incarnation IAAC of New York was established in 1890. Its expressed aim was to encourage manly sport and exercise, and develop sporting success among the Irish communities in the same way the Turn Verein did for German immigrants. As well as track and field athletics, this reincarnation of the club organized Gaelic football, baseball, and soccer. It achieved some successes, for instance, winning the first Gaelic football championship of New York, but once again the efforts of the instigators did not bear lasting fruit and the club finished up in 1894. It would be a case of third time lucky.

Founded in 1898, as the Greater New York Irish Athletic Association—a name reconstituted to the Irish American Athletic Club in 1904—under the guidance of Limerick native P. J. Conway, it would have unparalleled success during its existence. The club crest—a winged fist adorned with American flags and shamrocks under which was written the Irish motto, "Láimh Láidir Abú" (Strong Hands Forever)—would go on to strike fear into the hearts of competitors in track and field throughout the country. In addition to reflecting the patriotic sentiments of the founders, the emblem was designed to symbolize strength, fighting powers, speed, and athletic agility.

The IAAC had its famous fortress at Celtic Park in the borough of Queens, a seven-acre site purchased in 1897, for $9,000, when it was a suburban farming community known as Laurel Hill—today part of modern Sunnyside. New York's Celtic Park was named after the home of the Glasgow Celtic Association Football Club in Scotland, a similar hotbed of Irish nationalistic sentiment. It was frequently claimed that the IAAC facilities were deliberately built on the trolley line running to Calvary Cemetery, making it convenient to access for Irish immigrants already visiting their dearly departed in the city's largest Catholic cemetery—known as the "City of the Celtic Dead" to some wags—but as with the descriptions of the appetites of the Irish Whales, this most likely contains an element of hyperbole engendered by racial stereotypes.

At the time of its construction Celtic Park was one of the foremost athletic club facilities in the world. On May 30, 1898, the inaugural track and field meet at the stadium was held after a dedication speech by New York City magistrate Henry Brann—an Irish native—but the final touches were not put to the stadium until 1901, when the *New York Times* described it as one of the most "completely equipped places of the kind about the city" with a bowling alley, a restaurant that could accommodate 1,100 people, and a stand that could hold 2,500 people, as well as shower baths and dressing rooms. It was a remarkable achievement for members of an ethnic group who had long struggled against discrimination in their adopted home.

In 1908, Joe Fitzgerald of the *Gaelic American* newspaper interviewed P. J. Conway, founder and president of the IAAC, about the early days and development of the club. The opening of the piece by Fitzgerald was dramatic, eulogizing members of the club for their participation at the 1908 Olympic Games in London, which were ongoing:

> F-I-G-H-T! Irish! Natural enough to see those two words together, isn't it? Yes? Knew you were going to say that. But do you know what it means in this particular instance? No? Well, stick this one in your sweatband. It's the battle cry of the Irish American Athletic Club. It's the Celtic Park college yell. Twenty-one wearers of the Winged Fist, the emblem of the famous athletic organization, took it over to London with them, and judging by the way they are piling up points other nationalities now participating in the Olympic Games will have good reason to remember it.[2]

The journalist highlighted the importance of Conway to the development of the club and outlined his rise from humble apprentice blacksmith to owning one of the finest "equine shoe palaces" in the city on East 60th Street, where "his name is a byword wherever high-class horses hang out." Conway was self-deprecating when the journalist praised his role as the founder of the club, emphasizing that he was only one of a number of men who were involved. He explained that the club started in a back kitchen on East 66th Street and joked that the room was so mall each man could only bring one idea to the meeting. By the time of the interview in 1908, ten years after its establishment, the club had 1,230 members.

Conway attributed the success of the club to democratic principles; each man was treated the same regardless of his station in life.

In the original conception Celtic Park was to be a venue for the native Irish games of hurling and Gaelic football, but from the start it hosted athletic competitions under the auspices of the American Athletic Union (AAU); between 1902 and 1912, it hosted six of the All-Around Championships—the precursor of the modern-day decathlon. From the start, the IAAC was set up to accommodate the athletic needs of the working-class man in opposition to the elitist nature of the NYAC and its ilk. Apart from athletic pursuits, Celtic Park served a wider social and political role for Irish immigrants in New York. The *Gaelic American* noted that the Spanish War was insignificant compared to the foundation of Celtic Park because the formation of the Public Schools Athletic League, the Catholic Athletic League, the Military Athletic League, and the Irish Counties Athletic Union could all be traced directly to the sporting venue.[3]

The stadium also played a central role for the Irish county societies' benevolent associations, the GAA, and the Irish Volunteers, which regularly held events, meetings, and fundraisers there. The IAAC added immensely to the social and cultural fabric of the immigrant community, even providing a place of meeting and refuge for radical political elements involved in the ongoing fight against British imperialism and the quest for a free Ireland. It provided a bulwark of sociability and solidarity where the Irish could let down their guard among their own; however, it would be the sporting achievements of members of the IAAC that would bring the greatest pride to Irish America—none more so than John Flanagan, who took over the mantle of world's greatest thrower from Jim Mitchell.

Perhaps the most admirable achievement of the IAAC was its inclusivity and democratic nature. According to Jewish Olympic champion Abel Kiviat, it was a "kind of poor man's club and included policemen, firemen, sanitation workers, and other laborers and school kids like myself. If you could run or jump, you could try out."[4] Whereas the wealthy and elitist NYAC discriminated against Jews and other white ethnic, working-class people, the IAAC welcomed them.[5] Despite its name, it was open to everyone. Another Jewish athlete, Myer Prinstein, for example, won gold in the long jump and triple jump at the St. Louis games in 1904, a feat never equalled.

Perhaps the club's most profound legacy was the removal of the "color line," paving the way for the rise of black athlete John Baxter Taylor Jr. Taylor had graduated as a vet from the University of Pennsylvania, where he had come under the athletic tutelage of renowned Irish coach Mike Murphy. It was a brave move to allow Taylor, a child of former slaves, membership in the IAAC. If he wanted to join the NYAC, he would have had to wait until 1968, when it ended its color barrier. After joining the IAAC, despite some dissenting voices on the committee, Taylor became a hugely popular figure at the club. The *New York Mail* reported on the meeting during which the athlete's application for membership was discussed and quoted one attendee as saying, "We don't want a naygur in oor club."

It was the words of the "liberal-minded, genial, and democratic in the extreme" P. J. Conway that swung the meeting in favor of the "speedy smoke." Conway pointed out that the club already had Jewish and Dutch members, so there was no reason why a black athlete could not join:

> Our name is the Irish American Athletic Club, and under that wurrud, American, comes out our jutificableness in having these Dootchmin and Jews as our fellow members, an' where there's room for Dootchmin and Jews, there's no excuse in the wurruld for keeping out a man like this excellent naygur, more power to his lungs and speed to his legs.[6]

Tragically, Taylor would have a short-lived career in the IAAC, dying at the age of twenty-six in 1908, after contracting typhoid fever.

The IAAC prided itself on its appeal to the ordinary working man as opposed to the elites, who peopled associations like the NYAC. It provided a platform for other ethnicities to compete on a level playing field. Before the club took its first title, the NYAC had a stranglehold on the national championship for two decades.

The IAAC would go on to produce athletes who, between them, would win fifty-five Olympic medals between 1900 and 1928; at the 1908 London games members of the IAAC won ten of twenty-three gold medals, more than France, Germany, and Italy combined. Perhaps most notable was the gold won by John Baxter Taylor Jr. in the relay, making him the first African American to win a gold medal. Thirteen members of the IAAC competed as part of the U.S. Olympic team at the 1912 Olympic

Games in Stockholm, Sweden, winning 5 gold medals, 4 silver medals, and 1 bronze medal. It was truly an incredible level of sustained success.

Other non-Irish athletes who competed wearing the Winged Fist on their vests included Jewish men Harry Hyman and Alvah Meyer; Swedish Olympic gold medalist John Eke; the original "Flying Finn," Hannes Kolehmainen; Italian Emilio Lunghi; and Scot Lawson Robertson. Even Harold Wilson, an English runner who Mel Sheppard had beaten in the 1500 meters at the London games, preferred the IAAC over the Anglocentric NYAC.[7] The club also owed much of its success to foreign-born coaches like the famous Swedish American Ernie Hjertsberg, who outlined his innovative theories in his 1914 treatise *Athletics in Theory and Practice*.

There is no doubting the political role played by the IAAC in the lives of some Irish Americans. The *Gaelic American* regularly and enthusiastically reported crowds of 10,000 or 15,000 who paid twenty-five cents each to get into sports days organized for the benefit of Clan na Gael at Celtic Park. The ultimate wish of Clan na Gael was that some of the multitudes who attended the picnics in Celtic Park would be filled with thoughts of the national cause and be motivated to return to Ireland to fight for the freedom of their native country. John Devoy even advertised free rifles to any readers who had the desire to go back and fight, and explained that they could learn to shoot in the United States before returning to Ireland to put their newfound skills into practice: "In Ireland the people can't practice rifle shooting. In America, every man can have a rifle and learn how to use it. The riflemen that will free Ireland must be trained here."[8] The hoped-for Irish American freedom-fighting brigade did not materialize, but Tom Clarke did return to Ireland, taking some of the money raised by the IAAC to fund future military operations that would eventually allow Ireland to strike for freedom from Great Britain on Easter 1916. (Clarke was later executed by firing squad for his participation in the rebellion.)

Programs for the Clan na Gael annual sports days at Celtic Park are unequivocal in their support of violent insurrection in the pursuit of a free Ireland. In the 1905 program, for example, John Daly from Limerick gave a state-of-the-nation statement to Irish immigrants in an article entitled "How Is Old Ireland?" While he wished he could furnish some positive news about the old country, he could not, because the country was still under British rule; however, he believed the younger generation had it in their minds to rise up and end colonial power. Daly emphasized the uselessness of the constitutional nationalists who were representing Ireland in the British Parliament and willing to accept anything other than complete freedom from Britain. He believed the younger generation would rise up and condemn the half-hearted attempts of these lily-livered parliamentarians. While he bemoaned emigration, he also noted a positive side: "Emigration is taking away a great many of our young people—but there is one consolation, they are nearly all going to a land where the Gael has great power, and if they remain true to Ireland in exile they can exert immense influence against England when the time of her difficulty comes."[9] He advised readers to bide their time for a solution but assured them the opportunity would arise. England, he believed, was no longer the force it once was. The Irish people had never been found wanting when it was time to take on the oppressor, and he hoped that the "Irish beyond will lend them [those Irish living in Ireland] no small assistance."

In another article from the same program, the author challenged readers with the fighting words, "What Are You Doing for Ireland?" If you were doing nothing to further the cause, you were only a nominal Irishman and a reproach to the old country. He exhorted the reader in no uncertain terms: "Be a *worker* if you love the old land. Don't be a *shirker*." In another article, author "DhonFierna" railed against the stereotypical representation of the Irish on the American stage. It was the English who had started the ball rolling with the image of the Irishman as a "baboon face, wild whiskers, and lowering brow—dressed up in the garb of ignorance and buffoonery and poverty and presented to the Americans as a type," he believed. He urged readers to address the issue wherever they could.

In the 1909 program, an article entitled "Our Position and Our Hopes" started out by castigating politicians in Ireland who were only interested in lining their own pockets. It went on to fulminate against the Irish press, who ostensibly claimed to have a nationalistic ideology but did nothing to back it up and simply repeatedly expressed the opinion that Britain was moving in the right direction.[10] This, according to the author, was not at all the case. Unless there was a violent uprising, the British would do nothing to ameliorate the lives of those resident in Ireland. For those in the United States who were wondering exactly what Clan na Gael was doing with the money collected, he assured them it was doing everything possible to secure Ireland's freedom and defeat the colonial powers. He had no doubt that if they worked together, this could be achieved.

The IAAC was a unique part of the social and cultural history of the Irish in New York, and its achievements were astonishing; in the first two decades of the twentieth century, the club won the AAU Union National Outdoor track and field team championship titles in 1904, 1906, 1907, 1908, 1910, 1911, 1912, 1913, 1914, and 1916, as well as the AAU National Indoor track and field team championship titles in 1906, 1908, 1909, 1911, 1913, 1914, and 1915. Celtic Park hosted the AAU All-Around Championships on six occasions.

But it was not all plain sailing for the IAAC, and Celtic Park witnessed its share of arrests and crowd trouble throughout the years. In November 1903, for example, a Gaelic football referee was arrested at the Irish Volunteers Annual Field Day at the stadium for organizing sports on the Sabbath, an issue that preoccupied many Protestants. There was no further attempt to play the game, but the Volunteers held an "indignation meeting," at which they heavily criticized the New York Police Department commissioner and noted they had not broken any law, as no admission was charged to patrons.[11] The case was subsequently dismissed in court. Two years later, members of the Sabbath Observance Society came to Celtic Park on a Sunday to arrest violators of the Sunday Laws. Among those taken into custody were famous sprinter Lawson Robertson and renowned coach Ernest Hjertbert. Once more the case was thrown out of court. The same judge presided and told the members of the society they were wasting both his and their time.

Friction between the Irish Counties Athletic Union (ICAU), established to coordinate Gaelic games in the city, and the IAAC was also an issue. The ICAU argued that the IAAC charged too much for matches held in Celtic Park. When the fifty-cent admission charge to the Irish Counties Athletic Games of 1906 proved unpalatable to some of the patrons, they proceeded to smash down the gates; only $50 was collected from the estimated crowd of five thousand.[12] The ICAU and IAAC subsequently parted company. In a further example of the friction that was not unknown at Celtic Park, a fourteen-year-old boy was shot and badly wounded when he made a "tart reply" to an officer who had asked him to get off the wooden perimeter fence in April 1909.[13]

Notwithstanding the occasional difficulties, the Irish athletes who achieved so much with the IAAC helped their fellow Irishmen in the

United States in no small way. They were immense figures in the lives of their fellow immigrants, and their greatest triumph would come on the Olympic stage in London in 1908.

8

THE IRISH WHALES' GREATEST TRIUMPH

The 1908 London Olympics

> May joy and good fellowship reign, and in this manner, may the Olympic Torch pursue its way through ages, increasing friendly understanding among nations, for the good of a humanity always more enthusiastic, more courageous, and more pure.—Pierre de Coubertin

The 1908 Olympics—officially the Games of the IV Olympiad—were originally awarded to Rome after its bid was chosen over Milan and Berlin, but they were reassigned to London when it became apparent that the Italians would not be ready to accommodate the championships. Mount Vesuvius had erupted in 1906, and authorities claimed they needed to redirect the resources they had set aside for the Olympics to the reconstruction of Naples. London was then chosen because organizers believed its fame and ease of access would attract competitors from throughout the world. The International Olympic Committee (IOC), above all, wished not to repeat the mistakes of the 1904 games in St. Louis. Of all the Olympics that involved the Irish Whales, the London championships would throw the themes, tropes, and legacy of their lives and achievements into sharpest relief.

The complex tripartite relationship between Great Britain, the United States, and Ireland was embodied by the Whales who took to the world stage in London and would provide a lens through which the world could view the fractious relationship between the greatest power brokers on earth, as well as their differing views of a small island off the western coast of Europe. For radical Irish Republican nationalist John Devoy, the event would be similar to going to war for the American contingent. While they would not compete with arms, their "implements of combat are speed, strength, and confidence" would conquer the world in the London stadium. [1]

From the start, the games would prove tendentious and confrontational. Lord Desborough, chairperson of the British Olympic Association and a man of myriad achievements, was tasked with overall management of the project; among other adventures, he climbed the Matterhorn and swam across the base of Niagara Falls. Desborough did not take his duties lightly, believing England was the "motherland of athletics and sport" and should expend every effort to make the games worthy of the occasion and the country. [2]

Fortuitously for the British Olympic Committee the Franco–British Exhibition of the Sciences, Art, and Industry was also scheduled for London in 1908, and exhibition organizers generously agreed to finance and build a multipurpose stadium at Shepherd's Bush, adjacent to the exhibition site, even offering to share any profits. For the first time, a facility, later to become known as White City due to its ugly concrete structures, was specially prepared for the Olympic Games. It was built by George Wimpey in a remarkable ten months, at a cost of £44,000. The stadium included a 100-meter swimming and "diving pond" in the infield area; a 536-meter cinder running track surrounded by a 600-meter banked cycling track; and a grass area to accommodate football, hockey, rugby, lacrosse, wrestling, and gymnastics. It was designed to host 93,000 spectators but could hold as many as 130,000 standing. Luck, however, was not on the side of the organizers. During the summer of 1908, London experienced a significant amount of rainfall, which resulted in the infield area of the stadium being turned into a quagmire, while the swimming pool became clouded with dirt; by the end of the swimming schedule, competitors were colliding with one another.

Until the 1908 Olympics, British interest in the Olympic idea had been tepid, but attitudes started to change when London was awarded the games; many elements in the press portrayed Britain being chosen host as a tribute to the inherent superiority of the country. After all, it had been the British who first codified so many sports and consistently demonstrated their organizational abilities throughout the world. Despite such glowing endorsements it was an age of anxiety for the empire. The Boer War had surprisingly stretched its military capabilities; the Germans were producing two-thirds of Europe's steel, had caught up with British coal production, and were now in the ascendant in emerging chemical and electrical technologies. The United States was on a continuing upward trajectory in the new century. The Olympic Games stood as a chance for Britain to reassert its greatness on the world stage.

More than 2,000 athletes, 37 of them women, from 22 countries competed in 110 events in 24 sporting disciplines at the fourth official running of the modern Olympics. Finland and Turkey competed for the first time, as did athletes from New Zealand—albeit as part of an Australasian team. Diving, field hockey, and relay racing made their first appearances on the schedule, while powerboat racing was given its sole outing in the history of the championships. It was the first and only time in the history of the championships that Great Britain won the most medals, with 146—56 of them gold.

The games began on April 27 and finished on October 31, making them the longest in the history of the modern Olympics, lasting 187 days, surpassing the record set at St. Louis. The athletic standards of the games were much higher than the previous two official iterations, but that was hardly surprising given the shambolic organization of both of those. In swimming, for example, world records were established in five of the existing six events. Among the highlights of the championships were the performances of American Ray Ewry, who for the third games in a row took the title in the standing high jump and the standing long jump, becoming the only person to win a career total of eight gold medals in individual track and field events.

Despite such standout performances the games were beset by problems from the start. Dwarfed by swathes of empty seats, only thirty thousand attended the opening ceremony, while the weather proved inclement during the entire first week of the proceedings. From the outset, the relationship between British administrators and the American delegation was fractious; when James E. Sullivan saw the accommodations the British had provided for the U.S. team, he took immediate umbrage and moved his charges to Brighton. Before the games started, American officials objected to the participation of Canadian marathon runner Tom Longboat on the grounds that he was a professional athlete. Longboat—his original name was Cogwagee, meaning "everything" in the Onondaga Nation of the Iroquois Confederacy—was a member of the Irish Canadian Athletic Club in Toronto, and one of the favorites for the title. With Tom Flanagan (a brother of thrower John), Longboat had completed his preparations in Kilmallock, County Limerick. The IOC's decision to let Longboat compete contributed significantly to the disharmony between the American delegation and British officials. In the end, Longboat collapsed during the race, along with a number of other athletes. There were unsubstantiated rumors that Flanagan had drugged his athlete to collect on a bet, but it was more likely due to the unusual heat of the day.

More turmoil erupted before the start of the games when money was stolen from the bags of three American athletes while they were training in the newly constructed stadium. Each had £100 taken, a considerable sum at the time. Further trouble would surface once the competitions began.

The story of the role played by the American flag in the opening ceremony has long been part of Olympic folklore and a tale forever associated with the Irish Whales. The exact details of the story are disputed and the truth will never be known, but the various accounts of what transpired, particularly those of Arthur Daley and the American press, provide ample evidence of the mythology created around the Irish Whales.

The story goes that when the U.S. team noticed that their national flag had been inadvertently omitted from those flying at the stadium during the opening ceremony, American athlete Ralph Rose retaliated by refusing to lower the Stars and Stripes as it passed by the royal box. It was suggested that the incident was instigated by the Irish American contingent on the U.S. team, who objected to Ireland having to compete for the United Kingdom. The first shot in anger was fired when Irish American James E. Sullivan said it would be a shame if Ireland, which had supplied many of the world's finest athletes, should have to hide its identity behind the geographical description of Great Britain.

Meanwhile, the Gaelic Athletic Association (GAA) in Ireland issued a warning to its twelve competing members that they must not, under penalty of expulsion, take part in the games, unless the land of their birth received official recognition. There is no doubting the delicate political situation that underpinned the 1908 Olympics, and it certainly did not help that King Edward VII was on the throne. Before his accession he had been prince of Wales, but in Ireland—and in countries throughout the world that had a political sensitivity to recent Irish history—he was known as the "Famine Prince," as his reign as titular leader of the Welsh principality coincided with the decimation wrought on Ireland by the failure of the potato crop during the 1840s. Regardless of what he did or did not do, such an association was never going to sit easy with athletes with Irish nationalist sympathies. That they saw the opening ceremony as a way of demonstrating their loyalties is a strong possibility. Martin Sheridan held particularly passionate nationalistic views and was a member of Sinn Fein in New York; he, too, had expressed his disappointment in print that Irish athletes were competing for Britain.

Popular myth suggests it was the next emerging Irish Whale—Matt McGrath—who started the ball rolling by threatening Ralph Rose that he would require medical attention if he dipped the flag; McGrath supposedly uttered the words, "Dip that banner and you're in a hospital tonight."[3] This sparked a backlash among those with British sympathies, and according to most versions of the story it was Martin Sheridan who uttered the immortal rejoinder: "This flag dips for no earthly king."[4] According to some accounts, members of the U.S. team surrounded Rose to congratulate him on his bravery. The *Freeman's Journal* suggested Rose marched past the royal box a second time with his flag proudly aloft.[5]

In 1952, Arthur Daley wrote a speculative account of the flag-dipping incident in his "Sports of the Times" column in the *New York Times*, outlining what he thought took place the night before the opening ceremony. As was his wont, he peppered his narrative with generous helpings of his interpretation of the Irish accent of the athletes—no account of their doings by Daley was complete without the brogue dialed high. They were incensed that athletes resident in Ireland had to compete for Britain. These Irish Americans were Irish, too; Daley noted that "none of their ancestors came from Lower Slobodia," as they were much too close to the "Ould Sod." The plan the athletes hatched was, inevitably, conceived in a pub. Each passing hour and drink, so Daley wrote, intensified the nationalistic sentiments of the Irish American athletes.

"Tis a disgrace, it is," said Pat McDonald (another of the Irish Whales) in his soft County Clare brogue, "to think that our glorious American flag will be dipped tomorrow to the crowned head of a kingdom." "And him an English king, too," said Flanagan. "George Washington, the Lord have mercy on his soul, freed America from the yoke of a British king," said Sheridan. "We can't permit our flag to dip," said McGrath, pounding the table with brawny fist until the pewter mugs danced. "Ralph, me lad," said McDonald, drawing himself up to his full three hundred pounds and 6-foot-5 frame, transfixed huge Ralph Rose with baleful glare and told him that he was to carry the flag.

Rose may have been chosen because he was the biggest. Reportedly, McDonald told Rose he would "break him in half" if he dipped the flag. The threat had been laid down, and Rose was happy to acquiesce, according to Daley.

The fact that Martin Sheridan did not see fit to mention the event in his column for the *Evening World* newspaper, in which he wrote about the proceedings in London, raises questions about the entire episode. Instead of mentioning the opening parade, Sheridan was happy to provide accounts of the enormous appetites of his fellow Whales, playing into the mythology already created by the American press. He noted how Ralph Rose, John Flanagan, and Matt McGrath consistently caused a "panic in the pantry" where McGrath once tucked into "five plates of soup, four orders of fish, three broiled chickens, two steaks . . . seven cups of custard, three pieces of apple pie, four cups of coffee, and two pounds of cheese."[6] It was stretching it, and McGrath's stomach would have been well stretched, too.

Sheridan did, however, allude to the flag-dipping incident in a later column, when he noted that his "heart took a leap for joy" when he saw the American flag pass the reviewing stand without dipping.[7] Reports in the American press were various and contradictory. The *Philadelphia Inquirer* thought it hard to believe that Rose failed to dip the flag intentionally, but if he did, those with a combative nature would not blame him. The *Bookman* adopted a more pro-British stance, criticizing the choice of Rose as flag carrier, as it was well known that he was a hothead and had even offered to fight world heavyweight boxing champion James J. Jeffries after the 1904 Olympics. It also pointed to the termination of his studies at the University of Michigan for persistent rowdy behavior and criticized those who supported his act of "boyish patriotism."[8]

J. Ed Grillo of the *Washington Post* considered the incident "undiplomatic, ungentlemanly, and surely not in keeping with true sportsmanship," and believed that every true American would "deplore this exhibition of indecency and failure to observe the rules of good behavior."[9] The *Chicago Tribune* opined that Rose's lack of judgment was not easy to excuse and could only wonder what Americans would think if it was President Roosevelt who had been snubbed by British athletes;[10] however, it was left to the redoubtable Robert Edgren, sporting editor of the *Evening World*, to provide the most colorful and entertaining account of the incident to the American public. He described King Edward sitting in his royal box as "fat, happy, and smiling," surrounded by his thousands of subjects waiting for the parade to begin. He noted that the American contingent was different in their marching style than the other nations. They sauntered along with a "loose swinging step, light and airy, like the step of khaki-clad rough riders dancing up San Juan Hill." Compared to the military-like appearance of the others, the Americans were "free and easy and debonair." Ralph Rose, a "Goliath of a man," led the contingent past the smiling king with his flag aloft. A "sudden horrified silence" fell on the crowd, and a hundred thousand Englishmen exclaimed, "My word."[11] Edgren was one who often gilded the lily in his telling of stories and no other report mentioned a shocked crowd, but at the end of the day the full truth of what happened will never be known.

Talk of flags dominated the opening day of the London Olympic Games for additional reasons. British authorities were unable to come up with a Swedish flag, while, incongruously, the flags of China and Japan were flying proudly above the stadium, even though neither country was competing. Meanwhile, the Finns refused to carry a flag when they were told they would have to march as part of the Russian team. They did compete, but their medals were awarded under the standard of Tsarist Russia. British authorities later claimed the absence of the American flag was simply an oversight. Had they not put Imre Kiralfy, director general of the Franco–British Exposition and a man who for many years lived in New York, in charge of organizing the flags? Three of Kiralfy's sons had been born in the United States, and one was even on the U.S. sprint team. They were naturalized U.S. citizens to boot. Kiralfy had nothing but the highest respect for the Americans, the British argued. Was he not the very man who had brought New York to its feet with his two thousand–strong cast production of *The Fall of Rome* some years earlier? Was he not one of the most highly regarded impresarios of the Gilded Era? The American delegation did not buy the argument. Had not, they may have inquired, the Hungarian-born Kiralfy moved to England a few years prior?

Yet, further controversy erupted between the American delegation and British officials on the opening day of the competition when the preliminary heats were run for the "metric mile"—now the 1,500-meter race. The British held the drawings for heat assignments in private, a process that resulted in the best U.S. runners being bunched together in two heats, where they eliminated one another. James E. Sullivan immediately protested, but the British continued to hold the drawings in this manner for events throughout the games.

The first heat of the metric mile went to J. P. Sullivan of the Irish American Athletic Club (IAAC) of New York City; Mel Sheppard, also of the IAAC, took the second. But several other Americans had also run in the first two heats and were eliminated, while the Englishmen had been separated in heats three through eight; Sheppard and Sullivan found themselves facing five Englishmen and a Canadian in the final the following day. Two of the English athletes—Harold Wilson, the world record holder, and Norman Hallows—were considered the favorites to take the first two spots. The English duo ran a tactical race and looked like they were on their way to victory, but Sheppard put on an impressive finishing kick and won by a couple of yards, setting a new Olympic record. (In a bitter irony, a few months earlier Sheppard had been rejected by the New York Police Department (NYPD) because of what the department's medical examiners called a bad heart.) The IAAC and the U.S. team now had a gold medal, and the English were the ones left fuming.

The U.S. team was also highly critical of the high jump and pole vault areas, but it was the 400 meters that provoked the bitterest row of all; the countries had different views on interference between runners during the race, and the result of the final was hotly disputed. The British examined the footprints made by the athletes as they rounded the final bend and claimed their athlete, Wyndham Halswelle, had been hindered by American John Carpenter. The decision was made by British officials to rerun the race. Matthew P. Halpin, head of the U.S. track team, objected but was banned from the meeting where the race was reviewed by British officials. American Ray Ewry had been standing at the final turn when the alleged foul occurred and reported that he had seen Carpenter drift wide and contended that there was no interference. Halswelle, Ewry pointed out, had the option of going either on the inside or outside of the American but was unable to make up his mind. Carpenter said he had run wide, as was his usual style, and Halswelle had plenty of room to pass him on either side but could not keep up with the American's pace. A high-powered American delegation met that evening to discuss the proceedings, after which an incensed James E. Sullivan informed members of the waiting press that he had never seen such an outrageous example of unsportsmanlike behavior.[12] The race was rerun, but John Carpenter refused to participate, and Halswelle won by jogging around the track on his own. The only other finalists—three U.S. athletes—dropped out in sympathy with Carpenter. An article in the *New York American* fulminated that "instead of British fair play, our men encountered British foul play," while G. S. Robertson, a member of the British Olympic Council, responded in a postgames speech with an incendiary comment by saying that if the Americans were "both no sportsmen and liars then the lethal chamber at the Battersea Dogs Home was the only fit."[13]

The Americans were to have further quibbles with British authorities concerning the weight of the discus used, while the metal-rimmed shoes worn by the British team in the tug-of-war competition would become a cause celebre. Martin Sheridan, writing in the *New York Evening World*, said the British athletes in the latter event "had to waddle out on the field like a lot of County Mayo ganders going down to the public pond for a swim" because of their outsize footwear.[14] The British were having none of it. The rules stated that participants were required to wear everyday shoes, and the Brits claimed the footwear was the same as what was worn every day by their police force. They pointed out the significance of their superior technique and teamwork but, in the interest of goodwill, offered the American team a second opportunity to compete, this time without any footwear. The incensed Americans did not take up the offer and refused to attend a dinner organized in their honor by Lord Desborough later that evening. The American press made the most of the episode, with the *New York Evening Post* claiming the British athletes had boots with "six-inch soles" that were "heavier than those worn in the English navy" and fuming that the "headman had spikes fastened in his shoes"; not to be outdone, the *New York Evening World* described the Englishmen's footwear as "big as North River ferry boats."[15]

Despite the ongoing recriminations during the opening days of the games it soon became apparent that the American athletes were vastly in the ascendant. A week in, the *Observer* newspaper had changed its tune, ready to admit the British were no longer as great as their name suggested and that the "athletic spirit of England for foot-racing and feats of strength long ago decayed."[16]

However inauspicious the start of the London Olympics, they would go down in folk memory for a finish, while also providing further evidence of slipping British standards. In previous championships, the length of the marathon race had varied slightly, but in 1908, the king requested that the race begin on the lawns of Windsor Castle so his grandchildren could view proceedings. At a time when royalty invariably got what they demanded, the organizers duly obliged. This resulted in the race being run for a distance of 26 miles, 385 yards, thereafter the official distance for the marathon. By the twenty-fourth mile, it was a three-man race.

Charles Hefferon, an Irishman representing South Africa, led; Dorando Pietri, a diminutive Italian ice cream seller from Naples, was second; and Irish American Johnny Hayes was in the bronze medal position. Hefferon accepted a drink from one of the spectators and shortly thereafter developed stomach cramps and slowed dramatically. After a steep climb near Wormwood Scrubs prison, Pietri passed him. Hayes then began to close the gap. As the Olympic stadium beckoned, Hayes, the youngest man in the race, passed Hefferon—the oldest. Two Irishmen representing countries from opposite ends of the earth had just met in the Olympic marathon. Hayes later reputedly said that if he had known Hefferon was Irish, he would have spoken to him.

As he entered the stadium, Pietri was fifty seconds ahead of Hefferon, but with only 385 yards to the finish line, the Italian staggered and appeared delirious. He then started to go in the wrong direction and promptly collapsed. Officials lifted him to his feet and helped him on his way as Hayes entered the stadium. Just short of the line, Pietri collapsed for the fifth time, but Jack Reynolds, reputedly assisted by Sherlock Holmes creator Arthur Conan Doyle, grabbed and carried him across the line thirty seconds ahead of Hayes, cheered on by the crowd of one hundred thousand people. Unfortunately, the Italian was disqualified, and the gold medal was awarded to Hayes.

To add to the brouhaha, the Italian flag had already been hoisted above the Stars and Stripes, which given what had gone on during the course of the championships, further incensed the Americans. That evening there were false rumors that Pietri had died of exhaustion, but the stadium doctor later explained the Italian's heart had been displaced by a half-inch as a result of his exertion. The following day, Queen Alexandra presented Pietri with a gold cup as a consolation prize. The poor performance by British athletes in the marathon was a further disappointment to the nation, and the *Times* noted that the team was "hopelessly outclassed in the severest test of all."[17]

The Americans put on a spectacular show of sporting excellence for the British and the rest of the world in London; none was finer than that of the great Irish Whale Martin Sheridan. At the age of twenty-five, he was in his athletic prime and virtually unassailable. In 1907, Sheridan had once again won the American All-Round Championships; incredibly, this time his performance was even better than his previous tour de force. Of the ten events in the competition, he won nine, beating his own record with a score of 7,150 points—310 points ahead of his previous mark. Sheridan was now operating at a level barely thought possible a few years prior; just before departing for the Olympics he won eight medals at the American National Indoor Championships, scoring thirty-two points, a feat never again matched in the history of the competition.

When Sheridan had arrived in London, he was asked by the press about the chances of the U.S. athletics team and was bullish in his reply, claiming the Americans would take at least 75 percent of the medals and "knock the socks off the British."[18] He would do more than his share. Sheridan competed in both the Greek and freestyle versions of discus-throwing at the games. In the freestyle competition the winner of each of five preliminary groups proceeded to the final, and once again, Sheridan proved a slow starter in an elite contest, qualifying for the final phase in fourth position with a throw of 127 feet, 11 inches. The field ahead of him was loaded: Fellow American athlete Merritt Giffin, from Lockport, Illinois, only twenty-three years old and viewed as a great prospect in the sport, held the lead with an impressive 133 feet, 6.5 inches. Bill Hoff, another member of the U.S. team, entered the final set of throws in second place with an initial effort of 129 feet, 5 inches. Finnish competitor Werner Järvinin finished the preliminary session in third position, while Arthur Kent "Ding" Dearborn, yet another American athlete and a member of the country's ill-fated tug-of-war team, made up the final group of five, adding weight to Martin Sheridan's assertion that U.S. athletes would largely be competing against one another. With his now-characteristic ferocious competitive instinct, Sheridan was the only athlete to improve his distance in the throw-off when he landed a new Olympic record of 134 feet, 2 inches with his second throw. Giffin and Hoff had thrown consistently better than Sheridan in practice—as well as in the preliminary stage of the competition proper—but in the heat of battle the Irishman had triumphed.

In the Greek-style version—the last time the event was part of the Olympic schedule—throwers hurled the discus from atop a rectangular platform raised above the ground with the throwing style strictly prescribed by the rules. It had proved a disappointing event at the Athens games for Sheridan, but in the interim, as was his wont, he had made a close study of the biomechanics of the discipline and practiced until he was comfortable with the technique. His diligence was rewarded when he threw an impressive 122 feet, 8.75 inches on his first attempt. Only Hoff would come close to Sheridan's throw when one of his efforts fell just three inches shy of the Irishman's mark. It proved immaterial, as Sheridan powered back in the fifth round with an even better throw of 124 feet, 8 inches, securing his second gold medal.

He had still not finished his medal haul and was unlucky to come away with just a bronze in the standing long jump. The event was won by his peerless teammate, Ray Ewry, with a leap of 10 feet, 11.5 inches; Constantin Tsicilitras of Greece took the silver with an effort of 10 feet, 7.25 inches, a mere quarter-inch longer than Sheridan. If not for an injury in the first round of the triple jump that forced him to withdraw from the event, the Irishman could have added to his superb total of two gold medals and a bronze.

While Martin Sheridan performed majestically in the discus, it was the incredible proceedings during the hammer throw final that would prove the greatest-ever day for the Irish Whales in the history of their participation on the world stage. The imperious John Flanagan, who had joined the IAAC in 1906, was competing for his third Olympic hammer title in a row, but going into the games it was obvious he was not going to have it his way because by this time, two new Irish Whales had come into view—Matt McGrath and Con Walsh.

McGrath was born in Curraghmore, Portrane, near Nenagh, County Tipperary, on December 28, 1875, one of eleven children who made up the family of Tim and Pat McGrath. As a youngster he often walked ten miles to see John Flanagan perform and practice, after which he would go home and emulate his hero's moves with a homemade hammer. McGrath later implied that Flanagan was reluctant to pass along any tips to his protégé when asked for advice. The young McGrath labored hard on the land, a fact he later claimed stood him in good stead in his athletic endeavors. A later tribute to McGrath noted there was little to do except outdoor activities but that the young Tipperary boy was ingenious at devising his own entertainment and was wont to enter a paddock that contained a bull. He would tease the animal until it charged him and then leap over the surrounding wall to escape.

The only books in the family library were about the Olympics and the athletic feats of the ancient Greeks, according to the author. Matt was also partial to listening to his parents recount folktales and particularly attracted to a story in which a landlord challenged his tenants to a sledge-throwing competition—overwhelmingly likely to be the aforementioned *Knocknagow* by Charles Kickham. The tale inspired the young Matt to take up weight-throwing, and from the start of his career, the nascent thrower showed a strong competitive streak in everything he did, including competing in wrestling, boxing, and running.

Like the classical emigrant who eventually makes good, he traveled to the United States with only a carpet bag containing a shirt and a pair of stockings, his funds stretching to a mere sixpence. New York was a daunting proposition for the young immigrant; during the first few weeks he lived in fear that the buildings would fall on him, and if they missed, he worried that the trains would jump their tracks and kill him. Despite the impositions of his life in the New World, McGrath did not waste any time in developing his physical strength and started to visit a blacksmith to lift anvils, despite working thirteen hours a day, seven days a week. In addition to his workouts at the forge, the determined McGrath rigged an old mattress against a wall at his apartment and threw weights against it in an effort to further improve his hammer technique.

McGrath stood a fraction more than six feet and had a pronounced advantage over John Flanagan in height and reach. His square jaw and piercing eyes hinted at the fierce determination that would propel his successful sporting and professional life. Even though the Tipperary man showed great potential from the start of his career, he was a particularly exceptional athlete because he kept working on his throwing until he caught up with the other Irish greats who had come to dominate the field. After employment as a barman for a short time in Manhattan, McGrath joined the NYPD in 1902, the fourth of the Whales to don the uniform of the city's finest. McGrath would be a remarkably mature thirty-two years of age before his full potential was first realized, when he took the hammer title from the seven-foot circle with a phenomenal throw of 173 feet, 7 inches at the 1907 Canadian Championships, far exceeding John Flanagan's existing record of 170 feet. Yet, another great Irish throwing athlete had arrived on the scene, and despite his advanced age, McGrath would prove to be a hugely competitive force for a long time to come.

Unbelievably, the southern counties of Ireland would also provide the next great world-class thrower to North America, this time to Canada. Cornelius "Con" Walsh may have been born on April 24, 1885, according to his World War II draft card and naturalization certificate or it could have been April 30, 1882, if his World War I draft card is correct. Family sources believe it may have been 1881.[19] He was definitely born in Carrigaminna, County Cork—a small village halfway between Millstreet and Macroom—and both cards note he had dark brown hair and brown eyes. By the age of sixteen, the young Walsh was a behemoth—standing six feet tall and weighing fourteen stone—and a highly talented all-around athlete. Before immigrating to Canada, he played Gaelic football for his local club, Clondrohid, and had the honor of representing his village on the Cork county team, albeit on the losing sides in the 1901 and 1903 All-Ireland finals.

Walsh's throwing skills were also evident from a young age; he won his first medal in a senior competition at Macroom sports day in 1900, when he might have been only fifteen. As a further demonstration of the breadth of his talents, Walsh won the hugely competitive GAA football national placekicking title in 1901, 1905, and again in 1906. Such was his dominance on the day of the competition in 1906 that he captured five titles at the GAA national championships; in addition to his placekicking bauble, Walsh won the 56-pound weight throw for height and distance, the hammer throw, and the shot put. In capturing the 56-pound distance-throwing event, he set a new world record, while in the placekicking Walsh managed to land the ball 224 feet, 4 inches from where he placed it on the ground, a mark that is recorded as never having been beaten.

At the start of his hammer-throwing career some of the cognoscenti noticed that Walsh was somewhat ungainly in the circle. Tom Leahy, one of a famous family of brothers who competed in jumping events in athletics, reputedly advised him to take up step dancing to aid his technique; the footwork required for the intricate steps of traditional Irish dancing would help him "put his feet where he'd want them."[20] In May 1907, Walsh, wanting to compete for a country other than Great Britain—which he despised—immigrated to Canada, the first of the Irish Whales not to move to New York. Only five months after his arrival he became the Canadian hammer champion and broke the national record for height in the 56-pound weight throw. He improved his record for the latter with an effort of 15 feet, 9 inches at the 1908 Canadian Olympic trials but was not selected to attend; instead he paid his own way to the games. Walsh did not travel with the main body of athletes, nor did he stay with them at their official residence in London at 65 Sinclair Road in Kensington. He was also omitted from team photographs and did not march with the group in the opening parade.

A solid 215 pounds in his prime, Walsh was a naturally talented hammer thrower, but the general consensus was he did not put enough effort into his training. According to Paddy Ryan, the 1920 U.S. hammer champion (and another Irish American and Irish Whale), Con liked the good life, and as far as he was concerned training was not part of the good life. He could have beaten all the other Whales, Ryan believed, but never bothered with any serious training, and although lazy he thoroughly enjoyed competition.[21] Despite Walsh's reputed less-than-enthusiastic approach to his training, he provided a stiff challenge to the other athletes in London and gave an advance warning of his form just before the start of the games. On July 11, three days before competing in London, Walsh traveled to Edinburgh to represent Ireland in a competition against Scotland. He impressively took the hammer title with a throw of 162 feet, 7 inches, the best-ever throw recorded on Scottish soil up to that point. It was evident that the great John Flanagan could have serious competition in his effort to win his third Olympic hammer medal in a row, and that his fellow Irishmen, Matt McGrath and Con Walsh, were the most likely to provide it.

Sixteen athletes from eight countries took part in the hammer throw final on July 14—the first full day of competition. McGrath was leading with a throw of 167 feet, 11 inches as the throwers started their final set of throws; Flanagan was in second place, five inches behind. McGrath looked like he was set fair for victory, but Flanagan, ever the competitor, threw 170 feet, 4.5 inches with his final throw to take a third gold medal, capture a third Olympic title in a row, and set a new Olympic record. Con Walsh took the bronze as an independent Canadian athlete to complete the Irish treble. In later life, Flanagan considered it the sweetest of his Olympic victories and intimated that he was happy to get one over on McGrath because he believed his fellow Irishman was given to arrogance. He was, he said, also proud to see three Irishmen on the podium, albeit competing under foreign flags. It was the end of a wonderful Olympic career for the Limerick athlete, and his achievement in the hammer throw has never been bettered.

The 1908 hammer throw final was a remarkable reinforcement of North America as the preeminent hammer-throwing region—the continent took six of the top seven places—with British athlete Tom Nicolson managing to finish in the fourth position—and even he was of Scottish extraction. That it would prove a triumph for the U.S. team was almost inevitable; that the top three positions were occupied by Irish-born athletes was remarkable.

The 1908 Olympic Games garnered vastly more column inches in the press than the previous iterations and raised issues that would drag on for months thereafter. The overwhelming triumph of the Americans engendered a range of responses in the British press. The *Saturday Review*, for example, responded by dismissing the games as a futile exercise run by incompetents.

Nationalist elements of the Irish press inevitably sought to make political capital of the success of Irish athletes at the London Olympics. Some noted their physical prowess in comparison to the increasingly effete nature of the British competitors. This was not just a creation of the nationalist press; physical degeneration was a genuine concern of the British themselves and had previously been put into the public domain. Easy living and wealth generated by the Industrial Revolution, the school of thought went, was resulting in a nation of soft men, the sedentary nature of their work attenuating their vitality. Much of the employment in Great Britain no longer involved physical work, and the putative athlete did not have a chance to develop his athleticism on a daily basis by sitting in an office, the theory went. Wealth made people decadent, and the Industrial Revolution had exacerbated the process.

The Boer War of 1899–1902, in which British troops struggled to defeat an army substantially smaller than its own with a perceived limited technological and military ability, added to this concern and had resulted in the British government compiling a report on physical degeneracy. The public were shocked to learn that 37 percent of those who had applied to the army to fight in the war were rejected as unfit: Of the 84,402 applicants, 23,745 were turned down as unsuitable for combat.[22] This finding did not tally with the sense of racial superiority underpinning the previously ever-expanding British Empire. The report on physical deterioration also pointed to the poor working conditions of the urban working class, which combined with a bad diet, resulted in weak men unsuitable to defend the realm. The defeat of the English rugby team by the New Zealand All Blacks in 1905 had further enervated those concerned about the state of the nation. To be beaten by a mere colony in a game that they had invented was a significant cause for concern. In sporting terms it was particularly worrying as rugby was viewed as the greatest test of virility and a pursuit worthy of the elite Corinthian gentlemen born to lead the empire. Now the Olympics had provided further evidence that all classes of British manhood were on the decline. In contrast, elements in the Irish press inevitably suggested that the peasant lifestyle of the Irish man kept him strong and vital; a real man of the soil, typified by the magnificent physical specimens who were the Irish Whales.

The avidly nationalist *Irish and Belfast News* was quick to point out that of the 34,000 men who had sought admission to the ranks of Great Britain's army in the previous year a full 16,000 were rejected as "physically unfit" despite a lowering of the entrance standards previously required.[23] The *Freeman's Journal* took delight in the achievements of the Irish-born athletes despite the conditions imposed by the British on Ireland for so long and suggested that "plain food, and not too much of it, fresh air, and clean living" were instrumental in their success.[24] A letter to the editor concurred; when it came to Irishmen, "there is yet no sign of that physical deterioration, which is, and has been, noticeable in other races by those who have given attention to the subject."

The *Irish News and Belfast Morning News* took particular pleasure in the victory of Irish American Johnny Hayes in the marathon, an event the English press had believed they would dominate. The paper noted that Hayes was "typically Irish in his dark hairs and eyes and kindly expression" and his accent was more Irish than American. While the British congratulated him on his success with "lukewarm handshaking," his later reception in Ireland was "fit to kill." The London marathon marked the "Waterloo of English long-distance running," while the "physical vitality of Celt and Latin has been abundantly testified."[25]

Columnist "Jyaff" of the *Cork Sportsman* epitomized the bittersweet sentiments expressed by many at the achievements of Irish athletes. The "laurels of triumph which should rightly encircle Mother Erin's brow" were given to other lands that, however great and prosperous, "were not and cannot be as dear to us as our own Green Isle."[26] Jyaff believed

Ireland's request to compete as a nation would soon be recognized as a result of the success of Irishmen in London.

For the rabidly nationalist *Gaelic American* the poor treatment of the American contingent by the British was manna from heaven and reinforced its long-held belief that the English were a nation of belligerents with no concept of sportsmanship. They might pontificate about fair play, but they did not know the meaning of the word and "would go far out of their way to keep from learning it."[27] Editor John Devoy heaped praise on the great "Czar" Sullivan, who had so nobly led the American delegation into the breach against the despised and unsporting British. It was a perfect war by proxy for Devoy, and he did not spare the leather on the British when he got going, exhorting his readership to give the returning athletes a hero's welcome for their vanquishing of the "ever-perfidious Albion." They had "ventured with the American flag in the lion's mouth, while it snarled and growled." Remember the Civil War, he told the American public with glee.[28] Devoy had not been surprised by the treatment meted out by the British to the Americans because "John Bull knows no law but the intense selfishness and inordinate opinion of his own importance."[29] The debacle about the tug-of-war was further grist to the mill of Devoy. He dismissed Lord Desborough's argument that the British police team had merely worn their everyday shoes during the competition and considered it an equally pathetic excuse as saying the boots "were those that Lancashire men use to kick their wives with."[30]

Inevitably, James E. Sullivan was quick to condemn the British when he returned to New York and immediately set about writing a piece for the *New York Times* claiming that the British were friendly to every nation they could and raised their own flag upon the smallest pretexts but when an American won the raising of the Stars and Stripes was received in silence.[31] Sullivan, ever blustering and trenchant, brushed aside any dissenting voices and assured anyone who would listen that all criticisms of the British were valid and the Americans only complained when there was a genuine reason to do so.

To the delight of the Irish American contingent on the U.S. team, the party stopped off in Dublin on their way back across the Atlantic. It proved to be a great celebration. The *New York Times* reported on the ecstatic welcome received by the American athletes with the headline, "Dublin Honors Athletes: Tremendous Ovation for Irish American Winners at Olympiad," noting that the greeting accorded them was all the more remarkable because it was "entirely spontaneous" and the announcement of the hour of their arrival brought many thousands of people to the station to meet the athletes. The streets along the route to their hotel were completely blocked by "Dublinites."[32] When they arrived at their hotel, the Americans were met by influential nationalist Member of Parliament Joseph Devlin, who informed them that they would get a similar reaction wherever they went in the country. Sprinter Lawson Roberts said the team had expected an Irish welcome, but what they had received "quite took their breath away." No team of athletes had ever been welcomed in such a way, he declared. The crowds on the street did not start to disperse until after midnight, when they were told the reception had officially ended and they had to leave the vicinity.

There would be one disappointment for the Irish public. The GAA had declared the athletic meeting planned for the following Saturday by the IAAC illegal and asked the Irish American athletes not to compete. The *New York Times* thought it an unfortunate state of affairs and noted that P. J. Conway, president of the IAAC, had sent a cablegram to the president of the GAA ordering the team to withdraw from the Dublin meeting.[33] In the end, none of the Whales took part in the contest, much to the disappointment of the crowd. It can only be viewed as a statement of nationalist feeling. At the banquet held after the competition, the president of the Irish Amateur Athletic Association took aim at the stance adopted by the GAA, criticizing the "miserable clique" who he believed had deliberately set out to make the Americans feel unwelcome while lavishing praise on those athletes and officials who deigned to participate.[34] American representatives thanked their Irish hosts and expressed their distress about the complicated circumstances. One speaker's advice was to the point: "The less said about it the better."[35]

When the American athletes returned to New York they were welcomed as heroes with such banner headlines as "Big Welcome for Yankee Athletes," "Athletes Parade to Be Big Affair," and "10,000 to Parade for the Athletes" adorning the pages of the *New York Times*.[36] It was clear that the Irish contingent was considered a central part of the American team by the public. On the streets, Irish flags were being waved next to the Stars and Stripes, and spectators sang "The Wearing of the Green," an old Irish street ballad lamenting the repression of supporters of the Irish Rebellion of 1798. The Fighting Irish 69th Regiment was represented, while the first, second, and third regiments of the Irish Volunteers provided a bodyguard for the athletes, with the GAA represented by the Kilkenny and Sligo Gaelic football teams. James E. Sullivan, never one to be outdone, arrived at City Hall with a chained lion, an event Baron de Coubertin later described as a "minor incident [which] speaks volumes concerning the state of mind that prevailed" and one that "almost caused a diplomatic scandal."[37]

Johnny Hayes—born in New York to Tipperary parents—was particularly humbled by the welcome he received along with his teammates. It was the proudest moment of his life, and he waxed lyrical about his visit to Ireland, to the delight of the Irish Americans in attendance: "I have had a delightful trip . . . to Ireland, particularly at the former home of my grandfather in Nenagh, where they were just as happy over my marathon victory as here. I traveled from Belfast to Cork and will never forget the treatment accorded me."[38] As the first American to win the marathon and the first ever to win it at the new official distance, Hayes was feted wherever he went and contributed significantly to the development of long-distance running on the continent. He stood at only 5-foot-4 but became a cipher for American athletic know-how and the instigator of a marathon craze that would consume the nation for the next couple of decades.

Hayes became a darling of the American press, with numerous papers reporting that he was forced to do his training at night because he worked at Bloomingdale's department store six days a week. The story went that the job had been arranged for him by members of the IAAC when the athlete expressed a fear of developing arthritis due to the damp environment in the tunnels under the East River where he had been working. Hayes inquired whether the club would be able to get him a "dry job." The administrators took their brief literally and arranged a sinecure in the dry goods department of Bloomingdale's. After the London Olympics, the Bloomingdale family claimed they had built a running track on the roof of the department store where Hayes could conveniently train. Others suggested that his job was merely a ruse for him to train as a professional athlete and his days were more often spent training assiduously in the public parks and countryside adjacent to New York. The truth has been obscured by time and mythmaking, but it was publicity for Bloomingdales money could not buy.

After the welcome home parade finished a number of the athletes went to Celtic Park to compete in a sports event to aid the Fireman's Fund, and the following day President Roosevelt held a private event with the Olympians at Sagamore Hill, his summer home in Oyster Bay on the North Shore of Long Island. It may have caused him some equivocation of thought, as he had long been pursuing a subtly diplomatic course with the British government, and the harsh criticism leveled by the likes of Sullivan would have been at odds with his normal conciliatory approach. On the other hand, Roosevelt had been a founding member of the American Irish Historical Society and all too aware of the need for political support from Irish American voters. He had to walk a delicate line. A report in the *New York Herald* indicated that one of the athletes described the mistreatment they had encountered at the hands of the British, to which the president made "one or two strong remarks" but cautioned the group that he should not be quoted in the newspapers.[39]

As a former police commissioner, President Roosevelt took pride in the achievements of the officers in the party, he said, telling the team their performance had never been duplicated in the history of athletics. Roosevelt spoke with middle-distance runner Melvin Sheppard, winner of three gold medals. After describing his run in the 1,500 meters race at the request of Roosevelt, Sheppard took a Morocco leather case from his pocket and handed it to the president, saying it was his prize for winning the event. Roosevelt examined it carefully and remarked that it was a very pretty piece of work; Sheppard requested that the president keep it as a memento of the Olympic achievements of the U.S. team. Roosevelt demurred, but Sheppard insisted. It took some time for the president to be persuaded to accept the trophy, but he finally did with the remark, "This will be one of my most treasured possessions Mr. Sheppard, and I am very glad to place it in my collection."[40]

Sheppard's medal was not the only gift Roosevelt received on the day; following Sheppard's example, John Flanagan gave the president one of his medals, while P. J. Conway granted him honorary membership in the IAAC. Roosevelt graciously accepted both and posed for a photograph with the athletes; it hangs on the wall of the American Irish Historical Society on Fifth Avenue in Manhattan. James E. Sullivan's chest must have puffed out when Roosevelt said the U.S. team could not have done so well without his management skills.[41] Following the presidential reception, the team was ferried to a picnic organized by Alderman "Little Tim" O'Sullivan, a Tammany Hall stalwart.

One of the final tributes to the U.S. Olympic team was a gala banquet held by the IAAC at the Waldorf Astoria, where five hundred prominent citizens of New York gathered to lavish praise on the athletes—minus Martin Sheridan, who had decided to stay in Ireland for a holiday. Keynote speaker James E. Sullivan, in typical jingoistic style, stated that the American athletes "swept England off the athletic map."[42] Democratic Party candidate L. S. Chandler chose the occasion to launch his campaign for governor, an indication of the political colors of many there. With a menu that included roast guinea fowl, beef longchamp, and a selection of champagnes, the function was an indication of how far some members of the Irish immigrant communities had traveled.

Dissenting voices did exist. The *New York Evening Call*, one of the few left-leaning organs in the American press, had long been a trenchant critic of the Tammany Hall regime and became incensed when the *New York Times* reported that the Democratic Party had donated $10,000 to help fund the celebrations for the returning athletes. It predicted it would entail the public being coerced into making "voluntary" contributions that would result in a "sudden interest in the underpaid and hardworking employees," and deny their families the pleasure of a Sunday at the shore so that the athletes and their "bourgeois patrons" could celebrate in style.[43] It was, the paper fulminated, an attempt by a "bunch of ward heelers, political grafters, and artistic plunderers to steal city money."

There were also some in the press who questioned the appropriateness of immigrants and ethnic groups being part of an American delegation in the first place. The *Los Angeles Herald* termed the Irish Americans "ringing men" who should have competed for another country and suggested that many of the other native-born athletes did not want them on the national team. Their medals should have been credited to the British team, it argued.[44]

The *New York Sun* questioned the loyalties of those athletes from the eastern United States compared to those from the western states, insinuating that the former were more concerned with representing their ethnic groups than that of the country as a whole. The issue of representation by ethnic minorities on the U.S. athletic team also occupied the minds of a few letter writers to some of the nation's more august newspapers. "E. Pluribus Unum" wrote to the *New York Times* noting that, while he was proud of the American athletes, he could only wonder about the number of them that were foreign born and whether it was appropriate to consider them real Americans.[45] S. L. Harbinson of New York was moved to reply, arguing that only the "Indians" were real Americans if one was to follow that argument.[46]

It was a debate that cut to the quick of the United States: What exactly did it mean to be an American? Were the only "real" Americans the Native Americans who had their land taken by colonizers? Were the "real" Americans still only those who could trace their roots to the *Mayflower*? Could you be a proud member of your ethnic group and also be a proud American? These were questions the success of the Irish American athletes competing at the London Olympics, in particular, threw into sharp relief. America was changing, albeit incrementally and painstakingly. No longer did the white Anglo-Saxon Protestant dominate everything; no longer did those who could claim links to the original settlers have the right to be considered the only foundation stones of America. Accommodations had to be made for those immigrants who called America home, and the Irish Whales were at the eye of the hurricane-like debate. The general view was that the athletes were outsiders to a certain degree, but they were still America's outsiders. They were making the United States great, and anything that did so should be embraced. It was, after all, the century of America.

Inevitably some Irish American journalists with Irish nationalist sympathies were critical of the participation of Irish-based athletes on the British team, with John Devoy in the vanguard. In one of a number of articles on the topic he pointed out that members of the Owen Roe Club of New York condemned these Irish athletes, who had boosted the point total of Britain, and wrote that they were disloyal to the Irish athletic organization that gave them the opportunities for development.[47] Even P. J. Conway bemoaned the Irish athletes who had "disgraced themselves by making points for England that no Englishman could have made."[48]

In hindsight, it was easy to criticize these men from the privileged position of being across the Atlantic Ocean, but the political reality was that if those who lived in Ireland refused to compete under the British flag they could not take part at all. For athletes of world-class ability resident in Ireland it was a terrible and invidious position to find themselves in. Martin Sheridan suggested the men should have stayed at home in Ireland.[49] It would have been interesting to see how Sheridan would have responded if the shoe was on the other foot and he could have only competed for the Great Britain and Ireland team or not at all. Nor did

Sheridan consider why some of the Irish athletes stayed at home. Perhaps they had commitments to family or land, or just could not bring themselves to emigrate. On the other hand, an analysis of Irish athletes who competed under the British flag would indicate a preponderance of names from the Protestant Ascendancy class, gentlemen amateurs with time on their hands and a world removed from the tenant farmers who made up an overwhelming percentage of Ireland's population.

Whatever his criticisms of those who lived in his native land and competed for Great Britain, Martin Sheridan returned to a triumphant homecoming when he traveled back to Ireland after the games; everywhere he went he was treated as a national hero. On August 14, Sheridan arrived at Broadstone train station in Dublin, where he was met by the Blanchardstown Band and the Emmet Choir, which sang a selection of nationalistic songs in his honor. The famed athlete was then lauded in a series of speeches; among those who took to the podium were representatives of the Dublin County GAA Board, the Central Council of the GAA, the GAA Leinster Council, the Athletics Council of the GAA, and the political organization Sinn Fein. They praised Sheridan's nationalistic beliefs and pro-GAA stance. Sheridan assured the crowd that the principles of the GAA were close to his heart "because they were Irish and were for Irish men alone."[50]

He was brought to a reception in the Gresham Hotel held in his honor. Horse-drawn carriages transported the Emmet Choir, preceded by a detachment of the Dublin Fire Brigade, while a crew of hurlers escorted the group. When Sheridan was introduced to the crowd outside the Gresham, he had to wait several minutes before he could speak. He posed a rhetorical question to the multitude of admirers. People often asked him why he represented the United States in athletics. He said the answer was simple: Who had a better right than an Irishman to compete for the United States? Had America not been the country that found a home for the Irishman in freedom? They had treated the Irishman with the ultimate respect. The comparison to Britain was unspoken but obvious. He finished his speech by thanking the people for the reception "from an Irish heart" and wished "the people of Dublin and the Gaels of Ireland an Irishman's goodwill."[51]

While competing in London, Sheridan had expressed his wish to compete against fellow Irish athlete Thomas "Tom" Kiely on home soil. It would be a meeting of the two greatest athletic heroes of the nation, eagerly awaited by multitudes and recorded breathlessly in the press as the greatest individual athletic contest in Irish history.[52] Kiely, a fervent nationalist and a revered athlete, was born in 1869, in Ballyneale, outside Carrick-on-Suir, County Tipperary, and was an equally physically imposing specimen, standing 6-foot-2 and weighing more than fourteen stone. His athletic achievements were significant. In 1892, he won seven national titles in the GAA championships, where he beat world record holder Dan Shanahan in the hop, step, and jump (now the triple jump) with a mark of 49 feet, 7 inches, a distance not exceeded until the 1924 Olympics. In 1895, the first international athletics contest between Ireland and Scotland, held at Celtic Park, Glasgow, had made Kiely a national hero. With the meet tied at five wins each and Scottish jumpers leading in the final event, Irish officials appealed to Kiely, who was finished for the day and dressing in his tent, to come back to take part in the long jump. Rushing to the event without even lacing his shoes, according to contemporary newspaper accounts, Kiely took one leap to win the event and saved the day for Ireland. The Tipperary athlete went on to win the English hammer championships five out of six years from 1897 to 1902, losing only in 1900, to the great John Flanagan.

Kiely did not travel to the 1900 Olympics but took gold in the all-round event in St. Louis in 1904, returning to Ireland to a hero's welcome. Even though it was impossible to recognize Kiely as an Irish athlete representing Ireland, as the country did not exist, he was the first-ever man to wear a shamrock symbol on his vest—which he did illegally—at an Olympics. It is doubly ironic that his achievements were not recognized as those of an Irishman because Britain did not even officially enter a team in the 1904 Olympic Games.

Kiely had won a further gold at the American Athletic Union championships in 1906, but he had not competed against Sheridan, who was injured at the time. With Martin Sheridan having won the title in 1905 and 1907, their postgames meeting in 1908 was billed as the match of the two greatest Irish athletes of their generation, but it could have been equally promoted as the match of the two best all-around athletes in the world—such was their dominance of their sport. As Kiely had not attended the London Olympics, the stakes could not have been higher. After protracted negotiations, the men settled on Dungarvan, County Waterford, as the venue for a competition that would prove a contest for the ages.

The program consisted of five throwing events: the 16-pound shot from a seven-foot circle, the 16-pound hammer from a nine-foot circle, the 56-pound throw with an unlimited follow-through, a 29-pound throw, and a 7-pound throw. Sheridan had asked Kiely to include the discus as part of the competition, but the wily Tipperary man demurred, knowing he would have no chance of getting anywhere near the distances the Bohola man was capable of.

The 16-pound throw was the first event: Sheridan won it with surprising ease. His three best attempts landed at 47 feet, 9.5 inches; 47 feet, 11.5 inches; and 48 feet, 5.5 inches. The best Kiely could muster was 42 feet, and 8 inches. It was a clear and resounding victory for the Mayo man.

The athletes then moved on to the 16-pound hammer, a speciality for Kiely and one for which he was the overwhelming favorite. But it did not start well for the Tipperary man. He fouled his first throw, while Sheridan managed a relatively humble 130 feet, 2 inches. Kiely composed himself for his second attempt but only managed to throw 135 feet, 9 inches, a poor effort for a man of his abilities. His frustration mounted when Sheridan managed to slightly better him by throwing a little more than a foot longer, at 136 feet, 11 inches. With this being his speciality event, Kiely would have to do well if he was to have any chance of taking the overall title. On his third throw he found his rhythm with an impressive throw of 150 feet, 8 inches. That was as good as it would get for Sheridan. He fouled his final two throws, while Kiely consolidated his victory with an impressive throw of 153 feet, 3 inches—a new world record. The competition was all square after the first two events.

The 56-pound unlimited run and follow-through with one or both hands was up next and would be desperately close. With two throws remaining, Kiely was in pole position with a throw of 34 feet, 1 inch—three inches ahead of Sheridan. With his penultimate effort, Kiely advanced his best mark by four inches. Sheridan summoned all his energy and threw 34 feet, 3 inches, a mere two inches less. Once again it was an example of Sheridan marshalling his competitive instincts when they were most needed, but this time it would not quite be enough. Kiely had triumphed by a mere two inches and now led the day's proceedings by two to one; the competition had finely balanced out as they prepared for the 28-pound weight throw.

Kiely's opening throw reached 31 feet, 3 inches; with his first effort, Sheridan bettered him with 32 feet, 2 inches. Kiely took the weight in his hand for his second attempt, but the pressure was taking a toll and he fouled the throw. Sheridan improved his mark to 33 feet. In the remaining throws, neither managed to better their mark, and victory once more went to Sheridan. The proceedings were now tied at two victories apiece. It was down to the final event, the 7-pound weight throw.

By now onlookers were on their feet. The two great heroes of Irish athletics were slugging it out man to man, and it had come down to a final, winner-take-all event. After a short break, Sheridan and Kiely convened under the watchful eye of referee F. B. Dineen. The opening salvos proved anticlimactic when both men fouled their first throws. It was obvious the stakes were high; however, when both men fouled a second time it appeared there was a deeper problem. Dineen was not happy with their interpretation of the technicalities of the event and saw fit to give the men a further explanation of the rules and a demonstration of the desired technique. Each man took a further throw, but they too were deemed fouls. At this point the event became a fiasco. The referee, following his interpretation of the rules, declared the event over and a draw. The competitors had the impression that they were to have six throws each, but Dineen explained that they had misunderstood the structure of the competition; they had to qualify from the first set of three throws to go on and take a second set. As neither man had recorded a mark with their opening set of throws, they both failed to qualify for the next round and the competition was dead in the water. It was a draw and that was the end of it, according to the referee. Despite protestations, Dineen stuck to his decision.

Upon reflection, it was an acceptable decision for everyone: The two great heroes of contemporary Irish athletics retired from the field undefeated. Whether it was a plan hatched in advance is unclear; if it was stage-managed, it was done with notable aplomb, as the athletes were cheered with every step of their retreat from the arena, and it had proven a magnificent celebration of Irish athleticism. Later consultation of the rule book, as it pertained at the time, confirmed that the fastidious Dineen was correct in his interpretation of the laws governing the discipline. It was, despite being long lost in the mists of time, one of the greatest days in Irish sport.

Martin Sheridan was subsequently once again conveyed to the capital city and into the welcoming arms of the GAA establishment, which feted him with a dinner in his honor at the Thomond Hotel and presented him with a gold ring set with inlaid diamonds. Sheridan once more sang the praises of the organization, again expressing his trenchant opinion that it was the only body that should be allowed to represent athletics in Ireland because it was peopled by true Irishmen. He accepted the gift with thanks, knowing it came from men who were his true friends and Irish nationalists to boot. In a time-honored cultural motif—despite the general lack of mention of women—he likened Ireland to a woman. With the ring they had presented to him, he told the assembled dignitaries and guests, he would formally marry Ireland by placing it on his finger. He would return to the country of his adoption with Ireland in his heart and perhaps, some day, when the time was right, have the opportunity to fight for his native country in its quest for independence. The rest of the night was given over to song and dance, with Sheridan contributing a number of nationalist-inspired ballads he had committed to memory.

T. S. Moclair of the *Western People* interviewed Martin Sheridan at his home in Bohola in the dying days of August as his departure for the United States loomed near. The athlete gave a demonstration of his technique in the long and standing jumps to the impressed journalist.[53] Then Sheridan removed his clothing and took to the waters of the nearby river Moy. Sheridan emphasized the value of swimming in his training regimen, telling the journalist his knowledge of swimming had stood him in good stead throughout the years; on more than one occasion he had rescued people from the Hudson River. Sheridan spoke to Moclair about his love for his sport and plans to return to the United States to begin his training for the 1909 All-Around Championships, after which he would retire. If he had his way, he would spend all his time training, but, as he told Moclair, things did not work like that in the United States. It was a fast-moving and dynamic country where everyone had to pull their weight by giving their best to whatever position they occupied. Moclair finished by calling Sheridan a "genial, modest, and retiring giant whom Mayo in particular and Ireland in general esteems and admires," and an "Irishman to the core, in politics, and in sentiments, and aspirations, as well as in all matters pertaining to athletics."[54]

On the morning of Tuesday, September 10, 1908, Martin Sheridan traveled to Swinford train station to start the journey that would take him back to his adopted country for what would be the last time. From Swinford, he would make his way by train to Queenstown, where he would board the Cunard *S.E. Saxomia*, bound for New York, but first he would have to brave the crowds at the train station, where it seemed as if the entire town had turned out to wish the young athlete all the best for the future. He addressed his supporters: "Goodbye, boys . . . I thank you from the bottom of my heart, and I hope to be back again amongst you before this time twelve months."[55] But the great athlete would never see his native shore again. The country would go on to successfully fight for its freedom without the aid of Martin Sheridan, but he had made a lasting contribution to the spirit of the nation and reached the pinnacle of the world athletics stage. There would never again be another Irish athlete like him.

9

1912

The Swedish Masterpiece

Olympism seeks to create a way of life based on the joy found in effort, the educational value of a good example, and respect for universal fundamental ethical principles.—Pierre de Coubertin[1]

By the time the 1912 edition of the Olympic Games came around the makeup of the Irish Whales had changed significantly. Following his London triumph Martin Sheridan went on to compete domestically in athletics for another three years, winning the All-Around Championship of America for a record third time and improving the world discus record to 140 feet, 6.5 inches in 1909, and a further 141 feet, 4.5 inches in 1911—his last great athletic achievement. At his last appearance in the United States Amateur Athletics Championships, Sheridan won the all-around title for a record fourth time.

After the 1908 Olympic Games, Matt McGrath and John Flanagan continued their epic athletic battles in the United States. On September 12, the two greats met at the championship meet of the Metropolitan Association of the American Athletic Union (AAU) at Travers Island, where Flanagan took back the hammer throw title from McGrath with a throw of 117 feet, 4.5 inches. On October 11, the two adversaries locked horns once again, this time at the Fall Games of the Irish American Athletic Club (IAAC) at Celtic Park. Each man made four throws of more than 173 feet on a day conducive to hammer-throwing. With his last throw, Flanagan managed 173 feet, 10.75 inches, only to be bettered by

McGrath's final throw of 174 feet, 7.75 inches, but the Tipperary man would not have any luck on the day. His winning throw was marked ineligible because the wire handle was deemed to have stretched an inch on his hammer between the start and the finish of the competition, an occupational hazard of the discipline at the time. In the future, he would ensure this fate did not interfere with establishing records.

The long-standing duel between the two great Irish throwers finally came to an end when John Flanagan decided to return to Ireland in 1910. Why exactly he decided to leave the United States is not completely clear. One story at the time suggested he was no longer happy with the conditions of his job with the city police force. After the public-office squad of the New York Police Department was abolished in 1910, Flanagan was transferred to the West 68th Street station, where he was put to work walking a beat along Central Park West. This, the story went, did not sit well with the spirited Irishman, as it cut into his training time and ran counter to the favorable treatment the Irish American throwers had long been used to from their superiors.

Flanagan, it was said, duly resigned from the force, but reports in the press were at variance with the word on the street. The *New York Times* noted his departure but suggested that his leave was due to a family inheritance and bemoaned his loss for the coming American championships.[2] Whatever the reason, John Flanagan's departure would prove a harbinger of things to come; the production line of Irish American hammer throwers would not last forever. Flanagan was returning home to a country that was not yet independent, and he had no interest in competing for Great Britain. It was the end of an unparalleled hammer-throwing career; he had set a record that would never be equalled in the history of the event by winning three consecutive gold medals at the Olympic Games.

On Christmas Eve 1910, Matt McGrath was in the headlines, but not for his sporting achievements. He had allegedly shot a man five times in the abdomen and beat him on the head with his police-issue truncheon in his New York home. McGrath claimed that George Walker was an intruder in his home; Walker claimed that McGrath's wife, Loretta, had invited him to the house to fix a Christmas tree. A barman at a nearby hotel testified that McGrath's wife had been drinking with Walker in the hotel bar earlier in the day. McGrath was tried on a charge of causing grievous bodily harm, but the jury found him not guilty after a three-day trial in March 1911. On foot of the court case Police Commissioner James Cropsey dismissed McGrath the following month on a charge of conduct unbecoming a police officer, but Rhinelander Waldo ousted the commissioner a few weeks later and reinstated McGrath in May 1911.

A group of "concerned" citizens then took a civil case to prevent McGrath from being paid from the public purse. In response, his colleagues agreed to have money deducted from their salaries to pay McGrath, an indication of the high esteem in which he was held by his peers at the NYPD. All the while, McGrath was continuing with his burgeoning athletic career with an eye on the upcoming Olympic Games in Stockholm, the shenanigans surrounding the legal case having no apparent ill effects on his performances, nor did they have any long-term effects on his career in the police force, as he was promoted to sergeant in 1916, lieutenant in 1918, captain in 1927, deputy inspector in 1930, and inspector in 1936.

At Celtic Park on August 20, 1911, McGrath threw the hammer 179 feet, 3 inches; on August 26, he launched it 177 feet, 6 inches at the same venue. On September 23, he smashed Flanagan's Canadian record by throwing 182 feet, 4 inches at Montreal, and on October 29, he beat Flanagan's world figures by exactly 3 feet with a throw of 187 feet, 4 inches at the games of the Galway Men's Association at Celtic Park. McGrath, who had previously been denied records through technicalities, took no chances at Celtic Park on this occasion. Throwing the record on his first attempt and fearing the wire handle might stretch in succeeding throws, rendering the overall length of the implement longer than the stipulated four feet, he gave the hammer to a member of the AAU Committee to check that it had not broken the rules and opted to take no further throws, happy in the knowledge that the mark was unlikely to be beaten by any subsequent effort on the day.

In June 2012, McGrath was in good form at Travers Island, where he took the hammer title with a throw of 172 feet, beating Con Walsh by two feet. Going into that year's AAU championships, McGrath was the favorite, but he did not live up to his billing on that day at Forbes Field in Pittsburgh. Instead, the Cork man threw a new world record of 177 feet, 6.5 inches to beat McGrath by four feet. Walsh was now proving a worthy adversary of Matt McGrath, fully deserving of his membership in the Irish Whales group. McGrath, as was his wont, did not get discouraged and settled down to try and improve his throwing. It was a characteristic of his career; whenever he was bested, he went back to training and would return in better shape, a trait Con Walsh was not known for.

As well as being a champion hammer thrower, McGrath was a talented exponent of the 56-pound throw, long a popular event in Ireland. As a discipline that subsequently departed the sporting arena, McGrath still holds two world records—40 feet, 6.375 inches from a seven-foot circle and 33 feet, 1 inch from a standing position—using both hands in each case. Only two Olympic Games scheduled the event—Paris in 1904 and Stockholm in 1912. Today it lives on as a sport in the Scottish Highland Games and is still held at some indoor athletic championships in the United States as a replacement for the hammer—which can only be held outside—but it is not recognized by World Athletics (the IAAF until October 2019).

Con Walsh, despite performing well domestically, retired in 1912 and did not make it to the Stockholm Olympic Games of that year. On September 24, 1910, Walsh had set a new world record in the 56-pound throw for height with a throw of 16 feet, 6 inches at Travers Island, but his greatest victory had come in the American championships of 1912, in Pittsburgh, against McGrath. Later that same year, he set a new world record in the 56-pound throw for distance with a toss of 27 feet, 4 inches. Walsh retired at the height of his achievements. Thus, the U.S. team traveled to Stockholm without Con Walsh and John Flanagan: It was the chance Matt McGrath had been waiting for.

The 1912 Olympic Games, officially known as the games of the V Olympiad, took place between May 5 and July 27, and would later become known as the "Swedish Masterpiece" for their efficient organization and meticulous attention to detail, setting the standard for other venues to replicate for decades to come. Avery Brundage, International Olympic Committee (IOC) president from 1952 to 1972, later described the proceedings in Stockholm as follows: "The efficiency and almost mathematical precision with which the events were handled and the formal correctness of the arrangements made a great impression on me."[3] Electronic timing devices, podiums, photo finishes, and a public address system were used for the first time, while the modern pentathlon (at the insistence of Pierre de Coubertin), women's swimming, and diving and art competitions made their first appearance on the schedule.

De Coubertin had long believed a competition like the modern pentathlon would prove a true test of a gentleman and petitioned the IOC to include one. At Stockholm, his prayers were answered, and he was immensely satisfied when the three medals were won by officers of the Swedish army, the Frenchman's very ideal of the Corinthian amateur gentlemen athletes; however, the IOC was firmly in charge of the games, and the French founder did not have everything his way. Despite numerous requests, he was not allowed to hold a separate arts Olympiad in Stockholm. The athletics schedule in Stockholm also saw the addition of the 5,000 meters, 10,000 meters, the 4 x 100 meter relay, and 10km race walk. Boxing was omitted from the 1912 schedule because it offended Swedish sensibilities, a move that prompted the IOC to further curtail the role of local organizers from then onward.

Twenty-eight countries were represented by 2,407 athletes—of whom 48 were female—in 102 events in 14 sports. Seven countries made their Olympic debut: Chile, Egypt, Iceland, Japan, Luxembourg, Portugal, and Serbia. The participation of two Japanese athletes meant all five continents were represented on the world stage for the first time. De Coubertin still had not come to terms with female participation, which he called the "most unaesthetic sight human eyes could contemplate."[4]

Highlights of the games included American Jim Thorpe winning the pentathlon and decathlon, while twenty-two-year-old Finnish runner Hannes Kolehmainem completed a double in the 5,000 and 10,000 meters. The Finn also won a silver medal in the 12,000 meters team cross-country race and set a world record in a heat of the 3,000 meters team track event. Thorpe's Olympic success later turned to heartbreak when he was stripped of his medals because he had played professional baseball in 1909 and 1910, for the princely sum of $25 a week.

American Ralph Craig, a team alternate, won a double in the 100 and 200 meters sprints (he would return to Olympic action in 1948—thirty-six years later—to compete in a yachting competition), while the first death in the modern Olympics occurred in Stockholm when Portuguese runner Francisco Lazaro collapsed from sunstroke and heart trouble during the marathon, dying the next day. The games also saw a record that has never been beaten—and likely never will be—when a wrestling bout between Estonia's Martin Klein and Finland's Alfred Asikainen lasted an inconceivable eleven hours and forty minutes before Klein finally won. Endurance seemed to have been a defining theme of the games; the course for cycling was 320 kilometers long, still the longest race of any kind in Olympic history.

The needs of the spectators were at the forefront of the organizer's thoughts in Stockholm; from the numbered hats of the swimmers to the pleasure garden near the stadium, the Swedes were thorough in their preparation. Competitors and delegates were given a 50 percent discount on the national rail system, and a daily newspaper was printed for the duration of the games with nothing but coverage of the competition. The sun shone throughout, and the nation was entranced by the panoply of sporting endeavor. The Swedes were praised for the high quality of the 22,000-seat stadium designed by architect Torben Grut, which included an athletics track designed by Charles Perry—the world's first specialist in athletics tracks—and the 100-meter floating swimming pool built in the Bay of Djurgårdsbrunnviken.

Going into the games Matt McGrath was the overwhelming favorite for the hammer throw, a tag he would thoroughly justify in the final on Sunday, July 14. The police magazine *Spring 3001* later recounted an interesting story concerning McGrath's heroic performance in the competition. Obstacles were put in his place, the magazine claimed, but in typical fashion the resilient Irishman overcame them all. First, his proper competition shoes failed to turn up; later officials mistakenly gave him a two-handed hammer instead of the standard American one-handed version. These factors combined to throw Matt off his stride and resulted in his first two throws being fouls. This was not in the script, and spectators must have thought they were watching a favorite fall apart in front of their eyes. If he fouled a third time it would have been the end of the competition for McGrath.

According to the story printed in *Spring 3001*, Prince Gustaf Adolph of the Swedish royal family summoned McGrath to the royal box after the second foul and told the athlete he was greatly impressed with his technique and he would definitely take a medal if he composed himself and avoided throwing a further foul. The genial Prince Gustaf wished the Irish American luck on his next throw, and with his confidence restored McGrath went on to throw a new world record with his third effort.[5] It may have been an example of myth-making, but it made for a great story.

McGrath won the title with remarkable ease; with the retirement of John Flanagan and Con Walsh there was no one remotely near his quality in the field of fourteen athletes. The shortest of his six throws was more than 15 feet longer than any other competitor's best effort, and he set an Olympic record of 179 feet, 7.125 inches, a mark that stood for 24 years until it was eventually surpassed by Karl Hein of Germany at the controversial 1936 Olympic Games in Berlin. To put his achievement into further context, McGrath's throw was more than nine feet longer than the Olympic record held by John Flanagan prior to Stockholm. It must have seemed barely credible to the other competitors who had gathered in Stockholm that an Irish American had once again taken the most sought-after hammer title in existence. Despite a developing tradition of throwing in the host country, the other two medals also went to the continent of North America, with the fourth and fifth positions going to Robert Olsson and Carl Johan Lind of Sweden. Once more the North Americans had dominated the hammer-throwing event at the Olympics; the only disappointment was Ralph Rose's joint eighth position.

Matt McGrath was not the only Irish American thrower to gain worldwide attention in Stockholm. A new Irish hero—the biggest man of them all—emerged in Sweden to continue the great tradition of the Irish Whales. Born in 1878, in Doonbeg, County Clare—a small village perched on the edge of the Atlantic and now home to the Trump International Golf Links and Hotel—Pat McDonald's birth name was actually McDonnell, but when his sister immigrated to the United States prior to his own departure she had the name McDonald pinned to her by immigration officials in error, and her younger brother, considering it wise to avoid any undue complications, thought it best to keep the new name when he got to the point of disembarkation in 1901.

When McDonald first got to the United States, he worked sixty-six hours a week as a warehouseman for the princely sum of $12, a job he would later note—he became famous for telling stories of his past—was tantamount to slave labor but was instrumental in keeping him fit for his athletic endeavors. Four years later, he joined the NYPD in time-honored fashion. McDonald was an absolute giant of a man, standing 6-foot-4 and weighing more than 300 pounds. Ironically, he was given the nickname "Babe" by his teammates. Arthur Daley described him as the most massive athlete he had ever seen, with "arms and legs . . . like the boles of oak trees."[6]

In the early part of his career, McDonald had concentrated on the 56-pound weight throw, the hammer, and the discus, with some degree of success, but it was not until he started to compete in the shot put that he found his niche. He had hoped to compete in the 1908 Olympics in the 56-pound weight throw and was sorely disappointed when the event was not included on the schedule—an omission that, fortuitously, made him focus his attention on the shot put from then onward. McDonald served notice of his ability in the discipline by finishing second to the even more gigantic Ralph Rose at the 1909 and 1910 AAU championships; for an athlete who had come late to the discipline it was a notable achievement.

In Rose's absence, McDonald took the title in 1911, retaining it the following year. With his enormous frame and outsize NYPD uniform, McDonald stood out wherever he went and was a popular character with newsboys on the streets of Manhattan, whom he would stop to talk to while on patrol. Before he left for the Stockholm games a group of newsboys allegedly came up to him at his regular post at Broadway and 43rd Street, and presented him with a silver cup to wish him good luck in the upcoming international competition. Famously, renowned actor and comedian George M. Cohan noticed that McDonald was missing from his regular post one day and went to check that all was well with the gentle giant. When the celebrity found that the Irishman was fine, he was happy to report to his famous friends in the entertainment industry that McDonald was still in the land of the living.

In 1916, McDonald was prevailed upon by fellow Whale Jim Mitchell to contribute a chapter on "Training for Shot-Putting" to his famous book on weight-throwing. After an extensive dissertation on the technical aspects of the discipline, Pat addressed the issue of training, providing more than a hint of his limited personal regime. He recommended confining a session to just six throws, as this was the number required in competition.[7] There was no need to overextend oneself once the proper technique was in place. McDonald also provided the student athlete with some short advice on diet, noting that a man training for the shot could "eat anything he fancies," but on the day of the competition a "couple of chops, tea, and toast, about three hours before the competition" would be sufficient.[8] That is how the great Pat McDonald prepared for the 1912 Olympic Games. Coming to Stockholm, Ralph Rose was twice Olympic shot put champion, holder of the Olympic record, and the favorite for the title. McDonald looked to have his work cut out for him.

Twenty-two athletes from twelve nations were pencilled in for the final on Wednesday, July 10, but those who knew their throwing were well aware that, barring something totally unexpected, the laurels would go to one of two men. It proved to be a great competition between two colossal men, a true battle of the giants. With his first throw, Rose bettered his own record with a throw of 49 feet, 2 inches; with his third, the American extended his newly established record by throwing more than 50 feet. It looked like Rose was on the way to victory, although McDonald had thrown an impressive 48 feet, 4 inches. With the landmark distance of 50 feet having been reached for the first time ever, it was a daunting prospect for McDonald to overcome; only a few years prior it would have seemed an improbable distance in the discipline of shot-putting. That was the lie of the land after the preliminary round of six throws.

The three top athletes were then required to take a further three throws, with Lawrence Whitney taking the third position behind the two giants; neither Rose nor McDonald could have been overly worried about Whitney, as he had only managed 45 feet, 7 inches in the preliminaries. In fact, Whitney was lucky to even get that far in the competition, as it was the only legal throw he made in the preliminary round. There was no doubt that it was now a competition between Rose and McDonald.

With his first throw of the final round, Rose put the shot to a little more than forty-nine feet. Unbelievably, he had beaten the record he had brought into the competition with three separate throws. Rose was surely on his way to an impressive victory, but he had not reckoned with the fighting spirit of the Irishman. With his first throw of the final round, McDonald landed the shot just over the fifty-foot mark to break the record set by the American a few minutes earlier. None of the athletes managed a valid throw with their two remaining efforts: The gold medal in an Olympic throwing final would once again go to an Irish athlete from the IAAC. It would prove the best throw of McDonald's illustrious career. Once more the unfortunate Ralph Rose had been usurped by an Irish Whale—this time one almost as big as himself. It was a truly remarkable achievement. At the medal presentation ceremony, the 5-foot-11, 190-poind Whitney looked like a child beside the two gigantic men.

There would be a consolation prize for Ralph Rose when the 1912 Olympic Games witnessed the only appearance of the two-handed shot put as an Olympic event. Each thrower was required to throw the shot three times with each hand; the best distance with each was then added together to give a total score for the athlete. On Thursday, July 11, seven shot-putters from five nations took part in the event for the first and last time at an Olympics. The same four athletes who occupied the first four positions in the standard shot ended up in the top four positions in this competition, albeit in a different order. Rose threw the shot a little more than three feet longer with his stronger right hand to provide the platform for his victory. McDonald finished second, with the bronze medal going to Elmir Niklander of Finland, swapping places with Whitney from the conventional shot.

The American athletes returned home triumphantly after topping the medals table, although it was close competition. The home nation actually won two more medals, but the United States triumphed by having one more gold medal. The Americans took 25 gold medals, 19 silver, and 19 bronze for a total of 63. It was a striking return for the 174 athletes who had traveled from the United States. The Swedish team won 24 gold medals, 24 silver, and 17 bronze—65 in all.

The United States was at the zenith of its athletic powers, and triumphalism abounded. They were different—a class apart. Will T. Irwin noted that the European teams had marched around the stadium like military conscripts, but the Americans moved with the "loose, springy, natural step of men in perfect control of their bodies and in perfect condition." It was the "gait of the plainsmen who tamed our wilderness, of Jackson's 'foot cavalry,' of Sherman's army of athletes."[9] James E. Sullivan was mighty pleased as well. "Of course, the Americans went on a mission," he said. "This mission was to create a good feeling; to show the type of man this great country of ours produces; to bring them the type of sportsmen that come from this glorious nation of ours, and show the world that we play the game fairly."[10]

Once again, the Irish Whales had done their part in helping the New World dominate the Old. Little did the competitors in Stockholm know that many of their athletic careers would be finished by the next Olympics, nor did they know death would stalk the world, putting all thoughts of athletics aside. The Stockholm games may have been an example of benevolence replacing belligerence, but nothing could prepare the world for what was to come.

10

INTERREGNUM

1912 to 1920

Olympism is not a system; it is a state of mind. It can permeate a wide variety of modes of expression, and no single race or era can claim to have the monopoly of it.—Pierre de Coubertin[1]

While Baron de Coubertin was correct in stating that no race or era could monopolize the Olympic Games, both proved able to disrupt them. World War I involved twenty-eight countries and the deaths of nearly 10 million people between 1914 and 1919, and scuppered any thought of worldwide cooperation in a sporting contest. The Olympic quadrennial had been scheduled for Berlin in 1916—Berlin had been chosen over Alexandria and Budapest at a meeting of the International Olympic Committee (IOC) in July 1912, at Stockholm—and would have been the sixth running of the games, but in a world consumed by the horror of worldwide warfare, an international sporting contest dropped well down on the agenda, although it would be 1915 before the games were finally postponed.

While the geopolitics of the world were being redrawn in lines of blood both during and after the war, the Irish Whales also saw tragedy. In 1912, Martin Sheridan contracted blood poisoning from a small scratch on his head, and when inflammation quickly set in, doctors decided to drill into the side of his head to save his life. At the time he refused to take ether, and it was said he only survived because of his physical strength. Sheridan remained active as an advisor and coach to young athletes but never again competed. A little more than a year after his retirement one of his protégés, Jim Duncan, improved on Martin's world record in the discus with a throw of 145 feet, 9.5 inches. Sheridan was also involved in the promotion of athletics and responsible for organizing the first games in aid of the dependent families of policemen who had died while on duty. The event, held at the Gravesend Racetrack, was so successful it became an annual affair. It was a proud legacy.

On Friday, March 22, 1918, Sheridan, after working a double shift for an absent colleague, was taken to the hospital suffering from pneumonia. He seemed to stabilize during the first few days, and his friends were hoping the surprise party they had organized for his thirty-seventh birthday on March 28 could go on as planned. Sadly, it was not to be. His condition deteriorated rapidly on the Monday and Tuesday of his hospitalisation, and on Thursday—the eve of his birthday—Sheridan passed away peacefully. In retrospect, it is likely he may have been one of the first victims of the Spanish flu, the worst medical pandemic in the history of the modern world. Martin Sheridan had been struck down in the prime of his life.

Sheridan's funeral was a fitting send-off for an athlete who had achieved everything he set out to do. Members of the Irish American Athletic Club (IAAC), accompanied by a police escort of thirty of his New York Police Department colleagues, marched from the club grounds to Martin's house at 722 Lexington Avenue and on to Saint Vincent Ferrers Roman Catholic Church at 67th Street and Lexington Avenue on the afternoon of Saturday, March 31. Huge crowds thronged Lexington Avenue as the funeral cortege passed by. When it finally arrived at the church, there were seventy-five NYPD officers and fifty fire officers standing to attention as the casket was placed in the catafalque. The honorary pallbearers were a cross section of the great and good of New York society. Among them were Governor Martin Glynn; Police Commissioner Richard Enright; Judge Daniel F. Calahan; and P. J. Conway, longtime president of the IAAC.

Sheridan's death was a major shock to the NYPD, where he had served with distinction and been revered for his athletic achievements. At the time of his death, Sheridan was a first grade detective and had been acting as a special bodyguard to Governor Glynn. As the *New York Times* noted in Sheridan's obituary, he followed his profession of detective attached to the local bureau with the "same zest and zeal which had marked his efforts on the athletic field." The *Times* went on to describe him as "one of the greatest athletes that ever represented this country in international sport" and "one of the most popular who ever attained the championship honor."[2] The *New York Herald* poignantly emphasized the athlete's humanity:

> It is hard to believe that big, strapping, kindhearted Martin has been carried off. It seems only the other day that he was in here, with his good-natured laugh, and his hale and hearty way. Sheridan was one of the greatest athletes the world has yet known, but it was not on that account that he won so many friends. He was one of the finest characters we have known. He never had a bad word for anybody. We never know of his having an enemy, for even the malefactors, which he brought to justice, had to admire him. . . . Sheridan goes to Valhalla with a wondrous record, both as a doer of mighty deeds and a doer of kindness.[3]

The paper noted Sheridan's generosity: "Many is the man, both in and out of the police department, who could tell a tale of help and comfort in the darkest hours. Sheridan never had any too much himself, but his pocket always was open to the man in need of a friend." Every pay day he sent a remittance to his mother back home in Ireland.

The *Evening World* echoed these sentiments:

> To know Martin Sheridan was to love him. He was the kind of man who never knocked anybody. If he couldn't say a good word for a fellow, he wouldn't say a bad one. And what's more, Martin never got a swelled head. He was a young man when kings were breaking their necks to shake him by the hand, because of his prowess in competition. He was always modest, and when it came to the limelight thing, he wanted to be way back in the rear.[4]

The Irish press was equally eloquent, as exemplified by the *Western People*, the most-read regional paper in Sheridan's native Mayo:

> His death in the prime of his manhood grieved his countrymen and evoked regrets in the great community of international sport upon which he had shed the lustre of his deeds. He was one upon whose whole career his countrymen can dwell on with affectionate pride, and who can be commended to a younger generation as a man whose

ambition for self-assertion in a strenuous pastime never robbed of the grace of modesty nor warped by the fever of success.[5]

The *Weekly Freeman's Journal* wrote of the "genial, kindly, modest nature of the world's most notable all-round athletic champion." He had an "unspoilt character" and was a proud Irishman:

> Martin Sheridan, in all the glamour of the proud position he attained, never forgot the homeland and, unlike many other champions, refused to allow the universal plaudits he achieved to transform him into a cosmopolitan. He always remained a Gael, enjoying his exploits best when they redounded most to the fame of his race and the honor of his country.

Martin Sheridan was a role model to young American men, the *Wilkes-Barre Leader* reported: "Like every great athlete he was held up as a pattern for the youth of this country, and there is no way of estimating how much the young manhood of America benefitted by his example."[6]

The chaplain of the NYPD chose a text entitled, "I have finished my course. I have kept the faith," for the sermon at Sheridan's funeral mass, finishing his eulogy with the words, "And he did keep the faith. He kept it as a policeman; he kept it as a man. He was a magnificent athlete and a fine servant of the public. He remained on duty long after any ordinary man would have given up. He kept the faith."[7]

Sheridan's long-standing admirer, journalist Robert Edgren, was hit hard by the death of his sporting hero. It seemed impossible that he was now writing about the great athlete in the past tense, "one of those who have gone by, impossible to realize that his great fame and wonderful courage and vitality could fail to defeat the attack of any disease."[8]

The *Buffalo Enquirer* reported an incident that occurred at the 1906 American Athletic Union championships that demonstrated Martin Sheridan's caring side. The discus slipped from his hand as he was throwing it and hit a spectator on the shin. According to the journalist, it was the only time Sheridan was scared in his life: "While the doctor was examining the injured man Sheridan stood by as white as a sheet, and needless to say was much lighter of heart when the doctor said, 'Only a bad bruise.'"[9]

Shortly after Sheridan's death, efforts were made to decide how best to commemorate the athlete's life; only a week after his burial a special meeting was convened by the IAAC with the purpose of establishing a committee to devise a plan. The eminence of those chosen to organize a schedule of events was ample demonstration of the regard in which Sheridan was held. Among the high-profile committee members were Supreme Court Justice Barron S. Weeks; Dock Commissioner Murray Hulbert; Gustavus T. Kirby, president of the Public School Athletics League; and John J. McHugh, inspector of athletics of the Local Board of Education. Before the end of the meeting, $1,100 was contributed by those in attendance. The NYPD added substantially to the fund, after which the committee purchased a number of plots surrounding Sheridan's burial place in Calgary Cemetery for the purpose of erecting a memorial.

On July 10, 1918, Police Commissioner Enright issued a circular to members of the NYPD encouraging them to generously support a concert and games planned for Saturday, July 27, at Celtic Park, to gather money for the memorial's erection. The "greeting" printed in the official program for the day eulogized Sheridan as a "man of mighty muscles, dauntless courage . . . the personification of fairness and gameness—a man who was in every way a credit to his country, his race, and his profession."[10] The sports program for the day included a 16-pound hammer throw that featured Pat McDonald and Matt McGrath in a head-to-head matchup; a tug-of-war competition; exhibitions of weight lifting, fencing, and wrestling; and a hurling championship game between representative sides from Cork and Kerry. It was a fitting tribute to the greatest all-around athlete of his era.

The makeup of the Irish Whales was changing, as were the lives of many Irish immigrants in the United States, but it was a slow process. By 1900, 6 percent of Irish Americans were classified as middle class, while another 10 to 15 percent were recorded as lower-middle class. A significant proportion of the latter were saloonkeepers and owners of small businesses in working-class communities, and a substantial number of Irish were now working as teachers and clerks; however, two-thirds of the Irish American workforce was still employed in manual labor, and many of these jobs remained poorly paid, confining the many Irish who held them to an impoverished and precarious existence.

In 1900, 73 percent of Irish-born women worked outside the home, a significantly higher figure than in many other ethnic groups. More than 60 percent of them worked in domestic service, with an estimated 40 percent of the nations' 320,000 servants being Irish born, a remarkable statistic by any measure.[11] It was a difficult way to make a living: The days were long—many domestics worked seven days a week with few days off and frequently no holiday entitlements—and the wages were low. "Bridget" or "Biddy" the domestic worker was the female equivalent of "Paddy" the laborer and a frequent stereotyped character in vaudeville and theater. It is likely that this initial dependence on the slavery of domestic labor, with its inherent belittlements, spurred many Irish women to become educated, and educated they became. In 1900, 60 percent worked as domestics or waitresses; by the end of the second generation, the figure had fallen to 16 percent. Teaching and nursing were particularly sought-after occupations by Irish women. By 1908, more than 20 percent of New York and Boston public-school teachers were the children of Irish immigrants. With these jobs being largely the gift of the Democratic Party machine, the trust the Irish had placed in politics throughout the years was beginning to pay rich dividends.

While 2 million Irish entered the United States between 1871 and 1920, they only accounted for a little more than 2.5 percent of American immigrants from 1911 to 1920. A defining characteristic of Irish immigration to the United States was its permanence, in the vast majority of cases. In the era of mass movement to the United States, 40 percent of Italians eventually returned home, with the equivalent figure for Polish nationals at 50 percent and 60 percent for Hungarians.[12] Only 5 percent of Irish immigrants did so.

Gradually, the Irishman had come to be seen as an idealized American by other ethnic groups who had followed them to the United States. Newcomers encountering Irish policemen, politicians, bureaucrats, saloonkeepers, contractors, and teachers could be excused for thinking that "Irish" equaled American. The Irish were coming to the forefront in the United States at the same time the country was becoming a world power, magnifying their visibility. Their hard-won experiences and memory of oppression and starvation had willed them onward. In the great cities of the United States, the Irish had developed a coherent national identity and clambered their way to the top, helped in no small way by the Democratic Party machine.

Even organized criminals recognized the value of being considered Irish. Richie Fitzpatrick, who ran part of the criminal underworld on the Lower East Side, was actually a Russian Jew, while Paulo Vacaelli, largely responsible for muscling Irish gangs out of the Five Points area, was known as Paul Kelly. Kelly also traveled the familiar route of the Irish mob boss, having had associations with boxing, social athletic clubs, saloonkeeping, and dockside racketeers. The reputation of fighting ability of the Irish added to the advantages of taking an Irish moniker. The inherent masculinity perceived in the Irishman was a further attraction for gang members. Similarly, immigrants from many backgrounds took Irish names to work in specific jobs; there were Polish builders named Tim Murphy and Slovak factory workers named Paddy O'Shea.

Integration and assimilation took many forms in the United States. Etymology, the study of the origin of words, is not an exact science, but the claim for many words that became part of American urban street slang as having Irish underpinnings is strong. In the early days of Irish emigration, the addition of Irish to a phrase tended to be negative. "Irish evidence" was false evidence, "Irish promotion" was a reduction in pay, an "Irish theater" was a guardroom, and, curiously, an "Irish wedding" was the emptying of a cesspool. The list of words that have been claimed as having Irish origins is long: Speakeasy, slugger, dude, square (honest), turf, blocks, suckers, stool pigeons, squealers, phonies, swells, jazz, moolah, spunk, stiff, babe, maverick, ballyhoo, snoot, bud, mug, cop, beat, racketeer, joint, skedaddle, jiffy, dick, hunch, and slugged have all been suggested at one time or other. In the beginning, such slang was a useful commodity in the city slums as an oppositional code to formal English, but when it was appropriated by film and theater as representational of the dialog of gangsters and the streetwise, it gained kudos in the eyes of many young Americans; in modern terminology, it became cool and hip.

The Irish were not without their critics among other ethnic groups who had come to seek their fortune in the United States. It was sometimes observed by newer immigrants that hostility and racism seemed to be more prevalent toward them among the Irish than other nationalities. There was also a degree of anti-Semitism in some quarters of the Irish population. In 1902, for example, a group of young Irish and Germans working in a printing factory attacked the funeral procession of the most prominent local rabbi. Eyewitness accounts from Jewish mourners suggested that the police meted out more punishment to them than the original assailants and that the factory workforce had experienced previous anti-Semitic attacks.

Similar episodes occurred at theater and vaudeville shows, where Irish audiences attacked actors from other ethnic groups whose stage Irish impersonations they did not appreciate; such assaults often went unpunished by the sympathetic forces of law, dominated as they were by a strong pro-Irish sentiment and staff. The NYPD was also known to turn a blind eye to Irish nationalists demonstrating anti-British sentiment. In 1920, the elite Union Club in Manhattan was flying the Union Jack at a particularly delicate time during the Irish War of Independence. Supporters of the Irish nationalist group Sinn Fein were gathered on Fifth Avenue at Saint Patrick's Cathedral, having just departed a memorial mass, when they spied the offensive flag. Not pleased with what they considered an overt display of colonialism, the Irish attacked and badly damaged the Union Club building. Police officers in command of clearing the fracas were heard to order "no clubbing," while only four miscreants were arrested, two of them by Jewish and German American officers.[13]

Docks and construction sites continued to be interfaces where racial antipathies were expressed. In 1903, at an excavation for a building site at the corner of Broadway and 29th Street, for example, an Irish laborer and an Italian laborer got into a vicious fistfight. As John Kennedy and Lorenzo Vito went at one another, they were soon joined by the entire workforce of fifty Italian laborers and seventy Irish rock drillers; other Irish workers heard the commotion from above and started throwing stones on the Italians. Vito was arrested by a policeman and again attacked by a group of Irish workers when he got to ground level. That same year, the builders of a telephone exchange in Brooklyn employed a group of Irish laborers to carry out work. When Italian hod carriers came on site, the Irish employees immediately declared a strike. The elected representative of the Irish workers explained that it was "against their constitution and bylaws to work with Dagoes."[14] After the employer put several black workers on the job to replace the Irish, the Italians promptly declared their own strike. The *Brooklyn Herald* was of the opinion that the only way to have accord in the construction industry was to keep the different ethnic groups on different jobs.[15]

The role of the Catholic Church in the lives of Irish immigrants in the United States evolved throughout time, but the elaborate social networks engendered by the schools, hospitals, orphanages, charity organizations, and youth groups run under its auspices had enduring influence. In 1900, more than 90 percent of New York Irish claimed to be Catholic, and, of those, 90 percent claimed to belong to a particular parish. Thus, despite huge immigration from such Catholic countries as Italy and Poland, almost one of every two American Catholics was Irish American. With newer waves of emigrants from other Catholic countries, the Irish came to constitute a smaller percentage of the flocks of the great urban parishes of the past, but the Church hierarchy remained disproportionately Irish American; in the early twentieth century, the Irish controlled the important dioceses of New York, Boston, Philadelphia, Chicago, and Baltimore, and, by 1920, two-thirds of Catholic bishops were of Irish birth or descent. (The figure was an astonishing three-quarters in New England.) The preponderance of Irish people in positions of power in Catholic-managed educational facilities would have a long influence; immigrants in mixed neighborhoods often had no choice but to send their children to schools run by Irish Catholics, most frequently nuns.

There had been an anti-Catholic surge in the 1890s; members of the American Protective Association made a pledge not to hire, work alongside, vote for, or strike with Roman Catholics. The response of the Catholic clergy was virtually of one voice; Catholics were real Americans. The archbishop of New York, Michael Corrigan, put it trenchantly: "We are obliged to show that we Catholics are not opposed to the institutions of this country; that we are not subjects of a foreign potentate; and we are sincerely attracted to our land of birth and adoption."[16] In essence, Irish Americans came to be in the vanguard of pan-ethnic American Catholicism. A Worcester priest put it well in 1915: "It is a special blessing of the church in this country in that it has been founded along the lines of the Irish church, and no matter how great the flood of immigrants may be in years to come, the tradition and custom has been established and it will continue along the lines of the dear church of Ireland."[17]

The role of Irish Americans in New York politics was starting to change. On September 15, 1913, seventy-five thousand people had lined the Bowery for the funeral of "Big Tim" Sullivan, longtime political boss of the Lower East Side. Twenty thousand people visited the coffin as it lay in state at his former clubhouse in the Bowery. Sullivan had been born in the squalid tenements on Baxter Street in Five Points and, at the age of seven, gone to work as a newsboy and bootblack. He went on to gain election to the state legislature at the age of twenty-three and dominated politics in Tammany Hall at a time when the neighborhood increasingly accommodated newer Italian and Jewish immigrants.

Sullivan was a shrewd politician and sought to integrate the divergent groups in his bailiwick. While primarily identifying with his working-class Irish Catholic roots he employed Jewish and Italians to help him turn out the vote and was known to turn up at Jewish community events wearing a yarmulke. His move toward inclusiveness and recognition of other ethnic groups undoubtedly prolonged the influence of the Irish in Tammany Hall. It was a remarkable achievement. By 1910, the complexion of Sullivan's Lower East Side territory had changed hugely, with the combined Jewish and Italian residents accounting for 85 percent of the population, with the Irish reduced to a mere 5 percent.

The Irish-dominated political structures were gradually forced to accommodate the wider community. This new dispensation was personified by Al Smith, who opened the political process to Jews and pursued an agenda of social reform; although he identified primarily as an Irish Catholic, he was viewed by the *New York Times* as the "great composite."[18] Smith frequently spoke of his upbringing in the shadow of the Brooklyn Bridge, where Yiddish, Greek, Italian, and English were all spoken. As he moved up through the political ranks, he surrounded himself with a cadre of political advisors representative of the various ethnic hues whose support he sought. Smith also connected well with young people and was known for his ability to sing vaudeville and Broadway songs. Among the forward-thinking legislation enacted during his tenure as governor were rigorous new factory safety laws, antidiscrimination laws on the basis of religion—a policy that appealed to both his Catholic and Jewish constituents—and bills opposing the "Red Scare" and church-supported censorship efforts. Additionally, he presided over a regime in Tammany that opened up the city's legal department and judicial bench to some of his Jewish supporters. It was a long way removed from the flagrant corruption of the past.

Support for the war effort was a divisive issue among Irish Americans, but in the long run the desire for acceptance and respectability swayed the vast majority to get behind the country despite the inevitable alliance with Britain, a bitter pill for some nationalists to swallow. Spurred by the unwavering support of the Catholic Church—in a joint statement issued by cardinals Gibbons, Farley, and O'Connell, American Catholics were urged to "fight like heroes and pray like saints"[19] —Irish Americans joined the armed forces in huge numbers. Such was its level of support the Catholic hierarchy even founded a body called the National Catholic War Council to coordinate responses, while the Knights of Columbus opened field canteens and launched a massive Liberty Bond drive. Of the almost 5,000 conscientious objectors in the United States, less than 1 percent was Catholic. After the entry of the United States into the war, the number of Catholic chaplains increased dramatically—from 28 to more than 1,500—to cater to the needs of the faithful who had signed up with the forces.[20] Dissenting voices among the Irish American Catholic communities were closely monitored and quashed if considered an overt threat.

There would be one final addition to the school of Irish Whales. In 1910, Patrick Ryan—variously referred to as Pat, Paddy, or, for some unknown reason, Paddy "Chicken" Ryan—from the small village of Pallasgreen, County Limerick, arrived in New York. Ryan, born on January 20, 1883, had won eleven Irish hammer titles under the auspices of the Gaelic Athletic Association (GAA) and the Irish Amateur Athletic Association by the time he left for the United States, and created a massive shock in 1902, when he beat the feted Tom Kiely in the hammer title at the GAA championships in Limerick while still only nineteen years of age. Although a modest throw of 136 feet, it was the first time Kiely had been beaten for a number of years by an athlete other than the imperious John Flanagan. It was ironic that Kiely fell to Ryan because it was the great Tipperary athlete who first inspired the Limerick man to try his hand at the hammer. Ryan had seen Kiely dominate the opposition at a sports day in Old Pallas when he was fourteen and gone home to make his own makeshift hammer that evening. For the next seven years, Paddy Ryan won a host of Irish titles, his best result coming in the hammer throw in 1909, with a throw of 154 feet, 5 inches.

Famously, Ryan was another athlete little given to training, as William Dooley noted. If the athlete had lived a "more careful mode of life" and engaged in "systematic training," he might have done much better during his career, but like Irish American boxer John L. Sullivan, Dooley contended, Ryan "was one to speedily turn his trainers grey-haired." Perhaps because he was easily the best in the country he did not see any need to try harder, Dooley suggested.[21]

The emphasis placed on the limited training regime of the Irish Whales, particularly by William Dooley and Arthur Daley, deserves to be taken with a grain of salt, likely to have been another part of the myth-making surrounding the athletes. Here was a group of boisterous Irishmen achieving success on the world stage with limited training, the story went. What might have they done with a more rigorous regime? What records would they have set if they had lived more ascetic and disciplined lives?

They were fine representatives of their race, but like other Irishmen they were given to the finer things in life, primarily alcohol. It was a significant advancement from the cartoons of Thomas Nast and his simian, low-browed Irishman, but it was still a stereotype playing into the hands of the popular American imagination and certainly not true of all the athletes. Martin Sheridan, in particular, was known to live an austere life with a carefully controlled diet. America, however, was a land built on stereotypes, and the bigger and more outlandish the version of the stereotype provided by the individual member of the group, the more the press seized on it and the more mythological the characters became.

By the time Paddy Ryan immigrated to the United States in 1910, he had established a formidable reputation as a thrower. He found employment with the Consolidated Gas Company—the predecessor of Con Edison, the only one of the Irish Whales who was not a police officer (although it is frequently said and written that he was). By all accounts he was a magnificent physical specimen. William Dooley described him as follows:

> Nature endowed the 6-foot-3 Ryan with a magnificent frame, his build, from the knees up, depicting strength in every line and curve, while, together with this all-important attribute, he was possessed of a pair of small and shapely feet which would do credit to a ballet dancer . . . a rare combination. [22]

At an exhibition at the IAAC of New York in October 1910, Ryan threw the new-style hammer with a triangular grip and wire handle to 165 feet, 4 inches. Up until then he had only encountered the straight-handled hammer used in Ireland. Thus, his ability with the new implement was all the more impressive and served notice to the established throwers that a new talent had come on the scene. It was a remarkable transition from one great Irish hammer thrower to the next; it must have seemed to American athletic followers that the production line of Irish throwers would never end.

Ryan's first try for an American title was at Forbes Field in Pittsburgh on July 2, 1911, where he secured third place with a throw of 165 feet, 2 inches, behind compatriots Con Walsh, who threw 177 feet, 6.5 inches, and Matt McGrath, who threw 173 feet, 7.5 inches. Once again, a major hammer-throwing competition provided a clean sweep for Irish athletes.

A little more than a month later, Ryan came within inches of McGrath at Celtic Park with a throw of more than 179 feet. Ryan also took the 56-pound weight throw on the day, with Pat McDonald taking silver. Ryan went on to consolidate his authority by taking the New York Senior Metropolitan hammer title later that same year with a throw just shy of 175 feet. In 1912, Ryan retained his New York title at Travers Island on a day when Matt McGrath—who held the world record at the time—fouled each of his throws. With his best throw, Ryan threw 182 feet, 11.75 inches, managing to smash the bell at the finish of the 100 yards sprint. Two weeks later, he came in second to McGrath in the hammer at the U.S. championship but managed to win the 56-pound weight throw, ahead of Pat McDonald and McGrath, with a throw of almost 38 feet.

Ryan competed for both the New York Athletic Club and the IAAC, a sign that the tensions between the Anglo-Saxon elites and the immigrant communities were starting to dissolve. To his disappointment, and that of the U.S. athletics team, Ryan had not been able to compete at the 1912 Olympics Games in Stockholm because he was unable to establish citizenship in time, but during the next few years he would make up for this omission in considerable style. On February 8, 1913, Ryan established a new world record for the hammer with a throw of 189 feet, 6 inches at the unusually named Eccentric Firemen's Games, a mark that stood for twenty-five years on the world stage and remained the distance to beat for an incredible forty years in the United States. The "eccentric" games were well named; among other events they included a competition to hit a suspended ball with a jet of water from the back of a fireman's horse. Ryan later lyrically described his winning throw to Dave Guiney, a friend back home in Limerick:

> I spat on my hands and picked up the hammer, it was now or never, I put everything into that throw, and as the hammer left my hands I knew Matt McGrath's record was gone forever, the hammer soared up into the blue sky, glinting golden as the evening sun caught it in flight, dropped and tore into the green turf ahead of the world record flag. [23]

The great Matt McGrath had finally met his match. Only three weeks later, Ryan established new leading marks in the 35-pound throw with 57 feet, .875 of an inch and the 42-pound throw with a distance of 28 feet, 11.25 inches. On the same day, Pat McDonald put the 14-pound shot to 52 feet, 4 inches, incidentally eclipsing the mark of 51 feet, 6.375 inches made by Ralph Rose. Never before had there been such a "wholesale demolition of weight-throwing records," according to the *New York Times*.[24]

In July 1914, Ryan threw the 12-pound hammer to a record distance of 225 feet at Buffalo, but the athletic authorities did not see fit to record the result as an official mark. He had thrown 213 feet, 9.5 inches in the same event the previous autumn at Celtic Park, a mark never bettered in the rarely contested event. The competition between Ryan and McGrath further intensified as the year went by. The New York Senior Championships on October 3, proved to be a titanic struggle between the two greats of contemporary hammer-throwing; the day would see the highest-ever standard in one event on the American continent to that date. Ryan would get the spoils with a throw of 186 feet, 2 inches to McGrath's 181 feet, 11 inches. Later in the year, Ryan would throw the 28-pound weight for an American record of 36 feet, 8.5 inches.

The competition between McGrath and Ryan was now at fever pitch. In 1915, Ryan again took the American Championship title, this time held in San Francisco in conjunction with the Panama-Pacific Exposition. He threw 177 feet—two feet ahead of McGrath. Later that year, he improved substantially on that mark with a throw of 187 feet, 4 inches in front of his home crowd in Celtic Park, and, in 1916, McDonald once again took the American Championship in Newark, New Jersey—this time out-throwing McGrath by an impressive fifteen feet.

Despite the accusations of lax training and a marked propensity for the good life leveled at Paddy Ryan during his career, he saw fit to contribute a chapter to Jim Mitchell's 1916 book on weight-throwing, in which he wrote about training for the hammer. He discussed the technical aspects of the discipline at great length before warning the athlete that hammer-throwing is a particularly "tiring exercise" and a half-dozen throws a day is plenty. If an athlete finds himself "fagged out" he should skip training for a few days to "rest the muscles."[25] Ryan, according to numerous sources, was a man who avoided getting "fagged out" by his training regimen. He also provided advice on diet to the aspiring hammer thrower, noting that a "man may eat almost any healthy foods but must avoid the victuals that cause biliousness or cause any great exertion on the stomach during the progress of digestion." On the day of a competition "food should be partaken of sparingly" and the athlete should feel that his stomach is completely empty during a contest.[26]

In 1917, Ryan took the American titles in the hammer and 56-pound throw before departing for World War I in Europe, during which time he won numerous events organized for the armed forces. He became friends with fellow Irish American Gene Tunney, later conqueror of Jack Dempsey for the world heavyweight boxing championship. At the 1919 Enlisted Men's Olympic Games held at Camp Dix, New Jersey, under the auspices of the Knights of Columbus, Ryan won gold medals in the hammer throw and the 35-pound weight throw, contributing handsomely to the U.S. Army's crushing defeat of the U.S. Navy and the U.S. Marine Corps.

While on leave in Ireland in 1919, Ryan took the IAAC hammer title with a throw of 189 feet, and shortly after his return to the United States he won the American hammer title with a throw of 175 feet at Franklin Field, Philadelphia, in the absence of Matt McGrath. Ryan then joined the Loughlin Lyceum Athletic Club, as the IAAC did not start up again after the war.

Despite the continuing competition between the athletes the *New York Times* of August 19, 1915, recorded the disappointment expressed by the Irish American throwers regarding the lack of competitive outlets available in the United States.[27] Pat McDonald asserted that he was "through with the game" at the end of the year, as there were not enough competitions, and said Paddy Ryan and Matt McGrath felt the same way. Only one competition had included weight-throwing events in its schedule so far that season, and that was simply not enough, according to the athlete. If these men left the sporting arena it would be a serious loss for the United States should the Olympics by chance be held within the next few years, the journalist opined. He noted the achievements of McGrath and McDonald, and suggested that Paddy Ryan would be a serious threat to the other athletes in the next Olympics. Ryan, as it transpired, would have to wait a long time to see if he could prove himself on the world stage, and by then the end of a glorious era in the world of Irish American immigrant athletes would be nigh.

In 1916, Matt McGrath was also prevailed upon by Jim Mitchell to contribute to his instructional manual and did so in a chapter called "Training for the '56." McGrath started by extolling the virtues of the 56-pound weight throw as the best of the weight events for strength development; however, he believed that not everyone should contemplate taking up the discipline and that "weak men and especially those with defective

kidneys" should stay away from it. McGrath did not explain why those
with poor kidney function should refrain from taking part, but for those
men who were suited to the discipline he recommended throwing the
weight no more than a dozen times a day. He proceeded to give a lengthy
discourse on executing a double turn in the throwing circle, emphasizing
the difficulty and the need for practice with the provision of taking a
break for three days before a competition to give the muscles a "good
rest."[28]

After the catastrophic damage wrought by World War I, the IOC was
anxious to reestablish the Olympics and show the world, particularly the
main belligerents, that nothing could stop the greatest show on earth.
Belgium, Germany's near-neighbor, was the brave choice of location by
the committee. The games would prove one of the final great triumphs of
the Irish Whales.

11

LAST THROWS OF THE DICE

The Antwerp and Paris Olympic Games

The day when a sportsman stops thinking above all else of the happiness in his own effort and the intoxication of the power and physical balance he derives from it, the day when he lets considerations of vanity or interest take over, on this day his ideal will die.—Pierre de Coubertin[1]

World War I decimated the very constituency of the Olympic Games—young men from Western Europe and North America. Fifteen million perished worldwide, among them 890,000 British war-dead, 1.3 million French, and 1.7 million Germans. The British army alone had lost 13 percent of its recruits and 20 percent of its officers. It was utter devastation.

On April 5, 1919, at the eighteenth International Olympic Committee (IOC) Session, held in Lausanne, Antwerp was chosen to host the Games of the VII Olympiad in what Pierre de Coubertin later termed a "unanimous tribute to Belgium."[2] The choice of Belgium was symbolic: It had been occupied for four years by German forces during the course of World War I and suffered great privations. Giving the games to Antwerp was a sign to the world that the IOC was determined to thrive in the face of adversity, rise from its knees, and get on with the business of bringing a fractured world together in the sporting arena. It was, in this regard, a high-stakes Olympics.

Twenty-nine countries were represented by 2,626 participants (2,561 men and 65 women), with the program consisting of 154 events in 20 sports. The games ran between April 20 and September 12. Germany, Austria, Hungary, Bulgaria, and Turkey were not invited due to their role in the war, while the Soviet Union opted not to attend, as it was consumed by civil war, a harbinger of things to come in the later Cold War era. Anti-German sentiment ran so high that Swedish ice skater Magda Julin was not allowed to perform her routine to the music of Johann Strauss's "Blue Danube" on the grounds that it was "too Teutonic."[3] Baron de Coubertin did not countenance the participation of Germany and neither did the Belgians: An anti-German demonstration was held in Antwerp city center on June 13, before the games.

It was not an easy job for Antwerp to host the games. The preparations were hampered by bad weather and economic difficulties, while the construction time frame was overly ambitious; however, despite a limited budget, the Belgians managed to pull it all together in the end, albeit with some of the logistical solutions on the patchy side. The Red Cross and the Belgian army were supposed to have provided furniture and other material to the organizers, but both were overburdened trying to deal with the refugee crisis resulting from the war and the organizing committee was forced to fall back on their own limited resources. The financially straitened nature of the times was reflected in some aspects of the proceedings.

When the games started the main accommodation block had not been finished, and the athletes were forced to stay in crowded rooms with folding cots. Attendances were sparse because people could not afford the price of tickets; in the final days of the games authorities let schoolchildren in for free to fill the stands. The organizing committee went bankrupt in the middle of the games, and no final reports were prepared. Given the backdrop of the calamitous destruction wrought by World War I it was a major achievement for the Belgians to run the Olympics in the first instance.

Inevitably a thread of solemnity and sadness pervaded the games. The opening ceremony on August 14 was preceded by a requiem mass to commemorate athletes killed in the war. Cardinal Désiré-Joseph Mercier, a highly regarded activist in the Belgian war resistance, gave a sermon in which he stressed the importance of the games as a "preparation for peace and . . . for the awful possibilities which are still lowering on the horizon."[4] At the opening ceremony, King Albert symbolically wore his army uniform as commander in chief of the Belgian army, while an engraving of a Belgian soldier lobbing a hand grenade was made on the triumphal arch through which the athletes entered the stadium for the opening ceremony. Ordinarily there would have been an image depicting an athlete in the act of competing in a discipline like the discus, but these were far from ordinary times. While references to the war were kept in check, de Coubertin made a poignant acknowledgment of the legacies of the conflict when he wrote, "Here and there could be noticed a person whose gait was less elastic than usual, whose face looked older."[5]

Antwerp saw the introduction of the Olympic oath and the Olympic flag with its five multicolored intersecting rings, while doves, representing a worldwide hope for peace, were released for the first time. The sporting highlight of the games was the performances of twenty-three-year-old Finnish middle-distance runner Paavo Nurmi, who won gold medals in the 10,000 meters and the 8,000 meters cross-country individual and team races, and silver in the 5,000 meters. In a performance that has never been equaled in Olympic history, Nedo Nadi of Italy took gold medals in five of the six fencing events, while his brother Aldo won three golds and a silver. Albert Hill of Britain made his Olympic debut at the tender age of thirty-six and won both the 800 and 1,500 meters, while Oscar Swahn, aged seventy-two and sporting a long, white beard, became the oldest entrant to win an Olympic medal when he took silver in the 100 meters team running deer shots.

There were also outstanding performances by female competitors, with Ethelda Bleibtrey of the United States taking a gold medal in all three swimming events. In each final she set a new world record subsequent to also having done so in two of the three heats. Ice hockey was part of the Antwerp games, a sport that would not reappear on the Olympic schedule until 2016, while the 1920 yachting events provided some quirky additions to Olympic lore; the 12-foot dinghy event was the only event in the history of the games to be held in two countries, with the first race staged in Belgium and the other two in the Netherlands, as all entrants were Dutch. A further addition to Olympic sailing history was made on July 9, when Norway won seven yachting events, although they were the only competing nation in five of the races.

Having defeated Matt McGrath in the American Championships of 1920—which had doubled as the Olympic trials—Paddy Ryan traveled in confidence to Antwerp. The day of the hammer throw competition, August 18, was marred by heavy rain, and the grass throwing circle became badly torn up during the competition, an occupational hazard of the era. McGrath and Ryan were expected to duel it out for the gold medal, but the unfortunate McGrath injured his knee in the second round and was forced to withdraw. It was a disappointment for the spectators who were expecting a titanic battle between the two famous Irish Americans, and the cognoscenti knew McGrath's withdrawal meant the end of any meaningful competition. Paddy Ryan, aged 37 and weighing almost 20 stone, stayed true to form and took the gold with a winning throw of 173 feet, a full 15 feet longer than Carl Lind of Sweden—still the greatest winning margin on record in the event. Yet another American athlete, Basil Bennett from Dudley, Illinois, finished third with the best throw of his career. Ryan had thrown 181 feet the previous week, but conditions on the day dictated against a repeat performance. The unlucky McGrath finished a distant fifth after having only one throw counted before his forced retirement.

Colin Murphy told an apocryphal story of Ryan's weakness for drink, which, if true, could have cost him dearly in his pursuit of the gold medal in Antwerp. According to Murphy's tale Paddy Ryan insisted on going out the night before the final to sample the alcoholic delights of downtown Antwerp. Inevitably, he awoke the next day with a terrible hangover, greeting the U.S. coach with his hand to his forehead and the words, "I'm dyin'." The hammer thrower pleaded with the coach to take him for a hair of the dog—which the official obligingly did—where Ryan and an American teammate "shared enough cures to heal the dead."[6] After a struggle the benighted coach managed to extricate the athletes from the bar and rush them to the stadium. By the time they got there the other hammer throwers had made their first attempts; the Irishman had arrived in the nick of time. Flags marked the throws of the previous competitors, and Ryan asked an official if he would stand just beyond the farthest flag to act as a target. Although his vision was blurred by alcohol Ryan easily threw the hammer beyond the indicated flag. There is every chance that there is not an ounce of truth to this story, but once again, it fit perfectly with the narrative of Ryan and the stereotype of the jolly, bibulous Irish American.

Two days later there would be a consolation prize for McGrath when he finished second to McDonald throwing the 56-pound weight from the circle—the last time the event was part of the Olympic schedule. McDonald bettered the Olympic record with a throw of a little more than 36 feet with his first attempt, extending the mark to just shy of 37 feet in the final round, and as the event was never held again, the mark still stands as an Olympic record, the last great triumph for an Irish Whale.

The United States once again proved that it was the greatest sporting power on earth at the Antwerp Olympics, winning 95 medals, of which 41 were gold, 27 silver, and an equal number bronze. It was still the century of America.

In New York, further fundraising allowed the organizing committee to bring their commemorative project for Martin Sheridan to fruition when, on May 21, 1921, a magnificent Celtic cross was erected in his memory in Calvary Cemetery. Once again, the great and the good gathered to pay their respects to the famed Irish athlete. The unveiling was completed by Sheridan's close friend, P. J. Conway, by now retired from his longtime role as the president of the Irish American Athletic Club, and Thomas McQueeney, a captain with the New York Police Department. Among those who spoke were Police Commissioner Richard Enright, Reverend John Healy, and Dock Commissioner George Murray Hulbert. The inscription on the Celtic cross reads, "Martin J. Sheridan, an intrepid American; an ardent lover of his motherland; a peerless athlete; devoted to the institutions of his country and to the ideals and aspirations of his race." Shortly thereafter, the Martin J. Sheridan Award for Valor was established and awarded annually to a member of the NYPD who distinguished himself by an "act performed intelligently in the line of duty at imminent personal hazard of life and with knowledge of risk assumed."[7]

By the time the Paris Olympic Games of 1924 came around the pod of Irish Whales had further diminished. On July 3 1921, James "Jim" Mitchell—the first of the Irish Whales—passed away at the age of fifty-seven. Mitchell's final record of achievements bears favorable comparison with the greats: 17 Irish championships, 5 British titles, 20 American senior outdoor awards, 6 American indoor titles, 20 New York metropolitan titles, and 14 Canadian awards. Mitchell broke the world hammer throw record four times during his illustrious career, and although his Olympic medal tally was confined to the bronze medal he took at the 1904 games in the 56-pound weight throw he was forty years old and well past his prime. Should he have competed at either of the two previous championships there is every chance he would have added to his haul.

After retiring from the NYPD, Mitchell went on to become a sportswriter and covered the 1912 Olympic Games for the *New York Herald*. He had set in train the most incredible production line of throwers the world of track and field had ever seen. The first of the remarkable group of men who were later dubbed the Irish Whales is buried in Calvary Cemetery, New York.

A further changing of the guard occurred in 1924, when Paddy Ryan moved back to Ireland, where he and his wife went on to raise five daughters on a farm he bought in his native Limerick. The group was ever diminishing, and the next Olympics would see the very last of the Irish Whales.

Paris hosted the championships for the second time in 1924, with a firm view to making a better fist of it than the 1900 iteration. Officially known as Les Jeux Olympiques D'été de 1924—the Games of the VIII Olympiad—the second Paris games were the last organized under the presidency of de Coubertin and proved to be a notable legacy for the founder of the greatest sporting show on earth. The athletes stayed at an Olympic village that contained portable wooden houses complete with running water, a post office, a bureau de change, a hairdressing salon, and a restaurant where the athletes and officials were provided three meals each day—although the British, ever distrustful of the French and their strange food, brought along their own chef. The rising popularity of the games saw more than a thousand journalists present while they were broadcast on radio for the first time. The IOC further rationalized Olympic regulations; from Paris onward the rules and the Olympic program of individual sports were set by the international governing body of each sport, not the organizers of the games. If a sport did not have an international federation—archery, for example—it was excluded from the games.

Highlights of the games included the wins of the "Flying Finn," Paavo Nurmi, in both the 1,500 and 5,000 meters, his achievement made all the more remarkable by the fact that the races took place a mere hour apart. British runners Harold Abrahams and Eric Liddell won the 100 and 400 meters, respectively, and were later immortalized in the film *Chariots of Fire*, while the games saw the introduction of the first fifty-meter swimming pool, where future movie star Johnny Weissmuller won three gold medals. American William DeHart Hubbard became the first black athlete to win an individual gold medal when he took the long jump title, although some of the luster was taken from his performance when fellow American Robert LeGendre, who had failed to qualify for the U.S. long jump team, established a new world record for the event competing in the pentathlon the day before. Uruguay surprised the sporting world by taking gold in the soccer competition, while the Olympic motto "Citius, Altius, Fortius" (Faster, Higher, Stronger) was used for the first time. The Olympic program featured 126 events in 23 disciplines comprising 17 sports, and 44 nations competed. Held from May 4 to July 27, 1924, the games attracted 3,089 participants—2,954 men and 135 women.

Ireland competed as an independent nation for the first time in Paris. The country had been admitted to the IOC after the Irish Free State's 1922 independence from the United Kingdom of Great Britain and Ireland. The two medals the new team took home were a world removed from throwing: a silver in the mixed art competition and a bronze for poetry.

The great Matt McGrath, at the remarkable age of forty-nine, was back once more to compete in the hammer. On the morning of Thursday, July 10, at the Stade Olympique Yves-du-Manoir, fifteen athletes from ten countries took part in the preliminary round, with six proceeding to a final based on distance thrown: Fred Tootell of the United States, Malcolm Nokes of Great Britain, Erik Eriksson of Finland, McGrath, Ossian Skiöld of Sweden, and American James McEachern. Tootell and McGrath were significantly better than the rest of the field; between them they recorded eight of the top ten marks thrown. McGrath took the silver medal with a throw of 166 feet, 9 inches—his third Olympic award in sixteen years—behind Tootell, the first American-born athlete to take the title, who threw 174 feet, 10 inches. It was a remarkable achievement by Tootell, who had to wear a cast on his leg until the day before the final, having injured a tendon in his ankle on the journey to Paris. McGrath's achievement was equally admirable; he remains the oldest U.S. athlete to win an Olympic medal in track and field. Extant footage of the competition shows the slim and lithe Tootell throwing the hammer with considerable grace. The camera then moves to where the officials are noting the distance of a throw, and a number of athletes, one of them Matt McGrath, can be seen peering down at the mark to check it. McGrath is distinctly overweight and florid in the cheeks and by today's standards looks more like he should have been in the stands looking on.

At the Paris Olympics, American athletes were once again in the ascendant, winning ninety-nine medals, of which forty-five were gold, four more than the team had taken at Antwerp. In an unlikely coincidence they took the same number of silver and bronze—twenty-seven of each—as in the previous games. When Matt McGrath departed Paris the supply of Irish American Whale Olympic medal winners had finally come to an end.

12

A WHALE OF A STORY

Aftermath and Legacy

The immigrant's heart marches to the beat of two quite different drums, one from the old homeland and the other from the new. The immigrant has to bridge these two worlds, living comfortably in the new and bringing the best of his or her ancient identity and heritage to bear on life in an adopted homeland.—former Irish president Mary McAleese [1]

When Charles Kickham's novel *Knocknagow* was committed to film in 1917, by Fred O'Donovan, the event that had been described as "sledge-throwing" in the 1840s in the book was depicted and labeled as "hammer-throwing" in the movie adaptation, in keeping with the development of the discipline. When the film was released in 1918, it proved immensely popular. Reviewers described it as the "greatest attraction ever offered to Ireland's cinema-loving public" [2] and "Ireland's first big production." [3] The "famous story of the homely country folk of Ireland," as the special notice sent to exhibitors of the movie by the Film Company of Ireland noted, chimed with the great athletic feats of the Irish Whales. [4] The movie was also popular among emigrant communities. In Boston, David Walsh, the Democratic senator for Massachusetts, declared, "This film play . . . has started a movement to place the story of Ireland and her sufferings before the world for an unbiased verdict." [5]

In the United States, critical opinion was varied. The *Boston Globe* noted that the photography was the best yet seen from Europe. *Variety* was less complimentary: "It's just 'play-acting,' all the way, with no illusion to make the spectator believe he is witnessing anything more than a company of actors, impersonating human beings."[6]

The *Freeman's Journal* was effusive:

> It is common talk among exhibitors in Ireland that no picture was ever shown in the country that secured anything like the enthusiastic support given to *Knocknagow*. It is probably the only picture that is given repeats in nearly every village and town in Ireland, in the same picture house, in many instances four and five times.[7]

It was a case of art imitating life. Viewers were able to witness the fantastic throwing of Matt "The Thresher" O'Donovan as he defeated Captain French in the same era the Irish Whales bestrode the world stage as masters of the throwing disciplines in athletics.

The lives of the Whales played out in different ways. John Flanagan settled back into farming life after he returned to his native Limerick in 1910. When rumors circulated that he was going to compete for the Great Britain and Ireland team at the Stockholm Games, he quickly quashed them by writing the following to the *Gaelic American*:

> I saw where it was reported that I was to compete for England at the Olympic Games. *Never!* . . . If I were in form at the present time I would be only too glad to compete under the Starry Banner. Please give this all the circulation you possibly can as I want to refute statements in the press that I am competing for England.[8]

Flanagan was quite content to live out his days in the verdant countryside of County Limerick, where he had a "good slice of his father's wide acres."[9] According to the 1911 census, John Flanagan's home was "in the first grade of dwelling" and had "six front windows . . . surrounded by eleven outhouses." At the time of the survey, he shared the house with his parents, a brother Patrick, and four servants.[10] That same year, Flanagan attained a lifetime's ambition when he competed for Ireland. After taking the hammer and 56-pound titles at the Irish Amateur Athletic Association (IAAA) championships, he was chosen to represent Ireland against Scotland, and he defeated Tom Nicholson in the hammer. Flanagan made his final competitive appearance on May 27, 1912, at the IAAA championships at the RDS Showgrounds in Dublin, where he once again annexed the hammer title.

In 1933, the Gaelic Athletic Association (GAA) magazine *An Caman* took a retrospective look at Flanagan's career. Journalist "Celt" noted that Flanagan was utterly dominant in hammer-throwing and had raised the world record with sixteen incremental throws and extended it by thirty-seven feet during his lengthy reign. Flanagan, according to Celt, was a multitalented athlete who could have competed in many different disciplines and had brought weight-throwing to a "high pitch of perfection" by constantly seeking innovation. While praising Flanagan's supreme ability in the hammer Celt expressed the opinion that the athlete was not as proficient in throwing the shot from the shoulder for a good reason: The Irishman "loves the whirl of the more active event to the momentary concentration of the pushing pastime." The hammer was his forte, as it required a "man of battleship muscularity and light-cruiser activity." Flanagan's battle with Matt McGrath was "one of the epic tales of New World competition." Each excelled in turn until Flanagan finally retired, "weighted more with honors than years."

Republican John Devoy wrote one of his last letters to John Flanagan, in which he reminisced about the times he had seen the athlete perform in the United States: "It is one of my most pleasant memories to stand in Celtic Park watching your splendid figure as you whirled the hammer around and sent it flying in to space. . . . I always held you as the fresh type of the old Gallowglass . . . winning glory for Ireland."[11] Devoy emotively described an occasion when he saw Flanagan perform in Ireland, by which time the famous political activist was almost blind:

> It was a great pleasure to see you again, although my failing sight prevented me from getting a clear view of what was in front of me, but I was able to pick up your magnificent figure from the surrounding groups and recognized my old athletic demigod. I returned to America with renewed hope for the future of Ireland saying to myself—so long as Ireland produces John Flanagan's there is hope for her future. You have no better well-wisher in the whole world.[12]

In 1933, the year Celt wrote his article, Flanagan was still alive and working on his farm in Limerick, a "great figure of a champion whose presence should be an incentive to preserve the grandeur of the feats he accomplished and the tradition of which he was a superb embodiment."[13] His interest in athletics never declined, and he was a hero to everyone.

John Flanagan died on June 3, 1938, at the age of seventy at his home in Kilmallock. The *Irish Independent* described him as a man who brought an "old Irish pastime of the crossroads into the forefront of international athletics," a man who "created a cult which other nations were happy to copy," and a man who was "always anxious to instruct and encourage youth." The paper eulogized him as a man of the people who was "simple and modest—almost shy; hospitable in his home to a fault . . . loved and respected by neighbors at home and by sportsmen in far distant places . . . a shining star." An Irish American acquaintance had once spoken to the journalist about the athlete and got the answer that everyone loved the Irishman, and despite having had the "sunshine of America on his back for a dozen years," he never changed.

In 2001, a striking commemorative life-size statue of Flanagan was unveiled beside Martinstown Church—on the Kilmallock to Knocklong road—in the heart of the rich land of rural southeast Limerick. It depicts the athlete at the point of releasing the hammer, his well-proportioned physique and lack of height compared to modern athletes immediately noticeable. Among the many dignitaries present at the unveiling ceremony was Gregory Fried, executive chief surgeon of the New York Police Department. Fried brought greetings from Rudolph Giuliani, mayor of New York City; NYPD commissioner Bernard Kerik; and Joseph P. Dunne, the highest-ranking native Irish-born police officer in the force at that time, who said Flanagan was "the finest of the finest."[14]

Matt McGrath continued to compete up until 1934, by which time he was fifty-eight years of age. He and his wife Loretta would suffer a tragedy when their daughter Elvira died at the age of twenty-two. A few years later, the couple decided to adopt a Chinese boy in an unusual set of circumstances. While on holiday in the Adirondack Mountains in northeast New York State, the couple became friendly with a chef who was working in the resort where they were staying. The chef had a son who lived with him, while his wife had abandoned them both. The McGraths got on well with the father and son during the course of their vacation and told them to seek them out in New York if they ever needed help. Two years later, the Chinese man, who had come to the city with his son but failed to find employment and fallen on hard times, came to visit the McGraths at their home. The policeman and his wife offered to take care of the child while his father searched for a job. A couple of weeks stretched into a couple of years, and the McGraths were eventually appointed guardians of the boy, Bobby Low. Unfortunately, Loretta McGrath became seriously ill and was no longer able to cater to the needs of the child at home. The couple sent the boy to boarding school, and he went on to have a successful career in the military.

Matt McGrath was an exemplar of an Irishman who had made good through the offices of the NYPD and his sporting prowess. The 1940 U.S. Census records that he was the best-paid man in his neighborhood, earning a salary of $6,500.[15]

Whenever he got the chance, McGrath returned to Ireland, where he was always sought out by journalists. In July 1936, "Marathon" of the *Irish Press* noted that the athlete had lost none of his physical presence judging by the strength of his handshake. McGrath was "sixteen stone of bone and muscle, and six and a half feet of brawn." He had completed the required thirty years' service with the NYPD and was contemplating coming home to Ireland for good. He praised the available body of athletes in the country, hinting that he might return to lend his assistance to their development.[16] Alas, like so many other emigrants, McGrath's permanent return to Ireland did not come to pass, as he succumbed to liver cancer in 1941, at the age of sixty-four. The ebullient Limerick man had left an indelible mark on the landscape of the United States and world throwing, winning fourteen American championships and one Olympic medal during his long and illustrious career. He had a profound effect on the Irish American community, and according to William Dooley, much of the Irish population of New York had reason to mourn his death because McGrath had shown them how to succeed.[17]

Reverend Joseph A. McCaffrey gave the homily at McGrath's funeral, saying he had been a "moral, physical, and spiritual giant" and a "credit to the Irish race, to America, to the Catholic Church, to the police department, and to athletics." He had been an exemplary member of the NYPD who "gave his full share to make the department loved and respected by right-thinking people and feared by law breakers."[18] The *New York Herald-Tribune* described McGrath as a hero of four Olympic Games and "one of the finest craftsmen in the none-too-finely taught science of throwing weights for distance." It also wrote of his bravery as a police officer—a man who dived into ice-cold rivers to rescue would-be suicides, subdued a gunman by heaving a dinnick at him, and fought many fights under what he called the "Marquis of Kilkenny Rules."[19] He had been an "expert on how to untangle a fight on Eighth Avenue" and would be missed by every sportswriter who ever talked to him and the police and newsmen who knew him. McGrath was twice honored with a medal of valor, once for rescuing a man from drowning in the Harlem River and a second time for arresting a man who was fleeing from the scene of a shooting with a gun in his hand. The obituary finished eloquently: "As much for keeping alive the tradition of Irish strong men as for being an honest and decent policeman for forty years, Matt McGrath slips away, having a trail of goodwill and friendly recollection seldom left by any man."[20]

The police magazine *Spring 3001* returned to the subject of McGrath in 1994. It considered his professional achievements, emphasizing his ascension of the career ladder of the NYPD; McGrath was promoted to sergeant in 1917, lieutenant in 1918, captain in 1927, deputy inspector in 1930, and inspector in 1936. Matt McGrath "represented all the very best qualities a police officer could have in the sheer dedication he displayed in his professional work, as well as his personal health." He was a staunch proponent of a healthy diet and daily exercise, including jogging long before it became popular. McGrath's career was summed up by Hal Bateman of the United States of America Track and Field Federation:

> Without doubt, Matthew McGrath is an Olympic legend. For him to have competed as long as he did, in that day and age, is incredible. He was a very outstanding athlete on an elite level—a national champion in 1926, at the age of fifty—something almost unheard-of. To do this nowadays is almost unthinkable.[21]

In 1989, Matt McGrath was praised on the floor of the House of Representatives for being an outstanding athlete and a man who refused to dip the national flag to a foreign power, thus creating a precedent. In September 2002, the town of Nenagh in County Tipperary erected a statue outside the courthouse honoring McGrath's Olympic achievements.

Pat "Babe" McDonald continued to win American titles until 1933. Having won the gold medal in the 56-pound throw at the 1920 Olympic Games in Antwerp, at the age of forty-two years and twenty-six days, his place in history as the oldest-ever track and field gold medal–winning Olympian is unlikely to be usurped. McDonald was the grand age of fifty-three when he competed at the Centennial Exhibition in Chicago, where he threw the 56-pound weight 33 feet, remarkably only a foot shorter than his best effort at the 1920 Olympic Games. For this astonishing achievement—and his Olympic glory—the Irish American Athletic Club of New York gave him one of their rarely awarded lifetime memberships. He also had the high honor of carrying the American flag at the opening of the 1920 and 1924 Olympic Games, and, likewise, McDonald was held in such high regard by his fellow U.S. athletes that he was chosen to voice their concerns to authorities when conditions on board the ship SS *Princess Matoika* sailing to the 1920 games were adjudged to be substandard. The old troop carrier had been called into action at the last minute when it was ascertained that the more commodious *Great Northern* was not available for the trip. While the female athletes were given cabins on deck with the officers, 108 of the male athletes had to bunk in the troop quarters below deck, a far from ideal situation. As John Findling wrote, "The sea was rough, the food was terrible, and the cream of the athletic world turned slightly sour."[22] To exacerbate the situation, members of the American team who were employees of the U.S. Navy were brought across the Atlantic Ocean on the much more suitable SS *Frederick*. With his natural diplomatic skills, McDonald was able to negotiate a compromise to placate the U.S. team. The agitation on board the *Matoika* later acquired the dramatic title "Mutiny on the Matoika."

It was said of Pat McDonald that his Irish brogue and friendly banter were as familiar to New Yorkers as the best hotels, restaurants, and landmarks of the era. For fifteen years, from 1905 to 1920, McDonald, known as the "Living Statue of Liberty," held down the traffic beat in Times Square, where, according to *Spring 3001*, he "captured the imagination of the public and became a world-renowned figure," and "sightseeing bus 'holler boys' pointed him out as the cop who owns three Olympic titles, twenty-four national championships, and uncounted Metropolitan championships."[23] He went on to work for the NYPD until his retirement in 1946, after having given forty-one years to the service. *Spring 3001* noted that it was an admirable achievement that McDonald found the time to take the police departmental exams to reach the position of captain, all the while keeping himself in shape to compete at the highest level. It also pointed out that McDonald and his wife Mary raised their son Joseph to become an "outstanding physician." McDonald was still a "rabid track fan," attending as many of the big meets as he could each year, and he was not shy in expressing his opinion about what he perceived to be a relaxed interpretation of the shot put rules by officials in more recent years. Where officials always insisted on the shot being held at the ear in his throwing days, now they were allowing athletes to start the throwing action from behind the ear, "which permits greater leverage and hence greater tosses for more distance." Asked about his retirement by the journalist, McDonald replied, "That's what I did. I am doing nothing but having a rest, and a lot of fun with my wife and family."

Like Matt McGrath, McDonald had exhibited great courage in performing his duties. In an incident reminiscent of McGrath's heroics, he once reputedly displayed his colossal strength when he dangled a colleague by the legs over a bridge to rescue a drowning man, single-handedly pulling the two to safety.[24]

In August 1924, McDonald was back in Ireland, where he attended the first iteration of the revived Tailteann Games, an event designed as an expression of national identity of the recently independent state and first mooted as far back as the 1880s by Michael Davitt and his fellow cultural nationalists. The ideology behind the event was made clear at the opening ceremony when Irish president William T. Cosgrave informed those present that Ireland was no longer a colony, but the "home of a race of a historical lineage unsurpassed elsewhere."[25]

Pat McDonald was there to lend his support; a giant of a man sauntering onto the field from one of the dressing rooms "with the wonderful shoulders and chest and trunk that only Ireland can produce . . . the noble head crowned by a generous shock of silvering hair."[26] Despite being a giant and "ponderous in weight and bulk," McDonald "possessed a grace of carriage and a lightness of foot that spoke eloquently of perfect physical condition." Here was a returned exile proud to be back on his native soil despite the fame he had achieved on the other side of the world, a man whose name was known by "every turf fire in Eire, even if his face and figure were the face and figure of a stranger." He had come as a proud Irishman to attend the great celebration of his native culture. Despite the awards and titles the United States had brought his way, McDonald had traveled across the Atlantic to be present at this athletic rebirth of his native land. It was here that he would show his pride of race and the love he always had for his homeland. He may have been viewed as an American throughout the world, but on that day he was "as much an Irishman as he had been in the days of his youth in storied Dalcassia."[27]

There too was the great Matt McGrath standing shoulder to shoulder with Pat McDonald. It was a proud moment indeed. Two of Ireland's greatest athletes—"two of the men who had placed her name high among the sport-loving nations of the world"—back on their own shore to "act as sponsors at the rebaptism of their native land as an individual athletic entity."[28]

McDonald died in 1954, at the age of seventy-five. *New York Times* journalist Arthur Daley remembered him as a man who had gone through life "with a song in his heart, a twinkle in his eye, and laughter ever bubbling within him." In his obituary to the giant man from Clare, Daley eloquently recounted,

> Pat is dead now, that gargantuan laughter forever stilled and that lilting brogue no longer delighting the ear . . . when he laughed everything shook. It started as a low rumble down deep, like lava stirring in the pit of a volcano. Then came the eruption, and it engulfed everything before it in irresistible surge. He had the snow-white hair, the red cheeks, and the twinkling blue eyes of Santa Claus. He was twice as big, of course, but also left happiness behind him wherever he went.

Daley, never one to shy away from writing in his version of an Irish brogue, described Pat McDonald's account of a visit back home to Ireland:

> A pleasant visit it was. But when I got to the family cottage, glory be. Shure, what do I see but my sainted father, pitchin' a 56-lb. weight over the roof. A bit astounded I am. "Sire," I sez, "tis a dangerous thing you're a doin' with no one to watch where the weight falls." He spits on his hands and sez, "Git along with ye Pat. Is it not your grandfather I have on the other side catchin' the weight and throwin' it back to me."

After expressing dismay that he had beaten Paddy Ryan's record, McDonald settled down for dinner with the journalist. The champion thrower ordered steak but was not happy with the child's portion he received and ordered another. Daley contended that each was a fine piece of steak, and after consuming three of them McDonald had an "oversized order of roast beef for dessert."

Pat "Babe" McDonald is buried in the Gate of Heaven Cemetery in Hawthorne, New York, and there is a memorial to him at White Strand,

Doonbeg, County Clare, overlooking the wild Atlantic Ocean. In 2012, he was inducted into the U.S. National Track and Field Hall of Fame.

Compared to the rest of the Whales, Con Walsh retired early from competitive athletics—he was only twenty-six when he finished throwing in 1911—and subsequently attempted to launch an ill-fated boxing career. Some in the sport considered him a genuine heavyweight contender, but injury soon put an end to his hopes. His Gaelic games career had not finished, however; on a trip home in November 1911, he won a Cork county football championship medal with the Lees club. Walsh later moved to Seattle, where he joined the city police force, rising to the rank of inspector, and coached the force's track and field team. He died in 1961, and is buried at Holyrood Catholic Cemetery in King County, Washington. In 2009, residents of Carriganima, his native village in County Cork, erected a plaque to commemorate his athletic achievements at an event attended by the Canadian ambassador to Ireland, Patrick G. Binns, who noted in his speech the 4 million Canadians of Irish ancestry.[29] In September 2018, Con Walsh was inducted into the Athletics Ontario Hall of Fame.

On Independence Day 1921, nineteen years after winning his first Irish title, Paddy Ryan took his last American Championship at Pasadena, California, where he threw 170 feet to win the hammer; he was also the runner-up to Pat McDonald in the 56-pound throw in 1924. Ryan returned to Ireland and bought a farm near his native home in Pallasgreen in County Limerick. He got married at forty-eight and went on to have five daughters and live in quiet seclusion far removed from the scenes of his triumphs and the thunderous acclaim of tens of thousands. In 1952, journalist Seamus O Ceallaigh considered the career of Ryan. He met former champion hurdler Jack Eller, who had much in common with Ryan, as he was also a member of the NYPD and the IAAC, and a successful athlete, having taken the American Athletic Union (AAU) title in the 220-yard low hurdles five years in a row, as well as being part of the 1912 U.S. Olympic team at Stockholm. Eller was trenchant in his opinion of Ryan:

> Listen, the greatest weight thrower of all time was Paddy Ryan. The reason I say this is because he never trained properly. Let's say he trained like Freddy Tootell of Rhode Island State College, he would have set marks with the 35-lb. weight, 12-lb. weight, and the "56" that wouldn't be approached until my grandchildren had whiskers down to their knees . . . he didn't know his strength: He could turn in a three-

foot circle, and his speed and leverage made him the greatest athlete the world had known.[30]

Ryan died on February 13, 1964, at the age of eighty-two, and is buried in the Old Pallas cemetery, under the shadow of Knockgrean Hill. He won eleven Irish titles, ten American senior outdoor titles, and his Olympic medal. On July 24, 2004, a life-size statue was erected in his memory in the village of Pallasgreen on the main Limerick to Tipperary road. The local community produced a booklet in honor of Ryan that read as follows:

> He was just more than an Olympic champion and a great athlete. He had a rich, warm personality, was a glorious storyteller and an extremely lovable and homely character. He had a tremendous zest for living and missed the excitement and the glory of the days when he was known from one end of the world to the other. He said to his good friend and writer Dave Guiney: "Sure I miss every day of them, they were great days and I enjoyed them thoroughly. I'm sorry I can't live my life all over again."[31]

In another article, Guiney recalled speaking to Paddy Ryan at his Limerick home about his decision to return home from the United States, where he had been "lionized" and "loved by millionaires and bootblacks, and had he wanted to be, he might conceivably have become a millionaire."[32] Had he any regrets? "Why should I regret anything? I had a glorious time, great sport, great fun, enough to eat and drink, and now I have my family. Everything has been great. If I had stayed in America I would have been dead and buried many, many years ago." Guiney pointed out to Ryan that he had never lost his Irish accent, to which the Limerick man replied, "I went away with a yard of an Irish brogue, and I came home with a yard and a half." By Guiney's account Ryan's mode of expression was colorful:

> Paddy liked to talk and tell stories, and his accent, rich, melodious, and resonant, was pure Limerick. His vocabulary, to be mild about it, was profuse and explosive and liberally sprinkled with vigorous, unparliamentary expletives . . . he was the only man I met who used bad language beautifully. He was never offensive, although one or two old ladies, sipping tea in an old-world drawing room, might have quailed before the strength of some of his adjectives.

In 2015, Paddy Ryan was inducted into the U.S. National Track and Field Hall of Fame. The award was accepted by his daughter, Johanna, and granddaughter, Christine Killian, who had traveled from New York to the ceremony in Anaheim, California. Johanna remembered her time with her father when she was young. "I think he enjoyed reminiscing," she said. "When I came to America, every time my mother wrote to me there was a letter from my father enclosed. He never thought of himself as number one in the world. What he did, he did it well, and that was good enough for him."[33]

His daughter Catherine O'Grady now lives in Hospital, County Limerick, a little more than eight miles away from the original family homestead, which has passed out of family hands. I spoke to her on the phone. "He was a gentle giant," she remembered. "He was a happy man, an innocent, honest man. He really enjoyed his life. He was a very sociable man."[34]

What then was the legacy of the Irish Whales?

Where the amateur athletic scene in New York was once largely dominated by the patrician Protestant New York Athletic Club and similar groupings, the Irish Whales and others from such clubs as the IAAC helped democratize the sporting space and change the perception of amateur athletics as a sport for Victorian and Edwardian men of means to that of an accessible pursuit for the common working-class man of any ethnic group. They had brought with them from their native-shore sports of the common man, not the rarefied pursuits of hunting and fishing of the Anglo-Irish gentry and the landlord class. While Irishmen had found success in such sports as baseball, boxing, and pedestrianism in the United States, they were viewed as tainted by the Protestant elite, principally because of professionalism and gambling. Here now were Irishmen taking part in a discipline representing the Corinthian ideals of amateur sport, which brought them to the attention of governing bodies and, ultimately, to the world stage through being part of the Olympics. The vast majority of members who formed the U.S. national teams for the first few Olympics were students of the elite American universities—"college men," as they were called—but the addition of the Irish American Whales, men who ostensibly worked every day, helped change that.

During and after their careers the extent to which the Irish Whales were true amateurs was debated. There was no doubt that those who worked with the NYPD had certain latitude to develop their athletic abilities. In 1909, there was a major allegation of professionalism against Martin Sheridan and Matt McGrath when they were accused of receiving $500 and expenses for performing at a meet at the Gaelic Grounds in Chicago. According to a newspaper report, a noted marathon runner was offered $100 to compete at the same meet—an indication of the drawing power of the Whales.[35] The investigation could not find evidence of any infraction of the amateur code. As part of their defense against the allegations, the Chicago GAA published their accounts of the legal expenses paid to Sheridan and McGrath. This amounted to $100 each, of which $26 was for food per man. It was fitting that the two men consumed the equivalent of four men's weekly wage during their time in Chicago.

A journalist for the *Pittsburgh Press* noted that Sheridan consumed as much food in a day as other men would in a week. Even among the "valorous trenchermen" that comprised the Irish Whales, he was a "wonder at the training tables." Pointing out that Sheridan would not be a suitable candidate for a hunger strike, his typical breakfast consisted of "two oranges, two plates of oatmeal, ten eggs, one pound of potatoes, three cups of coffee, half a loaf of bread with three ounces butter"; for lunch Sheridan consumed "one pig's head, four pounds potatoes, three plates of cabbage, four ears of corn, two cups of tea, half a loaf of bread, [and] two pieces of pie," and for dinner he ate "two plates of soup, one whole chicken, one steak, hashed brown potatoes, three cups of tea, two pieces of pie and cheese, one loaf of bread, [and] one order of celery."[36]

The *San Francisco Call* reported the same eating regimen and noted Martin Sheridan's "perfect teeth and perfect digestion." The journalist suggested that it was lucky for Sheridan that he did not live at the Ritz Carlton, where police commissioner Rhinelander Waldo had his residence: "To buy at that hotel such meals as are given would cost $4 for breakfast, $6.70 for luncheon, and $7.85 for dinner." No policeman could do that, it contended. Even Mr. Waldo's annual salary of $7,800 would be decimated by an expenditure of $20.83 on daily meals. The paper also noted that Lawson Robertson, IAAC trainer, having seen the success of English boxer Fred Welsh and his colleague, five-mile runner E. R. Voight, became convinced that a vegetarian diet would be useful for his athletes. When Martin Sheridan was told of this newfangled diet he was aghast, according to the journalist: "About sixteen eggs, a couple of chops, and one potato disappear when Martin dines, and he feared Robertson would switch this to sixteen potatoes, one egg, and one chop, but the trainer reassured him."[37]

The *Evening Star* reported a comical interlude involving Sheridan at Celtic Park. The story went that P. J. Conway sent two dozen eggs to the club one morning to provide breakfast for a group of athletes who were in training. Sheridan was particularly partial to fried eggs and deliberately started an argument among the group, allowing him time to slip into the kitchen and devour the fresh eggs.[38]

In a similar vein, a story is told that Sheridan once turned up at the clubhouse kitchen to find that all the seats at the table were occupied. This did not please him, as there was a "steaming twenty-four-egg omelette . . . with pitchers of milk and plates of chops and other eatables ready to be consumed, and me standing there with my mouth watering for a chance to grab something. But no one would make room for me. I had to wait for the next table to be set."

Sheridan hatched a clever plan and went out and gathered some rubbish and built a small bonfire:

> When the fire was going full blast, I ran into the building yelling, "Fire!" at the top of my voice, and believe me, they heard that yell. Everybody made a beeline for the door except yours truly. I knew they would be back in a few minutes, so I had to get busy and do something very quick. I grabbed a loaf of bread, cut it in half, and made a sandwich out of the twenty-four-egg omelette and ran to one of the rooms and locked myself in. The crowd came after me in high rage, but I refused to be disturbed.[39]

He escaped through a window, telling the journalist that he would do it again if the same reward was there for the taking.

In 1912, Matt McGrath informed a journalist that he could not afford to go unpaid for the duration of the Stockholm Olympic Games.[40] The following month, the *Evening World* carried an article, complete with a photograph, explaining that Commissioner Waldo was granting sixty days unpaid leave to police athletes, including McGrath and McDonald, to prepare for and compete at Stockholm.[41] In 1913, the officers had the deducted salary reimbursed, despite the wishes of Mayor Gaynor.[42]

Unlike baseball and boxing, which were largely confined to North America, athletics were contested on the world stage, primarily at the Olympics. Through the achievements of the Irish Whales and other amateur athletes, the United States was able to demonstrate it had passed the Old World in sporting achievement. They bolstered the sense of identity of the United States while simultaneously showing the contribution the Irish were making to the melting pot. Sports had become a significant component of cultural nationalism throughout the world, and the international dimension of athletics put them in the spotlight.

The Irish Whales were a significant part of the story of the assimilation of Irish immigrants in New York in the early decades of the twentieth century. They were giants not only physically, but also in the psychosocial development of the immigrant. They were a bridge between the Old World and the New World, men of stature and substance. They were outsiders who had made good and, albeit grudgingly in some quarters, come to be considered insiders. The Irish Whales had demonstrated that amateur sporting success could be an important route to gaining acceptance in the American melting pot for ethnic groups.[43] By competing under the American flag, Irish Americans were able to demonstrate their loyalty to their new country. The pride the United States took in the achievements of its Irish American Olympians helped the process of assimilation. There is no doubt that they were at the privileged end of the immigrant spectrum. John Flanagan and Matt McGrath were both in the enviable position of being able to choose to return to Ireland.

The Whales had triumphed in an area of sporting pursuit that required strength and guile, reinforcing the long-held image of the physically powerful Irishman. These Irishmen were the acme of virile manhood and furthered the image of the Irish as fearless and tenacious athletes. In a country that was striving to define itself on the world stage and where sports played a significant part in popular culture, they found themselves at the nexus of interlocking strands that were knitting the very fabric of American society.

Their success came in an era of U.S. history when the tide was in favor of Irish immigrants. Other ethnic groups had come to take their place at the bottom of the social pecking order. Their currency had gained value through political and religious involvement. Irishmen had gained credit for fighting on behalf of their adopted country in the Civil War and Spanish–American War. They had shown their patriotism and proved their worth as members of the great republic. The once-maligned Catholic Church had provided invaluable infrastructure to the country, and such obstructionist factions as the Know Nothings were largely a thing of the past.

The Whales were also a significant component of burgeoning Irish nationalism fostered in the United States. When they were in attendance at athletic meets held under the auspices of Clan na Gael and similar organizations, they were the headline acts. The *Gaelic American* of July 2, 1904, for example, printed an article and advertisement for the Irish Volunteers of Yonkers Military and Athletic Tournament at the Empire City racetrack, noting that "John Flanagan, Champion Weight and Hammer Thrower of the World" and "Martin Sheridan, Champion Discus Thrower of the World" would compete in the "Weight-Putting Contest."[44] As far as their opinions have been recorded, Sheridan appears to have been the most trenchant nationalist of the group. His speeches during his time in Ireland after the 1908 games bear testimony to his strongly held political beliefs. In August 1909, Sheridan even played the role of Irish nationalist Robert Fulton at a concert at Carnegie Hall. Fulton was a scientist who worked with the application of steam to maritime transport and had close affiliations with the United Irishmen and other groups who agitated for Irish freedom.

The *Irish Independent* once wrote of Sheridan's nationalist leanings: "Ireland and her people's problems held first place in the exile's mind. Every time he won a big international event, he felt he was striking a blow for faith and fatherland. His patriotic ardor was his outstanding characteristic."[45] Sheridan was contemptuous of "shoneen" athletes like Con Leahy and Denis Horgan who defied the GAA ban and were happy to compete under the Union Jack: "Why, we Irishmen in the United States cannot understand how it is that any Irishman should wear England's flag as some did at the games in London . . . it is cruel to think after all those hundreds of years of persecution, to find some Irishmen still so slavish."[46] Sheridan also promoted his Irishness in his appearance. At the 1906 IAAC Games at Celtic Park, he took to the field "wrapped in a capacious dressing gown made of shamrocks" precipitating a "riot of cheers."[47]

That the Whales were painted as larger-than-life characters was inevitable in a society where ethnic stereotypes were everyday currency. Here were men who could perform in the sporting arena at the highest level but still enjoy life. They were straight from central casting heaven. Arthur Daley was as responsible as anyone for perpetuating the stereotype of the roistering Irish athlete. When researching one of his articles about the Whales, Daley consulted "Dapper" Dan Ferris, former secretary treasurer of the AAU, to see if his memory of the men was accurate:

> They were as good as they were big because they held all the world records. All were Olympians, and most were Olympic champions. The moderns train hard and lift weights to develop their muscles. The Whales never trained at all, and they never lifted things any heavier than glasses of beer, something they did quite expertly. They got more fun out of the sport than any athletes I ever saw.

Daley contended that some of the Whales kept competing for so long because they enjoyed the fun and camaraderie, and were practical jokers at heart. At the Stockholm games in 1912, for example, they were in their prime, and high jinks marked their trip. The Whales took such particular delight in playing practical jokes on a Colonel Conkwright, who, tired of their antics, hired Matt McGrath as a bodyguard. He had chosen badly. The Irishman started to stand guard one night but soon lost interest, according to Daley: "Matt stood guard one night protecting Conkwright from McGrath's own deviltry. He grew bored after a while, however, yanked the mattress out from under his sleeping charge, and left the colonel on the cabin floor."

They also played practical jokes among themselves. On the ship on the way back to the United States from Stockholm, Pat McDonald got seasick. Matt McGrath came into the Clare man's cabin "solemn as a pallbearer": "Old friend . . . tis your own wishes we want to respect. Will ye be wantin' your body shipped home or shall we be buryin' ye at sea?" This did not sit well with McDonald, who proceeded to chase McGrath to the top deck, "magically cured." Daley finished his article fondly: "They were a fabulous group of men, those Whales from the Irish American A.C. They since have faded into the legends of the past, but they were the best of their era. It is indeed comforting to learn, even at this late date, that their richly descriptive nickname was well deserved."

According to Abel Kiviat, a Jewish member of the 1912 U.S. team, the Whales were a kindly group, and he wrote movingly of how they looked out for him on his way to Stockholm:

> You know, those big Irishmen protected me, the only Jew in the Irish American Club. I remember I had a little run-in with the discus throw-

er, Jim Duncan, on the boat going over to Stockholm. He was a fresh mutt, about 225 pounds and ugly looking. He started calling me names and annoying me, so Matt McGrath and Pat McDonald grabbed ahold of him and dragged him to a porthole and threatened to push him through if he called me any more names. And then they made me track captain.[48]

In the United States, as time went on, the idea of competing for an ethnic subgroup and not the country as a whole gradually became obsolete. By the 1920s, the "No Irish Need Apply" racism of the nineteenth century was fading away, as some of the Irish gradually entered the white middle class and assimilation and acculturation progressed. The Irish Whales had played their part.

They did not lose their Irish identity; rather they added to the luster of America. Their love for Ireland was a complementary force to their American patriotism. They were Irish American with a firm foothold in America. P. J. Conway noted after the 1908 Olympics that those Irishmen who did so well were a credit to the Irish and American flags, both of which greeted them upon their arrival back in New York. Their Olympic success reinforced their Irish American aspirations and their loyalty to their new home, and gave their ethnicity enhanced value in the United States. Their competitive vigor and spirit, synonymous with the country of their birth, was part of what was making America great, and they became a valued part of American society.

In retrospect, two characteristics of the Irish Whales' careers stand out: the advanced age at which a number of them took to the world stage and the sheer competitive longevity most of them enjoyed. James Mitchell made his Olympic debut at 44 years of age, while Matt McGrath was 33 before he made his first appearance at the London Olympic Games in 1908. While McGrath was within striking distance of 50 in Paris, Pat McDonald remains the oldest athlete to take a gold medal in track and field at an Olympics by virtue of his achievement in the shot put at Antwerp in 1920, at the grand old age of 42 years and 26 days. John Flanagan continues to be the oldest gold medal winner in the Olympic hammer throw by virtue of his 1908 win in London at the age of 40 years and 168 days. By setting a world record there, he remains the oldest track and field athlete to outdo a previous leading mark.

The Irish Whales were finished as the dominant force in world throwing by 1924, but remarkably and appropriately, a now-independent Republic of Ireland took its first gold medal at the Olympics in the hammer throw when Pat O'Callaghan triumphed at the 1928 games in Amsterdam, following it up with a second at the 1932 Los Angeles games.

The ultimate decline of the IAAC occurred simultaneously with the gradual disappearance of the Irish Whales from the athletics arena. The outbreak of World War I was the initial catalyst for its gradual demise. Administrators decided to suspend sporting activities for the duration of the war and offered the facilities to President Woodrow Wilson for any purpose he might see fit to advance the national cause, but he declined the offer. After the war it proved impossible to get the crowds back. A prime factor was the adoption of the Volstead Act of 1920, which introduced Prohibition. Celtic Park had been notorious for the illicit sale of alcohol; according to the new dispensation it quickly became a high-profile target for law enforcement scrutiny and the object of unflattering media reports. The illicit sale of alcohol brought intense surveillance and sometimes ended in violent police raids. Bootleggers were viewed as a major threat and received summary justice when caught.[49]

World War I and Prohibition were not the only factors governing the decline of Celtic Park. Shrinking attendance forced the club to try and find other avenues for generating income. From 1928 to 1930, the IAAC held regular greyhound races, including a competition for the Martin J. Sheridan Trophy, but they petered out, in large part due to pressure from the growing residential community, which did not want gamblers and "riffraff" in the area.[50] The writing was on the wall: The end of Celtic Park was nigh. Like many other New York landmarks of the era it was razed in 1930, replaced by an apartment complex bearing the same name. An era in Irish American social and cultural history had finally come to an end.

The Democratic political machine continued to be kind to the Irish community in New York in the opening decades of the twentieth century. Between 1900 and 1930, the number of city employees jumped from 54,386 to 148,421; of these a remarkable 52 percent were Irish. By 1930, only 15 percent of the Irish population in the city had been born in Ireland, but somewhere between one-fourth and one-third of all first-, second-, and third-generation Irish worked in the public sector—fire and police departments, publicly owned subways and buses, waterworks and port facilities, and public schools.[51] It was this focus on what sociologists term *bonding social capital* that would ultimately cause the Tammany machine to break down. By not sufficiently sharing the spoils of political success with other ethnic groups, the seeds of its downfall were sown.

The privations imposed by the Depression compounded frustrations. While the Irish may have been willing to throw sops to other groups in the form of food and welfare programs, their unwillingness to spread the rich jam of city jobs was too much for others to stomach. It was under the leadership of Fiorello La Guardia, who harnessed the widespread discontent among the Italian and Jewish communities, that the death knell of Tammany Hall finally sounded. The resentment engendered by the extravagantly corrupt regime presided over by Mayor Jimmy Walker—and La Guardia's clever alliance with the rising American Labor Party— finally put an end to Irish dominance of Tammany Hall when Walker was chased from office in 1932. While the Irish remained firmly entrenched in the police and fire departments, the Irish politicos had been deprived of the thousands of other jobs that were once in their gift.

Like the political environment, hammer-throwing has changed since the glory days of the Irish Whales. A concrete circle replaced the previous cinder in 1955, providing a much cleaner and quicker surface, while tungsten balls were also introduced during the 1950s, further increasing records. American athletes almost disappeared from the winners' rostrum, as Eastern Europeans—the Soviets, in particular—came to dominate the event. The hammer throw lost popularity in the United States as the years passed by. Between 1900 and 1956, the United States had taken nineteen medals in the event at the Olympics, seven of which were gold, with the last title taken by Hal Connolly in the 1956 Games in Melbourne. Fittingly, he was of Irish extraction. From 1960 to 2000, only five male American hammer throwers made it to the final round of Olympic competition; Lance Deal was the sole athlete to medal during that period when he took the silver at the 1996 games in Atlanta. European domination of the event became absolute. By 1983, the sixty best male hammer throwers in the world all came from European countries.

Lane Dowell, a track official with United States of America Track and Field, and a retired hammer throw coach, penned "America's Forgotten Event: The Hammer" for the *Long and Strong Thrower's Journal* in 2003. In it he bemoaned the decline of hammer-throwing in the United States. Dowell's article appeared a year before the Olympic Games in Athens—a time when not one male American hammer thrower was within three and a half meters of the world championship–qualifying mark of

79.50 meters. The top American thrower at the time was ranked forty-seventh in the world. Dowell made an appeal to rejuvenate the discipline and argued that it is one of the best events in the track and field schedule, requiring intelligence, determination, and athleticism.[52] It is not a discipline to be afraid of, he said, and the "voodoo-like fears" expressed by some people would dissipate as more athletes participated in it.

On March 10, 2012, the street between 48th Avenue and 50th Avenue—the site where Celtic Park once stood—was renamed Winged Fist Way. On the day of the dedication ceremony, the NYPD and the Fire Department of New York pipe bands came to play in front of assembled dignitaries, members of the media, and the general public. The event came to pass after a long and sustained campaign headed by historian Ian McGowan. At the opening ceremony, dignitary after dignitary praised the Irish heritage of the club, and—appropriately in an area of New York City now considered one of the most diverse neighborhoods—a number of speakers emphasized that the club had always been open to all comers. Congressman Joseph Crowley noted that the renaming of the street was "not just great Irish American history, but great American history." The IAAC had made a massive contribution to New York by providing a refuge for athletes of every ethnic group and nationality who faced discrimination and hate. Its Winged Fist emblem served as a symbol of strength, perseverance, and triumph.

The Winged Fist organization had less luck when they asked to commemorate Celtic Park by placing a plaque on Celtic Park Co-op, the apartment block built on the location of the original stadium. After three years of negotiation, authorities refused the application "respectfully." Ian McGowan had persistently pointed out the diverse nature of the IAAC to authorities in his quest to have the plaque erected. The board of the apartment complex, however, had difficulty with the Winged Fist emblem. Some members felt that the IAAC's symbol resembled the Black Power protest at the 1968 Olympic Games rather than sepia toned athletes of another era. One even likened the clenched fist part of the crest to a swastika. McGowan tried to point out that the Winged Fist symbol predated the groups on their list. He argued that the symbol had no generalized meaning except as a demonstration of loyalty and unity. Peter McDermott, a journalist who covered the proceedings for *Queen's Gazette*, investigated the different uses the winged fist symbol has had throughout time and found that, among a raft of other things, it has been used to promote Northern Soul (a subgenre of soul music popular in the North of England), by Tommie Smith and John Carlos at their protest supporting black solidarity at the 1968 Mexico City Olympic Games, and as part of the rose and fist symbol used by the moderately left wing Socialist International, the largest political grouping in the world. McGowan later found out that a clenched fist was part of the image used by the International Brotherhood of Electrical Workers, members of which had worked on the original construction of Celtic Park. There is every chance that some of them were Irish. It is to the great credit of Ian McGowan and others that he established the Winged Fist organization and has worked to keep the historical legacy of the IAAC alive.

The Irish Whales and their throwing records have disappeared from the books. Why they have not endured as popular characters in the American imagination is an interesting question. Perhaps it is because the Irish have contributed to the United States in so many domains. The deep involvement of Irish Americans in political, labor, and religious issues may have resulted in their sporting pursuits getting less coverage in the history books. Perhaps the notoriety of boxing and the images of the Irishman that were built around the sport were considered best forgotten by some. Whatever the reasons, the accomplishments of the Irish Whales will never be matched and should never be forgotten.

APPENDIX A

Olympic Medals Won by the Irish Whales as Part of the U.S. Olympic Team

1900 PARIS

Hammer GOLD: John Flanagan

1904 ST. LOUIS

Discus GOLD: Martin Sheridan
Hammer GOLD: John Flanagan
56-pound weight SILVER: John Flanagan
56-pound weight BRONZE: James Mitchell

1906 ATHENS

Discus GOLD: Martin Sheridan
Shot put GOLD: Martin Sheridan
Stone throw GOLD: Martin Sheridan
Standing long jump GOLD: Martin Sheridan

1908 LONDON

Discus GOLD: Martin Sheridan
Hammer GOLD: John Flanagan
Hammer SILVER: Matt McGrath
Hammer BRONZE: Cornelius Walsh (Canada)
Greek discus GOLD: Martin Sheridan

1912 STOCKHOLM

Hammer GOLD: Matt McGrath
Shot put GOLD: Pat McDonald
Two-handed shot put SILVER: Pat McDonald

1920 ANTWERP

Hammer GOLD: Paddy Ryan
56-pound weight GOLD: Pat McDonald
56-pound weight SILVER: Paddy Ryan

APPENDIX B

Olympic Hammer Throw Medals, 1900–1932

Games	Gold	Silver	Bronze
1900 Paris	John Flanagan (USA)	Truxtun Hare (USA)	Josiah McCracken (USA)
1904 St. Louis	John Flanagan (USA)	John DeWitt (USA)	Ralph Rose (USA)
1908 London	John Flanagan (USA)	Matt McGrath (USA)	Con Walsh (CAN)
1912 Stockholm	Matt McGrath (USA)	Duncan Gillis (CAN)	Clarence Childs (USA)
1920 Antwerp	Patrick Ryan (USA)	Carl Johan Lind (SWE)	Basil Bennett (USA)
1924 Paris	Fred Tootell (USA)	Matt McGrath (USA)	Malcolm Nokes (GBR)
1928 Amsterdam	Pat O'Callaghan (IRL)	Ossian Skiöld (SWE)	Edmund Black (USA)
1932 Los Angeles	Pat O'Callaghan (IRL)	Ville Pörhölä (FIN)	Peter Zaremba (USA)

APPENDIX C

Multiple Medals Ranking, Hammer Throw

Rank	Athlete	Nation	Olympics	Gold	Silver	Bronze	Total
1	John Flanagan	United States (USA)	1900–1908	3	0	0	3
2	Yuriy Sedykh	Soviet Union (URS)	1976–1988	2	1	0	3
3	Pat O'Callaghan	Ireland (IRL)	1928–1932	2	0	0	2
4	Matt McGrath	United States (USA)	1908–1924	1	2	0	3

NOTES

INTRODUCTION

1. Brendan I. Koerner, "86.74 Is Going to Stand for a Long Time," *ESPN the Magazine*, June 27, 2011, https://www.espn.com/olympics/news/story?id=6656627 (accessed January 15, 2020).

2. Koerner, "86.74 Is Going to Stand for a Long Time."

3. James Mitchell, *How to Become a Weight Thrower, with a Chapter on Throwing the Javelin*, Spalding Red Cover Series of Athletic Handbooks, no. 70.R (New York: American Sports Book Publishers, 1916), 17.

4. Mitchell, *How to Become a Weight Thrower*, 18

5. Phil Conway, telephone conversation, March 25, 2018.

I. EXODUS

1. Sam Roberts, "Story of the First Through Ellis Island Is Rewritten," *New York Times*, September 14, 2006, https://www.nytimes.com/2006/09/14/nyregion/story-of-the-first-through-ellis-island-is-rewritten.html (accessed January 15, 2020).

2. Tim Pat Coogan, *Wherever the Green Is Worn: The Story of the Irish Diaspora* (London: Arrow Books, 2002), 253.

3. Fred Berri, *Ten Cents a Dance* (New York: First Edition Design Publishing, 2016), 3.

4. Clint Johnson, *A Vast and Fiendish Plot: The Confederate Attack on New York City* (New York: Citadel, 2010), 15.

5. M. Padden and R. Sullivan, *May the Road Rise to Meet You* (New York: Penguin, 1999), 102.

6. George Potter, *To the Golden Door* (Boston: Little, Brown, 1970), 372.

2. AMERICAN SPORTS

1. *Sporting Life*, September 19, 1896.

2. Patrick R. Redmond, *The Irish and the Making of American Sport, 1835–1920* (Jefferson, NC: McFarland, 2016), 59.

3. Caspar Whitney, *A Sporting Pilgrimage: Riding to Hounds, Golf, Rowing, Football, Club and University Athletics, Studies in English Sport, Past and Present* (New York: Harper, 1895), cited in Britt Peterson, "The Irish Whales: America's Gluttonous, English-Hating, Gold Medal–Winning Olympic Heroes of the Early 20th Century," *Slate.com*, July 26, 2012, http://www.slate.com/articles/sports/fivering_circus/2012/07/irish_whales_america_s_gluttonous_english_hating_gold_medal_winning_olympic_heroes_of_the_early_20th_century.html (accessed January 15, 2020).

4. Nat Fleischer, *The Boston Strong Boy: The Story of John L. Sullivan, the Champion of Champions* (New York: O'Brien Press, 1941), 35.

5. "About Some Whales, Human Variety," *New York Times*, June 12, 1942.

6. "All about Whales," *New York Times*, July 13, 1964.

3. JAMES "JIM" MITCHELL
AND THE IRISH INVASION

1. Paul Rouse, "When an American Invasion Cost GAA Money and Men," *Irish Examiner*, April 21, 2016.

2. Brendan Fullam, *The Final Whistle* (Dublin: Wolfhound Press, 2000), 32.

3. Rouse, "When an American Invasion Cost GAA Money and Men."

4. The sticks used to play the stick and ball game of hurling.

5. *Freeman's Journal* (Sydney), November 24, 1888.

6. This version of hammer-throwing subsequently became obsolete.

7. Lindie Naughton and Johnny Watterson, *Faster, Higher, Stronger: A History of Ireland's Olympians* (Dublin: Ashfield Press, 2008), 49.

8. Mike Cronin, Mark Duncan, and Paul Rouse, *The GAA, a People's History* (Cork: Collins Press, 2009), 13.

9. William Dooley, *Champions of the Athletic Arena* (Dublin: General Publicity Service, 1946).

10. Luke J. Harris, *Britain and the Olympic Games, 1908–1920: Perspectives on Participation and Identity* (London: Palgrave Macmillan, 2015), https://books.google.ie/books?id=UpGkCgAAQBAJ&printsec=frontcover&dq=luke+j+harris+perspectives+on+the+british+olympics&hl=en&sa=X&ved=0ahUKEwi6x5qZyfvlAhUSRBUIHZbMCXAQ6AEIKTAA#v=onepage&q=luke%20j%20harris%20perspectives%20on%20the%20british%20olympics&f=false.

11. Tom Hunt, *The Little Book of Irish Athletics* (Dublin: History Press Ireland, 2017), 20.

12. Hunt, *The Little Book of Irish Athletics*, 20.

13. Cronin, Duncan, and Rouse, *The GAA*, 19.

14. T. F. O'Sullivan, *The Story of the GAA* (Dublin: Middle Abbey Street, 1916), 9.

15. Hunt, *The Little Book of Irish Athletics*, 20.

16. Hunt, *The Little Book of Irish Athletics*, 22.

17. Hunt, *The Little Book of Irish Athletics*, 23.

18. Hunt, *The Little Book of Irish Athletics*, 23.

19. Colonel Red Reeder, *The Story of the Spanish-American War* (New York: Duell, Sloane and Pearce, 1955).

4. JOHN "THE MODERN HERCULES" FLANAGAN AND OLYMPIC GOLD

1. Stephen P. Erie, *Rainbow's End* (Berkeley: University of California Press, 1988), cited in Tim Pat Coogan, *Wherever the Green Is Worn: The Story of the Irish Diaspora* (London: Arrow Books, 2002), 278.

2. David Goldblatt, *The Games* (London: Macmillan, 2016), 5.

3. Some sources say there were 245 male athletes.

4. Goldblatt, *The Games*, 46.

5. John Hanc, "The Men behind the First Olympic Team," *Smithsonian*, June 25, 2012, https://www.smithsonianmag.com/history/the-men-behind-the-first-olympic-team-142232820/ (accessed January 15, 2020).

6. Pierre de Coubertin, "Paris 1990," *Olympic Memoirs*, https://www.olympic.org/paris-1900 (accessed January 16, 2020).

7. Goldblatt, *The Games*, 63.

8. "Americans Again Lead: Six More Gold Taken by Yankee Athletes in Paris Games," *New York Times*, July 17, 1900.

9. Theodore Roosevelt, "The Strenuous Life," a speech at the Hamilton Club, Chicago, April 10, 1899, quoted in Herman Hagerdom, ed., *The Works of Theodore Roosevelt, Vol. XIII: American Ideals, the Strenuous Life, Realizable*

Ideals (New York: Charles Scribner's Sons, 1926), cited in Mark Dyerson, *Crafting Patriotism for Global Dominance: America at the Olympics* (New York: Routledge, 2009), 331.

10. "Seven More Victories," *Chicago Tribune*, July 17, 1900.

11. Caspar Whitney, "The Sportsman's View-Point: Mug Hunters and Disregarded Agreements at Paris Games," *Outing* 36 (August 1900).

5. AMERICAN FIASCO, IRISH AMERICAN TRIUMPH

1. Mark Dyreson, *Making the American Team: Sport, Culture, and the Olympic Experience* (Champaign: University of Illinois Press, 1997), 72.

2. Carl Posey, *III Olympiad: St. Louis 1904, Athens 1906* (Toronto: Warwick Press, 1996).

3. Posey, *III Olympiad*.

4. *Official Guide to the Louisiana Purchase Exposition 1904*, cited in David Goldblatt, *The Games* (London: Macmillan, 2016), 65.

5. Bill Mallon, *The 1904 Olympic Games: Results for All Competitors in All Events, with Commentary* (Jefferson, NC: McFarland, 1999), 209.

6. Mallon, *The 1904 Olympic* Games, 209.

7. Mallon, *The 1904 Olympic Games*, 259.

8. Mallon, *The 1904 Olympic Games*.

9. Mallon, *The 1904 Olympic Games*, 17.

6. PEERLESS ATHLETE AND INTREPID AMERICAN

1. Robert Edgren, "Martin Sheridan, the World's Champion All-Around Athlete," *Munsey's Magazine* XLII (October 1909–March 1910).

2. Carl Posey, *III Olympiad: St. Louis 1904, Athens 1906* (Toronto: Warwick Press, 1996).

3. Edgren, "Martin Sheridan, the World's Champion All-Around Athlete."

4. Margaret Molloy, *Mayo's Famous Son, 1881–1918: The Life of Martin Sheridan* (Castlebar, Ireland: Mayo, 2018), 303.

5. Molloy, *Mayo's Famous Son*, 467.

6. Molloy, *Mayo's Famous Son*, 467.

7. Molloy, *Mayo's Famous Son*, 468.

8. Kevin McCarthy, *Gold, Silver, and Green: The Irish Olympic Journey, 1896–1924* (Cork: Cork University Press, 2010).

9. McCarthy, *Gold, Silver, and Green.*

10. James E. Sullivan, *Spalding's Athletic Almanac for 1907* (New York: American Sports Publishing, 1907), 218.

11. *New York Times*, May 27, 1906, cited in Redmond, *The Irish and the Making of American Sport*, 312.

7. THE IRISH AMERICAN ATHLETIC CLUB

1. Tom Hunt, *The Little Book of Irish Athletics* (Dublin: History Press Ireland, 2017), 51.

2. "Conway of the IAAC in Great Glee at the Club's Records at the London Olympic Games He Tells a Reporter How It All Came About," *Gaelic American*, July 25, 1908.

3. "Irish Athletes Made Splendid Records," *Gaelic American*, February 8, 1908.

4. Hunt, *The Little Book of Irish Athletics*, 52.

5. Allan Katchen, *Abel Kiviat—National Champion: Twentieth-Century Track and Field and the Melting Pot* (New York: Syracuse University Press, 2009), cited in Patrick R. Redmond, *The Irish and the Making of American Sport, 1835–1920* (Jefferson, NC: McFarland, 2016).

6. From the *New York Mail*, date unknown, quoted in the *Seattle Daily Times*, January 22, 1911, cited in Redmond, *The Irish and the Making of American Sport*, 313.

7. *New York Times*, July 11, 1909, cited in Redmond, *The Irish and the Making of American Sport.*

8. *Gaelic American*, May 12, 1906.

9. "The Clansman: Souvenir of Celtic and Emmet Clubs, Irish Picnic, and Games, June 17, 1905," *Wingedfist.org*, http://www.wingedfist.org/Clansman_1905.pdf (accessed January 16, 2020).

10. "Souvenir of the Monster Athletic Carnival of the Clan na Gael of Long Island, July 18, 1909," *Wingedfist.org*, http://www.wingedfist.org/Clansman_1909.pdf (accessed January 16, 2020).

11. *New York Times*, November 2, 1903.

12. *New York Times*, July 9, 1906.

13. *New York Times*, April 12, 1909.

8. THE IRISH WHALES' GREATEST TRIUMPH

1. *Gaelic American*, July 4, 1908.

2. Theodore Andrew Cook, comp., *The Fourth Olympiad, London, 1908: Official Report* (London: British Olympic Association, 1909), 241, available at https://library.olympic.org/Default/doc/SYRACUSE/28911/the-fourth-olympi-ad-being-the-official-report-of-the-olympic-games-of-1908-celebrated-in-lon-don-draw?_lg=en-GB (accessed January 16, 2020).

3. Roger McGrath, "Running Rings around the Empire: The 1908 Games," *Irish America*, August 2012, http://irishamerica.com/2012/07/running-rings-around-the-empire-the-1908-olympics/ (accessed January 16, 2020).

4. Mark Dyerson, "'This Flag Dips for No Earthly King': The Mysterious Origins of an American Myth," *International Journal of the History of Sport* 25 (2008).

5. *Freeman's Journal*, July 14, 1908.

6. "American Athletes Had a Busy Time on Way to Olympic Games," *New York Evening World*, July 15, 1908.

7. *Irish World*, August 1, 1908.

8. *Irish World*, August 1, 1908.

9. *Irish World*, August 1, 1908.

10. *Chicago Tribune*, July 26, 1908; *Irish World*, August 1, 1908.

11. *New York Evening World*, July 14, 1908, cited in Patrick R. Redmond, *The Irish and the Making of American Sport, 1835–1920* (Jefferson, NC: McFarland, 2016), 336.

12. "A Bitter Wrangle over Olympic Race, Carpenter of Cornell Easily Beats English Crack but Is Disqualified for Foul: Americans Protest Vigorously and Refuse to Participate in Run-off of Event on Saturday," *New York Times*, July 24, 1908.

13. "Objections, Disqualifications, Amazing Finishes, and No Fewer Than Twenty-Three Medals for Irish Competitors," *Irish Times*, August 4, 2008, https://www.irishtimes.com/sport/objections-disqualifications-amazing-finishes-and-no-fewer-than-23-medals-for-irish-competitors-1.926339 (accessed January 16, 2020).

14. Luke J. Harris, *Britain and the Olympic Games, 1908–1920: Perspectives on Participation and Identity* (London: Palgrave Macmillan, 2015), 288.

15. David Goldblatt, *The Games* (London: Macmillan, 2016), 81.

16. Harris, *Britain and the Olympic Games*, 288.

17. Harris, *Britain and the Olympic Games*, 288.

18. Harris, *Britain and the Olympic Games*, 288.

19. Redmond Walsh, grandnephew of Con Walsh, telephone interview, November 20, 2019.

20. Tom Hunt, *The Little Book of Irish Athletics* (Dublin: History Press Ireland, 2017), 65.

21. Hunt, *The Little Book of Irish Athletics*.

22. Inter-Departmental Committee on Physical Deterioration, *Report of the Inter-Departmental Committee on Physical Deterioration* (London: Darling and Son, 1905).

23. Harris, *Britain and the Olympic Games*, 58.

24. Harris, *Britain and the Olympic Games*, 114.

25. Harris, *Britain and the Olympic Games*, 66.

26. Kevin McCarthy, *Gold, Silver, and Green: The Irish Olympic Journey, 1896–1924* (Cork: Cork University Press, 2010), 187.

27. *Gaelic American*, July 25, 1908, cited in Redmond, *The Irish and the Making of American Sport*, 340.

28. *Gaelic American*, July 25, 1908, cited in Redmond, *The Irish and the Making of American Sport*, 340.

29. *Gaelic American*, July 25, 1908, cited in Redmond, *The Irish and the Making of American Sport*, 340.

30. *Gaelic American*, July 25, 1908, cited in Redmond, *The Irish and the Making of American Sport*, 340.

31. "Sullivan Flays Olympic Officials," *New York Times*, August 8,1908, cited in Redmond, *The Irish and the Making of American Sport*.

32. *New York Times*, July 31, 1908, cited in Redmond, *The Irish and the Making of American Sport*, 338.

33. *New York Times*, July 31, 1908, cited in Redmond, *The Irish and the Making of American Sport*.

34. Sean Whitney, *The Irish Whales: Winning a Place in the New World*, unpublished master's thesis, 2012, 31.

35. Whitney, *The Irish Whales*, 31.

36. "Big Welcome for Yankee Athletes: Official Reception Planned for Victors at London," *New York Times*, July 26, 1908; "Athletes' Parade to Be Big Affair," *New York Times*, August 18, 1908; "10,000 to Parade for the Athletes," *New York Times*, August 23, 1908.

37. Pierre de Coubertin, "Olympic Memories: The Fourth Olympiad," *Olympic Review* 114 (April 1977): 252, cited in Redmond, *The Irish and the Making of American Sport*, 340.

38. "Marathon Winner Gets Big Welcome," *New York Times*, August 20, 1908.

39. *New York Herald*, September 1, 1908, cited in McCarthy, *Gold, Silver, and Green*, 237.

40. *New York Herald*, September 1, 1908, cited in McCarthy, *Gold, Silver, and Green*, 237.

41. "President Greets Olympic Athletes: Tells American Team Their Performance Has Never Been Duplicated in History of Athletics," *New York Times*, September 1, 1908.

42. "Final Tribute to Olympic Victors, More Than 500 Persons at Dinner of Irish American Athletic Club at Waldorf," *New York Times,* September 22, 1908.

43. *New York Evening Call*, August 8, 1908.

44. Redmond, *The Irish and the Making of American Sport*, 334.

45. "Letter to the Editor from E. Pluribus Unum," *New York Times*, July 31, 1908, cited in Redmond, *The Irish and the Making of American Sport*.

46. "Letter to the Editor from E. Pluribus Unum," cited in Redmond, *The Irish and the Making of American Sport*, 342.

47. *Gaelic American*, August 1, 1908.

48. *Gaelic American*, August 1, 1908.

49. *new York Evening World*, July 22, 1908.

50. Margaret Molloy, *Mayo's Famous Son, 1881–1918: The Life of Martin Sheridan* (Castlebar, Ireland: Mayo, 2018), 249.

51. Molloy, *Mayo's Famous Son*, 249.

52. Frank Zarnowski, "Thomas F. Kiely: A Biography," *Journal of Olympic History* (August 2006), http://library.la84.org/SportsLibrary/JOH/JOHv14n2/JOHv14n2f.pdf (accessed January 16, 2020).

53. Molloy, *Mayo's Famous Son*.

54. Molloy, *Mayo's Famous Son*, 249.

55. Molloy, *Mayo's Famous Son*, 249.

9. 1912

1. "Pierre de Coubertin Quotes," *Quote Prism*, https://quoteprism.net/pierre-de-coubertin-quotes (accessed January 16, 2020).

2. "Flanagan Going to Ireland: Famous Weight Thrower Will Sail for His Old Home Saturday," *New York Times*, October 5, 1910.

3. Christopher Young, "When Pierre Met Adolf: The Olympic Games in the Age of Technical Reproduction," presented to the Conference on Globalization and Sport in Historical Context, University of California San Diego, March 2005.

4. B. Keys, *Globalizing Sport: National Rivalry and International Community in the 1930s* (Cambridge, MA: Harvard University Press, 2013), cited in David Goldblatt, *The Games* (London: Macmillan, 2016), 110.

5. "Police Athletes of the Past: Matthew J. McGrath," *Spring 3001 : A Magazine for Policemen* (March 1951).

6. "Last of the Whales," *New York Times*, May 18, 1954.

7. William Dooley, *Champions of the Athletic Arena* (Dublin: General Publicity Service, 1946).

8. Dooley, *Champions of the Athletic Arena*, 55.

9. Will T. Irwin, "The Olympic Games," *Collier's*, August 10, 1912.

10. James E. Sullivan, *The Olympic Games: Stockholm 1912*, Spalding's "Red Cover" Series of Athletic Handbooks, no. 17R (New York: American Sports Publishing, 1912), 101.

10. INTERREGNUM

1. "Olympism," *World Olympians Association*, https://olympians.org/woa/olympism/ (accessed January 16, 2020).

2. "Martin Sheridan Is Dead; Noted Athlete Succumbs to Pneumonia at St. Vincent's Hospital," *New York Times*, March 27, 1918.

3. Margaret Molloy, *Mayo's Famous Son, 1881–1918: The Life of Martin Sheridan* (Castlebar, Ireland: Mayo, 2018), 459.

4. Molloy, *Mayo's Famous Son*, 463.

5. Molloy, *Mayo's Famous Son*, 471.

6. Molloy, *Mayo's Famous Son*, 464.

7. Molloy, *Mayo's Famous Son*, 458.

8. Molloy, *Mayo's Famous Son*, 472.

9. Molloy, *Mayo's Famous Son*, 476.

10. "Grand Concert and Games under Auspices of Martin J. Sheridan Memorial Committee," *Wingedfist.org*, http://www.wingedfist.org/assets/Sheridan_Memorial_games.pdf (accessed January 16, 2020).

11. James R. Barrett, *The Irish Way: Becoming American in the Multiethnic City* (New York: Penguin, 2012).

12. Ray O'Hanlon, *The New Irish Americans* (Boulder, CO: Robert Rinehart, 1998).

13. "5,000 Irish in British Flag Riot on Fifth Avenue," *New York Times*, November 26, 1920.

14. Barrett, *The Irish Way*, 121.

15. Barrett, *The Irish Way*, 121.

16. Barrett, *The Irish Way*, 64.

17. Barrett, *The Irish Way*, 100.

18. Barrett, *The Irish Way*, 215.

19. Barrett, *The Irish Way*, 259.

20. Barrett, *The Irish Way*.

21. Barrett, *The Irish Way*, 69.

22. Barrett, *The Irish Way*, 69.

23. Pallasgreen commemorative booklet, "Unveiling of the Memorial Statue of Paddy Ryan," *Limerick City*, http://www.limerickcity.ie/media/lcBinder12.pdf (accessed January 16, 2020).

24. "World's Records at Celtic Park—Ryan and McDonald Annex Four Premier Marks at Weight-Throwing," *New York Times*, September 2, 1913.

25. James Mitchell, *How to Become a Weight Thrower, with a Chapter on Throwing the Javelin*, Spalding Red Cover Series of Athletic Handbooks, no. 70.R (New York: American Sports Book Publishers, 1916), 44.

26. Mitchell, *How to Become a Weight Thrower*, 44.

27. "Weight Men May Quit: Champions Disappointed over Lack of Interest in Competitive Events," *New York Times*, August 19, 1915.

28. Mitchell, *How to Become a Weight Thrower*, 61.

11. LAST THROWS OF THE DICE

1. "Pierre de Coubertin Quotes," *Quote Prism*, https://quoteprism.net/pierre-de-coubertin-quotes/2 (accessed January 16, 2020).

2. Pierre de Coubertin, *Mémoires Olympiques* (Lausanne: Bureau International de Pedagogie Sportive, 1931), 156.

3. David Goldblatt, *The Games* (London: Macmillan, 2016), 103.

4. Karla Anraepenbusch, ed., *Olympic Games 1920 International Encyclopaedia* (Berlin: Freie Universität Berlin, 2018).

5. Goldblatt, *The Games*, 55.

6. Colin Murphy, *The Most Famous Irish Men You Have Never Heard Of* (Dublin: O'Brien Press, 2012).

7. "Martin J. Sheridan: 'A Peerless Athlete,'" *Wingedfist.org*, http://www.wingedfist.org/Sheridan_peerless_athlete.html (accessed January 16, 2020).

12. A WHALE OF A STORY

1. "Full Text of Mary McAleese's Speech," *Irish Times*, November 11, 2004, https://www.irishtimes.com/news/full-text-of-mary-mcaleese-s-speech-1.994898 (accessed January 16, 2020).

2. *Irish Limelight*, February 1918.

3. *Irish Limelight*, July 1918.

4. Copy viewable at "The Film 'Knocknagow' (1918)," *Humphrysfamily-tree.com*, http://humphrysfamilytree.com/OMara/knocknagow.html (accessed January 16, 2020).

5. *Boston Daily Globe*, December 10, 1918.

6. *Variety*, September 30, 1921.

7. *Freeman's Journal*, January 28, 1920.

8. *Gaelic American*, July 20, 1912, cited in Kevin McCarthy, *Gold, Silver, and Green: The Irish Olympic Journey, 1896–1924* (Cork: Cork University Press, 2010), 264.

9. *Irish Independent*, July 22, 1936, cited in Sean Whitney, *The Irish Whales: Winning a Place in the New World*, unpublished master's thesis, 2012, 55.

10. "1911 Census of Ireland," *National Archives*, http://www.census.nationalarchives.ie/limerick/bulgaden/kilbreedy (accessed January 16, 2020).

11. John O'Shaughnessy, "Magnificent Career of Fine Sportsman," *Limerick Leader*, August 31, 1985.

12. Seamus O Ceallaigh, "Great Limerick Athletes (No. 13) John J. Flanagan of Kilbreedy," *Limerick Leader*, http://www.limerickcity.ie/media/flanagan-johnj13.pdf (accessed January 16, 2020).

13. O Ceallaigh, "Great Limerick Athletes (No. 13) John J. Flanagan of Kilbreedy."

14. "Olympian John 'the Finest among Finest,'" *Limerick Leader*, April 14, 2001.

15. "1940 U.S. Census, Bronx County, New York, ED 3-1368, p. 9, 5A 17292, 2477, Matthew McGrath household," *National Archives*, http//www 1940 census.archives.gov, cited in Whitley, "The Irish Whales."

16. "World's Greatest Weight Thrower, Matt McGrath in Ireland, What He Thinks of Ned Tobin," *Irish Press*, July 7, 1936.

17. William Dooley, *Champions of the Athletic Arena* (Dublin: General Publicity Service, 1946).

18. New York City Police Department, *Spring 3001: A Magazine for Policemen* (February 1941): 21. (*Spring 3001* was first published in 1930, for serving and retired members of the NYPD force. It takes its name from an old telephone number—SPring 7-3001—used by the organization.)

19. McCarthy, *Gold, Silver, and Green*, 261. The standard rules for boxing were known as the "Marquess of Queensberry Rules." This is presumably a play on words by McGrath signifying that he employed his own unique interpretation of these guidelines.

20. McCarthy, *Gold, Silver, and Green*, 261.

21. Mark D. Warren, "Matthew J. McGrath, the Olympic Legend Who Picked Up Where Martin Sheridan Left Off," *Spring 3001* (July/August 1994): 94.

22. John E. Findling and Kimberly D. Pelle, eds., *Historical Dictionary of the Modern Olympic Movement* (Westport, CT: Greenfield), 56.

23. "Police Athletes of the Past, Patrick McDonald," *Spring 3001* 20, no. 10 (November 1950): 27.

24. *New York Tribune*, November 5, 1922.

25. Ciara Meehan, *The Cosgrave Party* (Dublin: Royal Irish Academy, 2010), 46.

26. Flor McCarthy, *The Kerryman.*

27. An old name for County Clare.

28. McCarthy, *The Kerryman.*

29. "Carriganima Remember Their Olympic Medalist," *Irish Independent*, January 8, 2009.

30. "Great Limerick Athletes (No. 6), Paddy Ryan of Pallasgreen," *Limerick Leader*, December 20, 1952.

31. "Paddy Ryan: The Irish Whale of Pallasgreen," *Wingedfist.org*, http://www.wingedfist.org/Paddy_Ryan_Memorial.pdf (accessed January 16, 2020).

32. No date given. Article donated by Philip Conway.

33. Donal O'Regan, "Limerick Athlete Inducted into U.S. Hall of Fame," *Limerickcity.ie*, www.limerickcity.ie/media/sports%20people%20200.pdf (accessed January 16, 2020).

34. Catherine O'Grady, telephone interview, October 8, 2018.

35. *Chicago Tribune*, September 4, 1909.

36. *Pittsburgh Press*, March 9, 1913.

37. *San Francisco Call*, March 23, 1913.

38. Margaret Molloy, *Mayo's Famous Son, 1881–1918: The Life of Martin Sheridan* (Castlebar, Ireland: Mayo, 2018).

39. Molloy, *Mayo's Famous Son*, 479.

40. *San Francisco Chronicle*, May 18, 1912, cited in Whitley, "The Irish Whales."

41. *New York Evening World*, June 12, 1912, cited in Whitley, "The Irish Whales."

42. *New York Times*, December 13, 1913, cited in Whitley, "The Irish Whales."

43. Despite their avowed amateur ethos, which prevailed, some engaged in product endorsement. Sheridan, McGrath, and McDonald appeared in advertisements for Tuxedo Tobacco—Sheridan had the now-laughable lines, "Tuxedo is a strong card with me. I advise all athletes to stick to Tuxedo. It is the one tobacco that will help them, keep them in trim, [and] prevent them from going stale. Tuxedo leads—bar none." Matt McGrath's comments were equally ignorant:

"No athlete need fear to smoke as much as he wants if he uses Tuxedo. It's a general help to any man. A pipeful of Tuxedo puts new life in me." John Flanagan and Martin Sheridan appeared in advertisements for Spalding Sporting Goods, while Matt McGrath did work for Lifebuoy soap, for which he was introduced as "America's Most Famous Police Athlete." The faces of the Irish Whales—along with other members of the IAAC—also appeared in a 1910 set of trading cards that accompanied Mecca and Hassan cigarettes.

44. McCarthy, *Gold, Silver, and Green*, 91.

45. Molloy, *Mayo's Famous Son*, 484.

46. Molloy, *Mayo's Famous Son*, 331.

47. *St. Louis Post Dispatch*, May 31, 1906, cited in Molloy, *Mayo's Famous Son*, 90.

48. Lewis H. Carlson, ed., *Tales of Gold: An Oral History of the Summer Olympic Games Told by America's Gold Medal Winners* (New York: Contemporary Books, 1987), cited in Roy Tomizawa, "The Irish Whales: Living the American Immigrant and Olympic Dream at the Turn of the Century," *Olympians*, https://theolympians.co/tag/pat-mcdonald/ (accessed January 16, 2020).

49. "Celtic Park under Prosecutor's Fire: Queens District Attorney to Investigate Riot Sunday in Which Four Were Shot," *New York Times*, July 25, 1922.

50. "Protest Greyhound Races: Laurel Hills Associations Ask Patten to Bar Park Contests," *New York Times*, September 21, 1928.

51. James R. Barrett, *The Irish Way: Becoming American in a Multiethnic City* (New York: Penguin, 2012).

52. Lane Dowell, "America's Forgotten Event: The Hammer," *Hammer-Throw.org*, http://hammerthrow.org/training-resources/articles/americas-forgotten-event/ (accessed January 16, 2020).

BIBLIOGRAPHY

Anbinder, Tyler. *City of Dreams: The 400-Year Epic History of Immigrant New York*. New York: Houghton Mifflin Harcourt, 2016.

———. *Five Points: The Nineteenth-Century New York City Neighborhood That Invented Tap Dance, Stole Elections, and Became the World's Most Notorious Slum*. New York: Simon and Schuster, 2001.

Anraepenbusch, Karla, ed. *Olympic Games 1920 International Encyclopaedia*. Berlin: Freie Universität Berlin. 2018.

Bairner, Alan, and Gyozo Molnar, eds. *The Politics of the Olympics: A Survey*. London: Routledge, 2010.

Barrett, James R. *The Irish Way: Becoming American in the Multiethnic City*. New York: Penguin, 2012.

Bergvall, Erik, ed. *The Official Report of the Olympic Games of Stockholm 1912: Issued by the Swedish Olympic Committee*. Stockholm: Wahlström and Widstrand, 1913.

Berri, Fred. *Ten Cents a Dance*. New York: First Edition Design Publishing, 2016.

Bromell, Una. "Worlds Apart: The Gaelic League and America." In L. Irwin, ed., *Explorations Centenary Essays* (Limerick: Mary Immaculate College, 1998), 146–57.

Brownell, Susan. *The 1904 Anthropology Days and Olympic Games: Sport, Race, and American Imperialism*. Lincoln: University of Nebraska Press, 2008.

Bryant, John. *26.2: The Incredible True Story of the Three Men Who Shaped the London Marathon*. London: John Blake, 2013.

Casey, Marion, and J. J. Lee, eds. *Making the Irish American: History and Heritage of the Irish in the United States*. New York: New York University Press, 2006.

Clark, Kenneth. *The Nude: A Study in Ideal Form*. London: Folio Society, 2010.

Clarke, Joseph I. C. *The Fighting Race and Other Poems and Ballads*. New York: American News Company, 1911.

Connolly, Harold. *An Olympic Victor*. Stoughton, WI: Books on Demand, 2013.

Coogan, Tim Pat. *Wherever the Green Is Worn: The Story of the Irish Diaspora*. London: Arrow Books, 2002.

Cronin, Mike, Mark Duncan, and Paul Rouse. *The GAA, a People's History*. Cork: Collins Press, 2009.

Davin, Pat. *Recollections of a Veteran Irish Athlete: The Memoirs of Pat Davin, the World's All- Round Athletic Champion*. Dublin: Juverna Press, 1938.

de Coubertin, Pierre. *Mémoires Olympiques* (Olympic Memories). Lausanne: Bureau International de Pedagogie Sportive, 1931.

Delaney, Tim, ed. *Sportsmanship: Multidisciplinary Perspectives*. Jefferson, NC: McFarland, 2016.

Dixon, Peter L. *The Olympian*. Self-published, 1984.

Dolan, Jay P. *The Emigrant Church*. Baltimore, MD, and London: Johns Hopkins University Press, 1975.

Dooley, William. *Champions of the Athletic Arena*. Dublin: General Publicity Service, 1946.

Dowd, Christopher. *The Irish and the Origins of American Popular Culture*. London: Routledge, 2018.

Dyreson, Mark. "'This Flag Dips for No Earthly King': The Mysterious Origins of an American Myth." *International Journal of the History of Sport* 25 (2008).

———. *Crafting Patriotism for Global Dominance: America at the Olympics*. New York: Routledge, 2009.

Eisen, George, and David Kenneth Wiggins, eds. *Ethnicity and Sport in North American History and Culture*, Contributions to Popular Culture, no. 40. Toronto: Praeger, 1995.

Erie, Stephen P. *Rainbow's End*. Berkeley: University of California Press, 1988.

Ernst, Robert. *Immigrant Life in New York City, 1825–1863*. New York: King's Crown Press, 1949. Reprint, New York: Syracuse University Press, 1994.

Fleischer, Nat. *The Boston Strong Boy: The Story of John L. Sullivan, the Champion of Champions*. New York: O'Brien Press, 1941.

———. *The Heavyweight Championship*. London: G. P. Putnam's Sons, 1949.

Fullam, Brendan. *The Final Whistle*. Dublin: Wolfhound Press, 2000.

Goldblatt, David. *The Games*. London: Macmillan, 2016.

Golwoy, T., and M. Coffey, eds. *The Irish in America*. New York: Hyperion, 1997.

Greeley, Andrew. *Encyclopaedia of the Irish in America*. Notre Dame, IN: University of Notre Dame Press, 1999.

Guttmann, Allen. *Essays on Sport History and Sport Mythology*. Arlington: Texas A&M University Press, 1990.

Hamrock, Ivor, ed. *The Famine in Mayo, 1845–1850: A Portrait from Contemporary Sources*. Castlebar: Mayo County Council, 1998.

Handlin, Oscar. *Boston's Immigrants, 1790–1865*. Cambridge, MA: Harvard University Press, 1941.

Harris, Luke J. *Britain and the Olympic Games, 1908–1920: Perspectives on Participation and Identity*. London: Palgrave Macmillan, 2015.

Hunt, Tom. *The Little Book of Irish Athletics*. Dublin: History Press Ireland, 2017.

Inter-Departmental Committee on Physical Deterioration, *Report of the Inter-Departmental Committee on Physical Deterioration*. London: Darling and Son, 1905.

Isenberg, Michael T. *John L. Sullivan and His America*. Champaign: University of Illinois Press, 1994.

Jenkins, Rebecca. *The First London Olympics, 1908: The Definitive Story of London's Most Sensational Olympics to Date*. London: Hachette, 2008.

Johnson, Clint. *A Vast and Fiendish Plot: The Confederate Attack on New York City*. New York: Citadel, 2010.

Katchen, Allan. *Abel Kiviat—National Champion: Twentieth-Century Track and Field and the Melting Pot*. New York: Syracuse University Press, 2009.

Kirsch, George B., Othello Harris, and Claire Elaine Nolte, eds. *Encyclopaedia of Ethnicity and Sports in the United States*. Westport, CT: Greenwood, 2001.

Lucas, Charles J. P. *The Olympic Games, 1904: St. Louis*. St. Louis, MO: Woodward and Tiernan, 1905.

Maguire, John Francis. *The Irish in America*. New York: Arno, 1969.

Mallon, Bill. *The 1904 Olympic Games: Results for All Competitors in All Events, with Commentary*. Jefferson, NC: McFarland, 1999.

Matthews, George R. *America's First Olympics: The St. Louis Games of 1904*. Columbia: University of Missouri Press, 1999.

McCarthy, Kevin. *Gold, Silver, and Green: The Irish Olympic Journey, 1896–1924*. Cork: Cork University Press, 2010.

McNickle, Chris. *To Be Mayor of New York: Ethnic Politics in the City*. New York: Columbia University Press, 1993.

Mitchell, James. *How to Become a Weight Thrower, with a Chapter on Throwing the Javelin*, Spalding Red Cover Series of Athletic Handbooks, no. 70.R. New York: American Sports Book Publishers, 1916.

Murphy, Colin. *The Most Famous Irish Men You Have Never Heard Of.* Dublin: O'Brien Press, 2012.

Naughton, Lindie, and Johnny Watterson. *Faster, Higher, Stronger: A History of Ireland's Olympians*. Dublin: Ashfield Press, 2008.

O'Hanlon, Ray. *The New Irish Americans*. Boulder, CO: Robert Rinehart, 1998.

O'Riain, Seamus. *Maurice Davin (1842–1927): The First President of the GAA*. Dublin: Geography Publications, 1994.

O'Sullivan, T. F. *The Story of the GAA*. Dublin: Middle Abbey Street, 1916.

Padden, M., and R. Sullivan. *May the Road Rise to Meet You*. New York: Penguin, 1999.

Posey, Carl. *II Olympiad: Paris 1900*. Toronto: Warwick, 2015.

———. *III Olympiad: St. Louis 1904, Athens 1906*. Toronto: Warwick, 1996.

Potter, George. *To the Golden Door*. Boston: Little, Brown, 1970.

Rader, Benjamin G. *American Sports: From the Age of Folk Games to the Age of Televised Sports*. Englewood Cliffs, NJ: Prentice Hall, 1990.

Redmond, Patrick R. *The Irish American Athletic Club of New York: The Rise and Fall of the Winged Fists, 1898–1917*. Jefferson, NC: McFarland, 2018.

———. *The Irish and the Making of American Sport, 1835–1920*. Jefferson, NC: McFarland, 2016.

Reeder, Colonel Red. *The Story of the Spanish-American War*. New York: Duell, Sloane and Pearce, 1955.

Reiss, Stephen A. *Sport in Industrial America: 1850–1920*. Wheeling, IL: Harlan Davidson, 1995.

Riis, Jacob A. *How the Other Half Lives*. New York: Dover, 1971.

Roosevelt, Theodore. *Theodore Roosevelt: An Autobiography*. New York: Macmillan, 1913. Reprint, Fairfield, UK: Echo Library, 2006.

Ross, E. A. *Old World in the New*. New York: Century, 1913.

Seymour, Harold, and Dorothy Seymour Mills. *Baseball: The Golden Age*. New York: Oxford University Press, 1989.

Shannon, William V. *The American Irish: A Political and Social Portrait*. Amherst: University of Massachusetts Press, 1965.

Stivers, Richard. *Hair of the Dog: Irish Drinking and Its American Stereotypes*. New York: Continuum, 2000.

Tierney, Michael. *Eoin MacNeill: Scholar and Man of Action, 1867–1945*. Oxford, UK: Clarendon, 1980.

Toohey, Kristine. *The Olympic Games: A Social Science Perspective*. Oxfordshire, UK: CABI, 2007.

Wagner, Paul. "Letters Home." *World of Hibernia* (New York, 1995).

Wallechinsky, David, and Jamie Loucky. *The Complete Book of the Olympics*. London: Aurum, 2012.

Watman, Melvyn. *History of British Athletics*. London: Robert Hale, 1968.

Watterson, Johnny, and Lindie Naughton. *Irish Olympians, 1896–1992*. Dublin: Blackwater, 1992.

Whitney, Caspar. *A Sporting Pilgrimage: Riding to Hounds, Golf, Rowing, Football, Club and University Athletics, Studies in English Sport, Past and Present*. New York: Harper, 1895.

Whitney, Sean. *The Irish Whales: Winning a Place in the New World*. Unpublished master's thesis, 2012.

Young, Christopher. *When Pierre Met Adolf: The Olympic Games in the Age of Technical Reproduction*. Conference on Globalization and Sport in Historical Context, University of California, San Diego, March 2005.

Zarnowski, Frank. *All-Around Men: Heroes of a Forgotten Sport*. Lanham, MD: Scarecrow, 2005.

INDEX

ABOUT THE AUTHOR

Kevin Martin taught communications and cultural studies for twenty-five years at the high school and university levels. He is author of *Have Ye No Homes to Go To? The History of the Irish Pub* (2015), *A Happy Type of Sadness: A Journey through Irish Country Music* (2018), and *The Complete Guide to the Best Pubs in Dublin* (2019). He is married with two children and lives near Westport on the west coast of the Republic of Ireland.